P9-CNH-320

STOWAWAY

CAROL CÓRDOBA

Arte Público Press
Houston, Texas
1996

This volume is made possible through grants from the National Endowment for the Arts (a federal agency), the Andrew W. Mellon Foundation, and the Lila Wallace-Reader's Digest Fund.

Recovering the past, creating the future

Arte Público Press
University of Houston
Houston, Texas 77204-2090

Cover illustration and design by Scott Fray

Córdoba, Carol.
   Stowaway / by Carol Córdoba.
       p.   cm.
   ISBN 1-55885-166-6 (clothbound : alk. paper)
   1. Córdoba-Zapata, Nicolás. 2. Illegal aliens—United States—Biography. 3. Stowaways—United States—Biography. 4. Drug traffic—United States. I. Title.
JV6455.C583   1996
323.6'31'.092—dc20
[B]   96-12335
                                   CIP

The paper used in this publication meets the requirements of the American National Standard for Permanence of Paper for Printed Library Materials Z39.48-1984. ∞

Copyright © 1996 by Carol Córdoba
Printed in the United States of America

Acknowledgments

I would like to thank the many people who helped make this book possible.

For their help with the technical aspects of getting what was in my head into the computer, I want to thank Eric Roth, Stephanie Guttman, Josh Hillman, Joshua Guttman and Randy Spitz. A special thanks goes to the ever-patient reference-desk librarians at the Leon County Public Library who assisted me in my research, and Juanita Raymond at the Centerville Post Office whose empathy and encouragement helped me persevere.

For their suggestions, constant encouragement and faith in me, I wish to thank my three sons: Eric, Michael and Richard as well as Andrea and Howie Jacobsen, Marjorie and Mark Gross, Alisa and Ron Hutchinson, Dorothy and Norman Heyman, Sarna Strom, Bill Sokolow, and Matt Lawhon.

I wish to especially thank my brother, David Guttman, not only for his assistance in proofreading the many rewrites of this book, but also for his loving concern and support through the rough times.

In memory of Ana Teheran

"Only a man who has felt ultimate despair is capable of feeling ultimate bliss.... Wait and hope."

—Edmond Dantes in *The Count of Monte Cristo* by Alexander Dumas

STOWAWAY

PREFACE

2 AM
Thursday, January 24, 1991
New York Harbor

Cold.

Cold that seeped into his bones. Cold that made his arms and legs ache.

It was surely not the coldest day in that first month of 1991. The temperature was 17 degrees that morning, as an arctic front moved over the region, causing flurries that lasted until noon. With brisk winds accompanying the front, the temperature hovered in the teens as the frigid air settled in.

It was not the coldest day of the year, nor was it the worst day of the year, but for Nicolás Córdoba-Zapata, sleeping fitfully in a nylon mesh hammock suspended two feet above the Atlantic Ocean, it would prove to be both.

PART ONE

Not knowing the distance already traveled or the miles of ocean yet to be traversed, he finally slipped into the oblivion of dreamless sleep only to awake with a shiver, thinking to himself that he would never feel warm again.

To Nicolás, born in Turbo, Colombia, five hundred miles from the equator, hell was no fiery inferno. Hell was a frigid, windowless underwater compartment, known as a rudder trunk, inside a 660-foot oil tanker. Hell had a ceiling eighteen inches above his head that condensed the moisture in the air into icy drops of water which dripped onto his head and into his eyes and soaked his shirt and jacket. Hell had four walls of riveted gray steel, slick with sea slime, six feet apart. Its only floor was the ice-filmed surface of the Atlantic Ocean.

There was no escape from this watery hell. The only way out was the 15" x 18" oval steel hatch in the ceiling which had been sealed shut by twenty-four bolts on the deck of the steering gear room above him before the ship had left port.

With nothing to do but wait, as he had occupied himself for the past six days, he sat with his legs dangling over the side of his hammock and gazed into the water three inches below his feet. This opening was his window, his only connection to the outside world, and although a grisly death awaited him if he should fall into its depths, it provided him with information and diversion during the long voyage.

The compartment was faintly illuminated from time to time as the stern rose and fell and he was able to distinguish day from night. As the color of the water changed, he mentally plotted the ship's course, from the brilliant aquamarine coastal waters of Colombia to the vibrant blue of the Gulf Stream and finally to the deep green of the Atlantic as the ship made its way northward.

With his gaze fixed downward from his precarious perch, he suddenly realized that both the color and clarity were changing. The water was becoming more and more opaque with each passing minute. The massive propeller blade, which he had occasionally seen churning below him, now became increasingly difficult to see as the vessel made its way into the murky water of New York Harbor.

Nicolás strained forward as he tried to figure out exactly where the ship was heading. He was oblivious to his sea-soaked clothes, his rubbed-raw skin and the salty spray in his eyes now that he appeared to be approaching his destination.

It was 2:30 A.M.

Suddenly, for the first time in nearly a week, the deafening noise of the propeller diminished and the whine of the machinery in the bowels of the ship lowered in pitch as the propeller slowed down.

At the same time, almost imperceptibly at first, and then at an increasingly faster rate, the water level in the compartment began to recede. As the space between the ceiling above his head and the water below his feet expanded to three feet, four feet, five feet and finally eight feet, the flashing brightness of the propeller blades slashing through the water became duller and duller.

Nicolás' heart beat faster as the ship's engines slowed down.

His pulse throbbed in his ears as he impulsively yanked the ear protectors off his head and threw them into the rapidly receding water. They had been more of an annoyance than anything and had only slightly diminished the noise. He wondered briefly if he would suffer from permanent hearing loss, but thought to himself that becoming deaf was certainly the least of his problems right now.

All at once he realized that he could hear horns in the distance.

Although he was still imprisoned in the bowels of the ship, at least eight feet below the surface, the sounds of other ships, in what he was certain was a large harbor, was a welcome signal that his ordeal was finally coming to a close. As one ship and then another passed by, the blasts of their horns approached and then receded in the distance.

Darkness became almost absolute now as the propeller slowly turned. The rotations of the blades which had not only churned the sea water releasing life-giving oxygen, but had also occasionally reflected the light of phosphorescent sea life into the compartment, now provided neither.

Trying in vain to peer through the darkness into the abyss below him, he gave up, realizing that he could not even see his hand in front of his face.

He decided not to remain in the hammock which for the past six days had scarred his buttocks, back and thighs with its crisscross design. Grabbing onto the cord that was tied several times around his waist and attached to a steel ring set into the wall of the compartment, he pulled himself over to one of the narrow planks of wood that he had placed as a bridge over the span of the rudder trunk. The strong nylon cord assured him that any misstep on his part or sudden movement of the ship would not plunge him into the water and its awaiting propeller.

With his heartbeat hammering in his chest, he waited and tried to prepare himself for whatever would happen next.

Suddenly the propeller stopped completely. The only thing Nicolás could hear above the constant ringing in his ears was the muffled resonance of the idling engines.

When the noise abruptly ceased, Nicolás contemplated the courses of action available to him. The water level was at its lowest point since the tanker had started to take on its cargo of oil at the port of Mamonal on the night of January 17, but he knew that the stern of the ship still had not risen high enough in the water to expose the entrance to the compartment.

"Should I inflate the raft and attempt to leave immediately, now that the engines have slowed down and that murderous propeller has stopped turning?" he asked himself.

"No, it might start up again without a second's warning, and I won't be able to escape from it once I'm trapped in the whirlpool of its suction. Besides, with the stern of the ship not completely out of the water, I'll have to swim underwater with the inflated raft until I can get out from under the ship."

Although that wasn't an insurmountable obstacle, there were other things to consider.

First of all, he had no idea where he was. He knew that he was near a coast, because he had seen the water turn cloudy before his eyes, but he had no idea which coast it was or how far away the ship was from a pier. It could be a few hundred feet, a few hundred yards, or even a few miles away from any pier or dock from which to step ashore.

There was another problem that was more difficult to overcome. The water temperature at this time of year was thirty-six degrees, but to Nicolás, accustomed to tropical waters, it might just have well been absolute zero. He realized that if he swam out of the compartment, his chance of survival in his already weakened condition would be very slight.

"No," he thought to himself, "I'll wait until the stern is completely out of the water, and then I can stay relatively dry in the raft and row towards land."

He waited, sitting on the rough plank, ears straining for any sound that would indicate how close the ship was to shore. One minute, two minutes, three minutes...all he could hear was the thudding of his heartbeat and the muted horns of ships fading in the distance.

Though normally very patient, always considering all the options before plunging ahead, he now realized that his very life might depend upon the decisions that he would have to make in the next few hours. He nervously tapped his foot quietly and listened.

Four minutes...five minutes...six minutes.

Suddenly the propeller churned into life again, this time spinning in the opposite direction. A huge wave surged into the compartment and Nicolás was swept off the board and into the water.

He grabbed the rope that tethered him securely to the bulkhead and wondered if the ship was about to resume its journey. He thanked God that he had not attempted to leave a few seconds earlier.

The water receded immediately, and he remembered that in order to secure the anchor in the ocean floor, the engines have to be reversed. That the solitary wave meant the ship had cast anchor.

It was time to take action.

Outwardly tranquil, his face showing none of the excitement and elation that he felt, Nicolás waited for the pounding of his heart to subside.

"I made it...thank God, I made it at last," he repeated over and over again. He could not get on his knees, but he silently mouthed a prayer of thanksgiving to God for watching over him and for bringing him safely to the United States.

It was 3 A.M.

He debated with himself about what to do with the four bags of cocaine that he had found in the compartment. He could just leave them exactly as he had discovered them, lashed onto the platform above his head. Whoever had placed them on the ledge before the ship left Colombia surely had someone waiting at the other end of the trip to remove them. If someone did show up to retrieve the bags while he happened to still be there, the fact that the bags were untouched would hopefully enable him to plead for his life. Knowing that drug traffickers were merciless and would kill with impunity anyone in their way, he realized that his life was probably in more danger now that the trip was over than it had been for the previous six days.

He gingerly extracted the inflatable raft from the confines of the bag, making sure that it did not catch on the edges of the zipper. Although he had brought a patch kit with him, he didn't want to travel the final part of his journey in a mended raft of dubious seaworthiness. He carefully removed the four sections of oars that were packed along with the raft; when he was ready to leave, he could quickly snap them together and be on his way.

After taking out the portable air pump that he had bought just a week ago for this occasion, he fumbled around in the darkness until he finally located the valve on the raft. Then he attached the nozzle of the pump to the valve and positioned the entire rear end of the raft across his lap. He braced the handle of the pump against his chest with his right hand and held the raft in place with his left hand as he rhythmically pressed and released the handle of the pump.

For a few anxious minutes it didn't seem like he was making any progress, and he wondered if there were any pinholes in the raft which were caused by being compressed in a bag all week.

Patiently, he kept pumping for fifteen minutes.

He passed his hand over the part of the raft that was hanging over his legs and was relieved to feel a slight resistance to the pressure of his fingers, which meant that air was entering the raft's chambers. Not increasing his pace, but slowly pressing and releasing the handle of the pump in the same rhythm as before, he decided to wait before leaving the ship. He sensed that he had at least a few hours of darkness still ahead of him.

It was 5 A.M.

Finally he finished inflating the raft and lowered it until he heard it hit the water with a soft splash.

Nicolás held his heavy eyelids open with his fingertips, forcing himself to stay awake. He hoped that morning would cast a little light into the water below him. He strained his ears to hear anything at all that could guide him once he was outside the ship as he scrutinized the water in a futile attempt to see anything in its depths.

Crawling along the board on his hands and knees, he returned to the hammock. He crossed his arms and tucked his hands under his armpits. Then he squeezed his legs tightly together, brought his knees up close to his chest, and tried to brace his body against the bitter cold.

He closed his eyes and remembered the voyage.

It seemed more like seven weeks than seven days ago that he had entered the rudder trunk of the Bright Eagle. As a seaman since the age of eighteen, he had known that there was an air pocket in the stern where the rudder shaft connected to the steering-gear mechanism. Seeing the tanker sitting high in the water, he had realized that someone could easily enter the rudder compartment before the ship was loaded and its access sealed off by the ocean. Without a doubt, he had thought to himself, it was the ideal location to stow away.

As soon as a crewman on the dock had told him that the ship was bound for the United States, Nicolás knew that it was now or never. Nicolás thanked the man for the information and then hurriedly left the pier. He had only a few hours to prepare for the most important and probably the most dangerous undertaking of his life.

Although his heart was racing with anticipation and his mind was leaping from one idea to another, he forced himself to calm down as he sprinted home to begin his preparations. He packed warm clothing in a small gym bag and took all the money that he had saved in anticipation of leaving in a hurry, just like this, one day. It wasn't much, just a little over two hundred dollars in Colombian pesos and American dollars, but it was all that he had. He flung the bag over his shoulder and

without even a backward glance, closed the door to his small
room and bolted down the stairs.

Once on the street, he hitched a ride into town and headed towards the beach. He knew that in the shops along the
shore, he would find exactly what he needed for his journey.
Twenty minutes later, he left the brightly-lit avenue with his
purchases: a rubber raft with collapsible oars, a large knife
with a compass set in its handle, ear protectors, a blue nylon
mesh hammock and some other small items he thought would
be necessary for the trip. He also bought some food and two
plastic gallon jugs filled with fresh water.

It was nearly midnight when he returned to the dock.

After stashing everything away inside two vinyl bags, he
placed them at the edge of the pier. He turned around and
silently lowered himself feet-first into the warm water. Steadily treading water to keep his upper body straight and as high
as possible above the surface, he raised his arms, grabbed the
two wooden planks that he had placed at the edge of the dock
and put them into the water. Then he reached up and
retrieved his two bags, slipped his left arm through the handles of one of them and held on tightly to the other which he
had set on top of the boards. With his chest resting on the
planks of wood, he slowly kicked and paddled his way towards
the Bright Eagle. The rudder compartment was nearly invisible in the looming shadow of the tanker. Not wanting the
ship's lights to reveal their reflection in his eyes as he swam,
he kept his head down low as he dipped his free arm sound-
lessly through the water. When at last he was within the
shadow of the ship, he turned around and took one last look at
the lights twinkling on the shore and, swallowing the lump
that had unexpectedly appeared in his throat, swam the last
few yards to the stern.

The leviathan tanker towering above him had not yet
taken on all its cargo of oil and was still sitting high in the
water. In less than a minute he found himself at the entrance
of the rudder trunk. He paused for a second and then swam
directly into the empty space. Holding on tightly to the
boards, he extracted his flashlight from one of the bags and
turned it on. The first thing he noticed was a narrow metal lip
that ran around the perimeter of the compartment, a few
inches above the water line. After returning the flashlight and

grabbing his two bags in one hand, he hoisted his body out of the water and stood precariously on the narrow strip of metal.

He took out the flashlight again and directed its light toward the walls and corners of the six-by-six-foot compartment in order to determine where to attach his hammock, where to stow his gear and where to position the two wooden boards.

He knew from his own experience and from the accounts of his companions that worked on the docks and ships, that although the rudder trunk had no floor, there was the narrow ledge that he was standing on at the bottom and a similar but narrower ledge near the top. There was also a two-feet-by-three-feet steel shelf that protruded into the compartment about three-quarters of the way up. He would be able to use this shelf not only to rest on when he got tired of the hammock but also to stow his gear. He would also be able to place the edge of one of the wooden boards on this ledge, thus providing himself with additional seating space. In the constricted confines of the compartment, these boards would also serve as a bridge over the bottomless span, and it was for this particular purpose that he had taken them with him. Although one of the boards was partially cracked and not exactly the same size as its companion, it would be serviceable enough when placed over the better piece of wood.

Nicolás swung his flashlight towards the top of the compartment in order to find a place where he could wire the boards securely. The beam of light illuminated the small platform.

"Oh, my God!" he said to himself as his heart plummeted precipitously to his stomach.

Somebody had already entered the rudder trunk.

With a trembling hand, he redirected the flashlight's rays around the perimeter of the compartment, about three feet below the place where the ceiling and the walls joined. His second investigation of the room confirmed the fact that somebody else had taken advantage of this perfect hiding place. However, it wasn't the sight of another person in this compartment that had shocked him and forced him to question his decision to stow away in the Bright Eagle. No, finding another person in the rudder trunk would have been a relatively easy matter of sharing space and probably provisions as well.

No, it wasn't that simple. Instead of sharing the compartment with another person, he would now have to share this space with the four large bags that were tied to the platform with crisscrossed yellow and pink nylon ropes.

The bags occupied nearly every available inch of space on the ledge, space that now he would be unable to use. The bottom three duffel bags were of shiny brown vinyl, stacked carefully one on top of the other. They were neat, yet bulky, about thirty-six inches long, eighteen inches wide and twelve inches high. Tied on top of the uppermost bag was a slightly smaller white nylon bag which nearly reached the ceiling and the underside of the manhole cover.

He wasn't certain what was in those four bags, but he wasn't naive. He guessed that they contained drugs that somebody had stashed in the rudder trunk for the very same reasons that he had chosen it.

"There's still time to change my mind," he told himself. The tanker was not yet as low as it would be when fully loaded, and he could still get out just as easily as he had gotten in. He could paddle back to the shore and remain unseen in the sheltering shadow of the ship.

"But I've come this far!" he argued with himself. He had gotten into the ship without anyone raising an alarm.

Nicolás could almost hear the laughter and derision of his companions ringing in his ears, ridiculing him for his weakness and lack of character. He had thought about, dreamed about, and talked about going to the United States for such a long time that he would never be able to live down the disgrace if he changed his mind and returned after actually entering the rudder trunk.

"No! I'm not going back," he decided. With only seventy dollars of American money and twenty pesos of Colombian money left after buying the supplies for the voyage, he realized that he had no choice. He had to follow through with his hastily-conceived plan to stow away, whether the bags that he discovered in the compartment contained drugs or not.

It was close to four o'clock in the morning by the time Nicolás finished tying up the hammock and wiring the boards to the ledge that ran around the perimeter of the rudder trunk. Impatiently wiping the sweat that cascaded over his eyebrows and stung his eyes, he searched for a good location to stow his gear.

There weren't many choices available.

He noticed that luckily there was still a space remaining above the duffel bags that occupied the ledge. Cutting off a few feet of the pink rope that crisscrossed several times over, under and around the bags, he divided it into several pieces. Then, after threading the pieces through the straps of his two gym bags and through the handles of the water jugs, he tied his gear on top the duffel bags.

He looked around one last time and pulled at all the ropes to make sure that everything was securely fastened. The water level was far below him and, although he realized that it would rise once the ship was fully loaded, he felt confident that he had tied everything high enough. He knew that it would be impossible to make any adjustments once the ship was underway. Right now, with the engines off, the huge propeller lay stationary and he could remain in the water of the compartment safely, but once the engines started, the whirlpool and suction that the propeller created would pull him inexorably under the water, and he would be torn to pieces by its massive blades.

Satisfied that everything was secure, he climbed into the hammock, switched off his flashlight and tucked it into his waistband. Although he was only wearing a pair of shorts, in the ninety-five degree heat of the sultry Colombian night, his body was shiny with sweat. He closed his eyes and breathed a long sigh of relief.

At last he was on his way to the United States.

The increased pressure inside his ears woke him up six hours later and he sensed instinctively that something had changed. He flicked on his flashlight and was surprised to see that the water level had risen substantially while he had been sleeping. With mounting alarm it rose higher and higher even in the few short minutes that he was watching it. His heart started to hammer in his chest as it rose still higher than ever.

He sat up in the hammock and hung his feet over the side. Leaning forward, to get a better look, he aimed the flashlight on the once cavernous space beneath him as he stared with disbelief at the advancing water.

"There's supposed to be an air pocket in this compartment," he told himself. "Everybody knows there's supposed to be an air pocket here."

He unconsciously held his breath as the water gradually reached his toes, lapped at the soles, inched up until it covered the tops of his feet. It finally stopped its ascent when it reached his ankles.

With an audible sigh of relief, Nicolás crossed himself and voiced a brief prayer of thanksgiving.

"I'm going to be all right," he assured himself. "I just hadn't figured on the water rising this high...that's all...I'm going to be okay."

Suddenly with a deafening roar, a tidal wave of water inundated the compartment. Unbeknownst to Nicolás, the captain had just given the order to start the engines in reverse in order to weigh anchor.

Torn out of his hand in the onslaught of water, the flashlight swept into the maelstrom while Nicolás clutched the mesh sides of the hammock with both hands, trying to cling onto the only stationary object at hand. He stretched his neck upwards as high as he could and found a few inches of air above the water with just enough space for his head.

Gulping a few strangled breaths of air, he was certain that he had reached the hour of his death. Panic-stricken and wondering if he was going to drown or be torn to pieces by the propeller, he inhaled deep shuddering breaths, sure that each one was his last. He had faced death several times before in his life, but never as imminently as right now. Even in the pitch-blackness of the compartment, he realized that if the water rose any higher, he would be a dead man. As he tried unsuccessfully to calm himself to conserve the little air that remained, the propeller abruptly stopped and the water miraculously started to recede. When his shoulders breached the surface, he groped around with his hands until he located the end of the rope that he had used to secure the hammock to the wall of the compartment. He quickly tied it around his waist.

He held on to the sides of the hammock as the water receded to his waist, to his knees, and finally halted at his feet.

"Thank you...thank you...thank you, God," he repeated over and over again in a litany of gratitude.

With a sudden roar like a dozen airplanes all taking off at once, the propeller started up again and another wave, as gigantic as the first, reared up into the rudder trunk.

Praying that there was still an air space remaining at the top of the compartment, Nicolás struggled against the suction of the whirlpool as he half-swam, half-leaped upwards towards air and life.

"How can I survive in here if it's going to be like this for the next seven days?" he asked himself.

His heart was still clamoring in his chest, but he felt slightly calmer than the first time the wave had washed into the compartment. Maybe it was because the first time he had been sure that he was going to die. But he hadn't.... Maybe it was because he refused to abandon the last remnant of hope that remained in his heart.

The noise of the propeller diminished ever so slightly as the tanker's engines reached their cruising speed. The revolutions slowed down and the water in the rudder trunk started to recede as well, inching down slowly until it was just under his feet that dangled over the side of his hammock.

Nicolás felt something warm under his nose and wiped it away, only then realizing that his hand was covered with blood. Now in addition to the fear of losing his life by drowning, he feared that he might slowly bleed to death due to the inescapable fluctuations of the air pressure inside the compartment. Every twenty seconds, as the water rose and then receded in response to the forward motion of the ship and the swell of the waves, the air in the compartment was compressed and released as well. The pressure was bearable when the water level was at its lowest point, but as the water started to rise, the increased pressure caused the blood vessels in Nicolás' middle ears and sinuses to dilate, and as they dilated they leaked and blood oozed out into the surrounding tissue. By the time the water reached its highest level in the compartment, Nicolás was at his highest level of agony, with the blood vessels bursting and blood flowing into his ears and out of his nose.

Grabbing his throbbing head in one hand and maintaining his grip on the hammock with the other, he cautiously stepped onto the crossed boards below him. He hadn't stood on them since the wave had rushed into the compartment, and he wasn't sure if their moorings were still secure. With legs that were shaking due to both his narrow escape from death and the pounding in his skull, he inched over to the spot where he remembered he had stowed his two bags. Feeling around in the darkness, he finally located them and extracted his ear protectors. He immediately placed them over his ears, hoping that they would diminish the pressure of the air as well as the noise of the propeller.

They did neither.

He kept them on just the same, reasoning that they were better than nothing.

When he checked the rest of the items in his bags, he discovered to his dismay that everything that wasn't in a can or in its own separate plastic or cellophane bag, was completely saturated. He tossed all packages of wet food into the vortex below, where they were instantly sucked into the propeller.

"Let the sharks eat that instead of me," he chuckled to himself.

Walking more confidently on the boards now, he returned to his hammock and lay down, attempting to relax. It was difficult enough to breathe in the heat and almost ninety-nine percent humidity of the rudder trunk, but the increased pressure of the air compelled him to consciously force air into his lungs. After less than twelve hours in the compartment, his skin had already started to peel, due to the high temperature and salinity of the water as well as the sweat that poured off his body. This produced a fierce itch that threatened to drive him crazy, and it was all he could do to resist scratching his skin to shreds.

Finally, he slept.

By the second day of the voyage Nicolás had lost all track of time.

In the almost total darkness of the rudder compartment, he squinted at the watch on his wrist. "As soon as I get back to Colombia, I'm going to get that thief that swindled me," he vowed. The luminous-dialed, highly touted, very expensive watch that the shopkeeper had claimed was resistant to water and capable of keeping perfect time under very deep pressure could do neither.

Tossing it into the water, he wondered what else would go wrong.

He was soon to find out.

Climbing very carefully out of the hammock and onto one of the wooden boards that crisscrossed below him, Nicolás inched his way over to the bag of food. He felt around until he located it and pulled out a jar of cheese. His intestines, which had started to rumble and cramp two days before he had entered the compartment, were now even worse. His lack of physical activity combined with a slight case of nausea did not improve their condition. With something in his stomach, Nicolás reasoned, they would start working again and he could relieve himself and feel better.

Scooping out the soft yellow cheese with his index finger and popping it into his mouth, he decided that the cheese would taste better, as well as be more filling, with crackers. But just as he was reaching into the bag to retrieve them, his intestines started to work again, this time with a vengeance to make up for the days that they had been inactive.

Doubled over with a spasm that ripped through his bowels, he knew he had to do something in a hurry. He hastily threw the cheese back into the bag, dropped to his knees and not trusting himself to walk upright, crawled on the board until he reached his hammock. He stripped off his shorts and tied an additional rope tightly around his chest, securing its other end to the same steel ring on the wall.

Slowly and cautiously and still holding on to the side of the hammock with both hands, he lowered himself into the violently raging vortex below him. With the two ropes tightly wrapped around his body he wasn't too worried about being sucked into the propeller-generated whirlpool; he just wanted to relieve himself.

With a sigh of pleasure as he slipped into the water, he realized that he had also relieved himself of the suffocating heat and near asphyxiation that had been wearing him out.

"Why didn't I think of this before?" he asked himself. "Here in the water it's cooler and I can breathe more easily and my skin doesn't itch. I can relax here until the ship gets to the United States."

But after less than ten seconds, Nicolás launched himself out of the water and back into his hammock, clawing at unseen jellyfish tentacles that had attached themselves to his skin during those few seconds that he had been in the water. Frantically scraping them off, he only succeeded in spreading their glutinous toxin all over his skin, which was now a vivid red color instead of its normal dark brown.

He desperately searched the compartment for the sack of lemons he had brought with him. He finally located it and ripped the lemons open with his nails and squeezed their juice over the red burns that covered his entire body. Although the acidic juice of the lemons burned his skin, it somewhat alleviated the agony of the jellyfish burns, and he returned to and sank back into his hammock, breathing raggedly from the exertion and pain.

After a while, when his breathing had returned to normal and the pain had subsided, he fished out the jar of petroleum jelly he had brought and spread the ointment over his cracked lips and raw skin. Then he pulled a pair of grey sweat pants and a sweatshirt from his bag and put them on. They were as soaking wet as all the clothes in the bag, but he knew that the ship was heading north and he could feel the temperature starting to drop already.

He settled back down into his hammock and, laying on his side with his hand supporting his head, he gazed down into the water from which he had recently emerged. In its depths he could see the phosphorescent threads of thousands of luminous glow worms and jellyfish, their scintillating lights reminding him of a million flashes of fireworks at Christmas, spiraling and sparkling in the wake of the propeller. "How could anything so beautiful be so painful?" he wondered.

He closed his eyes and fell asleep.

A change in the pulsations of the motor awakened him with a start and he realized that the water which had been a few inches below his feet since the ship had gotten underway, now was halfway up his back as he lay in the swaying hammock. He sat upright at once and was horrified to feel the water splashing around his waist.

"What's going on out there?" he asked himself rhetorically. But he already knew the answer.

What Nicolás could feel but not see was the Bright Eagle plowing its way through the thirty-five foot waves of a tropical storm.

The walls of water crashed over the supertanker's bow and washed over the deck, which now that the ship was almost fully loaded with its cargo of oil, lay low in the water. The ship was built to withstand a storm like this and, although the waves buffeted the superstructure at the stern containing the crew's and captain's quarters as well as the bridge, it was in no danger of floundering.

The keening winds heaved the waves high into the air and hurled turbulent towers of water over the ship. With

winds between forty-five and fifty-five knots, the storm wasn't
technically a hurricane; there had to be winds of over sixty-
three knots for that. But for Nicolás, trapped in the constricted confines of the rudder compartment, it was a moot point.

Stretching his arms high in the air and touching the wall
of the compartment above him, he found a place where he
could tie his hammock even higher. After a half a dozen
attempts, he finally secured the ropes to their new position. It
was not too soon, because by now the ship was heaving mighti-
ly through the waves and the water in the compartment had
reached his chest as he sat clutching the sides of the hammock.

He started to pray.

It was the only thing he could do. He prayed more pas-
sionately than he had ever prayed in his life, and although he
couldn't even hear his own voice above the din of the propeller, the words had a calming effect and restored his tranquility.

He knew that the waves that surged and receded in the
rudder trunk echoed the rhythmic intensity of the storm that
the ship was passing through. He had been a sailor long
enough to know that this storm would last for hours and
would increase in intensity and that the water inside the compartment would rise higher and higher until the ship finally
navigated through the tempest. Praying that the water would
not reach the top of the compartment before that occurred, he
closed his eyes against the splashing water that was now over
his shoulders. He prayed more fervently than ever, knowing
that he was trapped and that his life was in God's hands.

It was his fourth day at sea.

Shivering in his saturated clothes, Nicolás sat on one of
the boards near the wall of the compartment.

He hadn't slept at all for the last fifteen hours, but his
back ached from remaining in one position for so long and he
wanted to sit up for a while. Although he still had one rope
tied around his waist, he hadn't wanted to release the grip of
his hands from the hammock during the storm. He had been
afraid that if he closed his eyes, he would never open them
again.

The ship sailed swiftly through the now gentle waves and,
as the water splashed against his feet, Nicolás felt his eyelids
getting heavy at last. He folded his arms across his chest,
leaned back against the wall and closed his eyes.

Suddenly he shrieked out in pain.

As soon as he had fallen asleep, the back of his neck had grazed the wall, which was covered with the remnants of jellyfish tentacles that the storm had splashed on them. He reacted reflexively to the intense burning sensation on his skin.

Deep in sleep and blissfully unaware of the fact that he was sitting on a plank of wood suspended over nothing but a propeller and the Atlantic Ocean, he fell off the board. He awakened immediately, screaming more in terror than in pain as he plunged headfirst into the water. Luçkily, the rope around his waist had not snapped.

With both hands, he grabbed onto it, praying that the other end would stay securely fastened. The rope had never been forced to carry his full weight before and his one hundred-and-seventy-five pounds combined with the suction of the whirlpool was creating an even greater strain on its fibers.

Hand over hand he pulled himself upwards until finally he reached his hammock and flipped himself gratefully inside. The water splashing against his feet was getting colder by the hour and Nicolás realized the ship was in northern waters, although he had no idea where he was. He had thought that the Bright Eagle was headed for Florida and was therefore surprised how cold the water was. Believing that he was almost at his destination, he tied himself even more tightly into his hammock and with a euphoric smile on his face, fell into a deep sleep for the first time in the five days since his odyssey had begun.

Five and a half hours later, a shudder coursing through his body woke him up. His teeth started chattering audibly, and he started rubbing the wet sweat suit that covered his arms and legs with his stiff fingers. He had never been so cold in his life.

It was the morning of the sixth day.

"We should have reached the United States by now," he thought to himself, wondering when he would be able to get out of the rudder compartment.

But the only thing he was reaching was the end of his body's capacity to withstand much more. He felt flushed with fever in spite of the cold, and while the burns caused by the jellyfish had faded and his skin had restored itself to its normal color, the saltwater had covered it with a rash of fine pimples.

When he had awakened, he found his face, neck and chest covered with blood. His nose, which had never stopped dripping blood, was now an open faucet. "I have to do something to stop this bleeding," he told himself with alarm. But he couldn't stop the ship, and that was the only thing that would stop the flow of blood from his ruptured membranes.

"Here I am," he berated his body that was about to betray him, "about to reach success at last and my body's falling apart."

He tried to lift his spirits by reminding himself how different his life was going to be. "Soon I won't have to put up with hunger like a rat or a dog. Soon I won't have to listen to my friends telling me that my family's so poor that in my house when the stork came to bring my little sister, we cut its neck off, fried it and ate it because we didn't have money to buy food.... I won't have to listen to them joking that when the garbage man stops in front of our house, my mother tells me, 'Nicolás, take three bags.' No, I won't have to listen to them anymore...I'll come back from the United States rich...and their mouths will drop open when they see me.

"First, I'll try to get a job around the docks...cleaning the bathrooms in bars or restaurants...that will also solve the problem of eating. Then, when I've learned enough English, I'll get a better job and a decent place to live. My grandmother always said that each new language that you learn is an open door to a new life...and that's what I'm going to have... a new life."

6 A.M.

John Paul Cummings, a sergeant with the New York City Police Department, arrived at work and went straight to his office. As the supervisor of the twenty-four-man scuba team, he wanted to get an early start on what he was pretty sure was going to be a busy day.

He had been in the NYPD for ten years, and he was especially proud of his work on the scuba team. Not only was he in charge of the men, but he was also responsible for the entire operation of the scuba team. In spite of the cold weather, he eagerly looked forward to today's investigation.

John Conti of the United States Customs Service had telephoned him before dawn to inform him of the day's assignment. An oil tanker, the Bright Eagle, had just anchored off Staten Island in New York harbor, and U.S. Customs wanted to get a search underway first thing in the morning. Although there had not been any tip-off that there might be contraband on board, the very fact that the ship had come directly from Colombia made an inspection almost mandatory.

With at least eighty percent of the world's cocaine being produced, manufactured and exported from Colombia, U.S. Customs tried to inspect ships coming from Colombia as often as possible. Conti was a member of FIST, the Freighter Interdiction Surveillance Team of the U.S. Customs Service, that searched commercial vessels for contraband and held meetings regularly with personnel from shipping lines. As the special agent in this case, Conti was responsible for the investigation from the beginning to the end.

Sgt. Cummings mentally reviewed the facts about the assignment that Conti had told him earlier that morning.

There was to be a two-prong inspection of the tanker. A team of eight Customs inspectors led by Jack Lane, the supervisor of CET, the Customs Enforcement Team, would board and search the interior of the ship, while at the same time, Cummings' team of divers would make a visual inspection of the surface and exterior of the hull and those compartments, or voids, that were accessible only from the outside of the ship.

Conti had informed him that Jho Tae Ho, the captain of the Bright Eagle, was Korean, as was his entire crew. The captain could speak and read English, but the members of his crew were not able to speak or understand any language other than their native tongue. The Bright Eagle was registered in Monrovia and had been loaded with its cargo of oil during the night of January 17 at the port of Manomal, Colombia. Immediately afterwards, the tanker had left the fueling station at two o'clock in the morning and had proceeded non-stop to the United States where it had arrived in the early morning hours of January 24. Its final destination was Roseton, a small town north of New York City on the Hudson River, where its cargo of oil was scheduled to be unloaded.

Sgt. Cummings called his men together in the squad room and briefed them on the day's assignment.

8 A.M.

The men of the scuba team went to the storage room and started removing all the gear they would need that day.

They realized that they would have quite a few problems with this assignment. For one thing, it was 17 degrees at one o'clock in the morning, which meant that the water temperature would not be above 36 degrees, and even with a dry suit to insulate them and protect them from the temperature, they would not be able to withstand the cold water for more than a half-hour before they would start to feel the effects of hypothermia.

Another problem that they were going to have to deal with was one they could not change: the visibility of the water around the ship. The waters of New York harbor were notoriously murky. Not only was there silt, marine life and debris that normally reduced visibility, but there were also all the products of pollution in the water. Because the Hudson River emptied into New York harbor, its current agitated all the particles, which virtually prevented light from penetrating more than a few inches.

In addition to the near-freezing temperature and almost zero-visibility of the water, the men knew from past experience that there would be a third obstacle in their assignment today: the reverse tide, also known as a rip tide, that was present in New York Harbor. They knew that it could be fatal. Although most scuba deaths were caused by panic, carelessness, poor judgment and practices that were clearly unsafe, rip tides contributed highly to the mortality statistics.

The rip tide occurred because the Hudson River, which was constantly discharging its water into the Atlantic Ocean, created a current that was always running towards the sea. This current was on the surface of the water and was not dangerous. However, when the tide from the ocean was coming in, it created a current that flowed under the outgoing current and headed towards the land. This created a very dangerous situation for anyone swimming or diving in the water at the time, because either of the two opposing currents could pull someone in the opposite direction from which they headed.

The usual early morning banter was subdued as the men mentally reviewed the briefing while getting their gear ready for the day's assignment. Removing thermal underwear, heavy insulated socks, neoprene gloves and boots and the orange and blue dry suits from the shelf in the closet, they stacked everything neatly in a pile outside the door.

Turning to the next closet, they took out their scuba gear. They removed the adjustable fins and masks and then the weight belts, which they checked to see if the quick-release mechanisms were working smoothly. They made sure that there were enough underwater watches, depth gauges, compasses, decompression meters and knives for all divers. The divers left all the gear inside the building while they went outside to the storage shed to remove the air tanks that they would be taking with them. They checked the pressure in each tank and made sure that the air was good. Then they double-checked the regulators, making sure that the main valves were open and that the reserve valves were in the "OFF" position.

The last item removed from storage was the Zodiac, a large black and red inflatable craft that was propelled by an outboard motor. It would ferry the divers back and forth between Police Launch 8 and the dive site. After checking its condition, they prepared the lines, cables, shackles and winches they would need. They stacked them to the side of the Zodiac in preparation for their departure.

Then they went back into the building to suit up for the dive.

The divers entered the locker room, removed their street clothes and donned their diving clothes, scrutinizing the dry suits for any hairline cracks or pinholes. They examined their masks and regulators. Before they put on their neoprene rubber boots, they checked them also for any pinholes or cracks which would allow the icy water to penetrate. They picked up the rest of their gear and carried everything outside to the van and stowed it neatly inside.

Now that they were suited up, they were anxious to get over to the ship and eager to get the search underway. They took their seats in the van and waited for González to join them. He had been preparing everything and going over the details of the operation with Cummings and Conti since the seven o'clock briefing had ended. González was the certified dive master of the Harbor Unit Scuba team and had been part of the scuba team for the last four of his eight-year police department career. He took pride in the fact that he had reached his present position and had acquired his certificates mostly through on-the-job training and not just by formal instruction.

González stepped into the van and took his position behind the steering wheel as he joked with the men to lighten the tension. The apprehension that he also felt was not apparent in his voice, although he could feel it in his gut. He had lost count of how many dives and searches he had undertaken in the last four years, but he still experienced the same sensation before each dive.

He drove through the nearly deserted streets until he got to the pier where Police Launch 8 was waiting. Some of the divers clambered aboard while the rest handed over the gear from the van. Sgt. Cummings and Agent Conti arrived at the pier, climbed on board the police launch, and silently watched the scuba team get ready.

Police Launch 1 started its engine and the eight U.S. Customs Inspectors standing on deck braced their legs in anticipation of any sudden movement. As members of CET, they had received special training and had extensive experience in the investigation of vessels and cargo shipments. Their assignment that morning was to inspect the interior of the tanker while, at the same time, the scuba team made a search of the exterior.

9 A.M.

Police Launch 8 pulled up to the Bright Eagle, and Sgt. Cummings and Agent Conti walked up the narrow gangway and came on board. They nodded curtly to the crewman on deck, who then accompanied them to the captain's quarters.

Captain Ho awaited them on the bridge along with his chief engineer. The engineer pulled out the blueprints of the ship and showed them the underwater compartments. The captain pointed out the rudder-trunk area and other places located towards the stern of the ship.

Cummings told the engineer to make sure that all the engines were shut down so that no propellers would be turning while the divers were underwater conducting the search. After briefly conferring with Cummings, Conti remained with Captain Ho in his quarters and then returned to Police Launch 8.

The eight Customs inspectors disembarked from Police Launch 1 and climbed up the metal steps onto the tanker. Waiting for them on deck were the eight members of the crew who were selected to accompany them. Because none of the crew members understood English, the agents were forced to use hand gestures until finally everyone was teamed up. The pairs headed in all directions, each assigned to a different part of the vessel, and started to methodically search all the areas on deck.

Nicolás squeezed his thighs together, crossed his arms across his chest, and placed his fists under his armpits. The narrow board that he sat on vibrated with the uncontrollable shaking of his body as he mouthed a silent prayer that his ordeal would be over soon.

He didn't know how much longer he could stand it.

Suddenly he heard the sound of small motors approaching the ship.

The level of the noise increased and seemed to be getting closer and closer with each second. Nicolás' heart audibly pounded in his chest as he sat there, shaking now more from fear than from cold. As the rumble of a motor got closer to the stern of the ship, he could distinguish the sound of men's voices talking and shouting to one another.

His fear turned to sheer terror.

He was trapped!

The frigid water and other obstacles that had convinced him to stay in the compartment now seemed like minor incon-

veniences compared to the threatening presence of men in
boats, hovering close to the hull. Although Nicolás did not
understand a word that the men were saying to each other,
waves of panic washed over him as the adrenaline in his body
instinctively told him that he was in great danger.

At the same time that the U.S. Customs agents were fan-
ning out to begin their search of the Bright Eagle, the men of
the scuba team on Police Launch 8 completed their final
preparations. Sgt. Cummings went over the details of the
underwater compartments that he had just learned from Captain Ho and the ship's engineer. Once again he reminded
them to take extra precautions because of the rip tide and
the near-zero visibility.

He informed officers Kevin Brodley and Mike Rivedinera
that they would be the first team in the water and that
González would remain in the Zodiac as their safety tender.
Brodley and Rivedinera grinned at each other, glad to be
working together again. Each had the utmost confidence in
the other's ability and knowledge.

González helped the other divers get the gear together
and then started to set up the lines and equipment in the
Zodiac. Brodley and Rivedinera walked over to the side of
Police Launch 8. They held onto the railing and swung around
and down into the large black and red raft. González started
up its motor and immediately turned it around and headed
toward the bow of the ship, where the search would begin.

As the Zodiac skimmed along the icy surface of the water,
Brodley and Rivedinera got ready to dive. They sloshed some
water into their open-heeled fins and firmly pulled them over
their boots. Taking even greater care and more time with
their masks and regulators, they spread a thin film of saliva
over the inside surface of the mask and inserted the mouthpieces of the regulators into their mouths and clamped their
teeth on them. Although they had already examined the air
cylinders, they checked the pressure again, just in case the
valves had opened up slightly on the way over from the police
station.

Each diver made sure that his own harness and that of his partner was adjusted properly. Then, after they had attached their regulators to the cylinders, they listened for any sound of escaping air which would indicate that there was a leak around the high-pressure block of the cylinder. Finally, after they inhaled and exhaled through their regulators to make sure that the units were functioning properly, they removed their mouthpieces and waited to get into position.

Brodley turned to Rivedinera, seated across from him in the raft, and gave him a "thumbs-up" sign when González pulled alongside the hull and unfurled the red and white diver's flag that indicated to anyone in the vicinity that a dive was in progress. After uncoiling the nylon safety line, González attached one guide line to each diver and made sure that all the knots and buckles were securely fastened. Because of the zero-visibility of the water, these lines were the only links that he would have with the divers once they entered the water.

Finally González attached the six-foot-long "buddy line" between Brodley and Rivedinera. The buddy system was not just a good idea, it was a mandatory safety procedure that held that no diver, regardless of proficiency or experience, should dive alone, but must be accompanied by another qualified diver.

In good visibility, ten to twelve feet were recommended, but that morning the divers wanted to remain closer together not only in case of an emergency, but also to double-check each other's examination of the hull. They would only be able to communicate with each other by pulling on the rope, utilizing the same signals that they used when they sent messages to the surface.

Brodley sat quietly on top of the Zodiac's inflated side, his feet resting inside the raft, while Rivedinera, sitting next to him on the gunwale, made sure that his neoprene hood was sealed tightly around his face and neck. Then each diver donned his mask by first placing the mask over the upper part of his face and enclosing his eyes and nose. After making sure that the flange was sealed tightly against his face, each man pressed the mask to his face, pulled the strap over his hooded head, and checked the fit.

The two divers saluted González with a "thumbs-up" sign, inserted their regulators and clamped their teeth on the

mouthpieces. They locked eyes through their masks and wordlessly nodded in agreement. Holding their faceplates with one
hand and securing all other equipment with the other, they
took a deep breath and let themselves fall backwards off the
side of the Zodiac.

With a quiet splash, they entered the icy water of New
York harbor.

As soon as they were submerged, they immediately tilted
their heads backwards towards the surface of the water a few
inches above them. With one hand still pressing against the
top and both sides of the mask's faceplate, they exhaled force-
fully through their noses into the mask, expelling all the
water out of the mask and assuring a tight seal. The imperme-
able outer layer of the dry suit prevented the frigid water from
reaching their bodies; the warm air trapped between the layers of their clothing added extra insulation against the cold.
They could feel the water on the parts of their faces that were
not protected by their hoods or covered by their masks, and
they were thankful for the insulation that their suits provided.

They switched on their powerful waterproof flashlights
and turned towards the massive hull of the Bright Eagle
looming beside them. They could see almost nothing except
the light from the flashlights reflected back to them by the
particles of silt and debris that were suspended in the nearly
opaque water. They realized that they were going to have to
search the hull of the vessel by feeling the sides of the ship
with their gloved hands.

The eight Customs inspectors, each accompanied by a
crew member, continued to search the interior of the ship. The
Bright Eagle was longer than two football fields and, although
it was basically just a huge floating container for the oil stored
in its hold, there were many places where contraband could be
concealed. Therefore, the agents searched every inch of the
ship's interior.

First they checked the crew's personal living quarters and
all their related work areas; then they examined all the storage rooms on deck and below deck. Drawing on their extensive
training and experience, the agents systematically investigat-
ed all the known locations that had been utilized in the past
by experienced drug dealers, who daily seemed to be using

more and more sophisticated locations and techniques to bring contraband into the United States.

10 A.M.

Conti, who had remained in the captain's quarters on the bridge, held a mug of steaming black coffee in his hands as Captain Ho delicately sipped tea from a similar mug. They spoke mainly of the search and inspection. From time to time, Conti pulled back his cuff to check the time on his wristwatch. There had been no news from either the Customs agents on board nor from the NYPD scuba team below.

Captain Ho sat back in his chair and reminisced with Conti about his seventeen years at sea, ten years of it working as a captain of a merchant ship. Since July of 1990, he had served as captain of the Bright Eagle. Although the captain had been born in Seoul, Korea, he spoke English fairly well. In fact he had studied English in Korea since junior high school and had obtained his radio-telephone operator's license, which required communication in English. In addition, as captain of a vessel, he was required to communicate in English over the radio. Conti and Captain Ho traded stories back and forth, each looking at his own watch every five to ten minutes, each wondering how the search was proceeding.

Brodley spread both arms backwards in a slow breast stroke and gently flicked his ankles as his fins propelled him along. Rivedinera, tethered to him, fluttered his fins as the nylon rope and the propulsion generated by his kicking moved him along a few feet in back of Brodley. They were searching for something unusual. From past experience and from the information at the briefing that morning, they knew that there was a good chance that they would find drugs somewhere on board the ship.

Carefully feeling the hull with one gloved hand and holding the flashlight with the other, they searched for a torpedo-shaped metal object that might have been magnetically

attached to the ship. They moved along the starboard side of
the ship towards the area known as the sea chest, a large
compartment located underwater in the bottom of the ship
that provided access to the intake of sea water that cooled the
engines while the ship was moving. The plan was that each
team was to carefully search the sea chest because contraband
had been discovered there in other vessels. There was no danger of going near it now. Cummings had been assured by Captain Ho and his chief engineer that no engines would be
running while the search was underway.

Brodley and Rivedinera directed their flashlight beams
onto all the walls and into all the corners of the sea chest and
ran their hands over the cold steel. They discovered nothing.

Suddenly, as Brodley was going under the ship to check
the area one last time, the rip tide grabbed him and he started
flailing his arms in front of him as he tried to halt his backward motion. He struggled for a few terrified minutes, trying
to fight the reverse current, when with a dull thud he bumped
the back of his neck on the bottom of the ship.

Rivedinera, a few feet away and attached to Brodley, felt
himself being tugged in the opposite direction from which he
was heading. He realized at once what was happening as he
was propelled backwards by the current over to his partner.
By the time Brodley looked up and saw Rivedinera peering
into his face mask to see if he was okay, he had regained control over his direction. He gave the thumbs-up sign to his partner, and together they started moving forward again along the
hull of the ship.

After making their way back to the bow, the two divers
continued their search on the port side of the ship. González,
in the Zodiac, followed them, watching their stream of air bubbles in the water as the inflated raft bumped the flank of the
massive ship beside him.

Nicolás sat shivering on the wooden board, his heart
hammering in his chest and his mind searching wildly for a
solution as he fought to overcome his feelings of fear and fore-
boding. Although the noise of the small motors had faded
away in the distance and he could no longer hear the sound of

men's voices calling out to each other, he knew that it would be foolish to assume that the danger had passed. With this realization, a wave of despair washed over him, and he sat there, staring into the void below him as he awaited with dread whatever would happen next.

11 AM

Rivedinera gave the buddy line three short pulls to signal to Brodley that he was ready to ascend. Then he yanked the safety rope that was attached to the Zodiac with the identical signal so that González, on board in the raft above them, would realize that they were coming up.

Brodley's head broke the icy surface of the water, followed immediately by Rivedinera's. Brodley shook his head from side to side and jerked his thumb down in a negative response to the questioning glance of González, who was busy pulling the safety rope, hand over hand, into the bottom of the Zodiac. Both divers had already removed their mouthpieces and began telling González about their fruitless search as he extended his right hand, first to one man and then to the other, and helped them climb back into the raft.

Brodley and Rivedinera sat down in the bottom of the craft and removed their face masks. The dive had not lasted long, but they were both physically tired and emotionally drained. There was always danger during a dive due to the water conditions, the current and the location of the dive site itself, and they were especially glad that this one was over.

They were disappointed that their careful inspection of the hull had not uncovered anything unusual. It was always a great feeling when a dive resulted in the discovery of a hidden cache of drugs, weapons or other contraband that someone had attempted to bring into the United States. Although both Brodley and Rivedinera liked scuba diving for its own sake, they were dedicated members of the New York City Police Department and they realized that it was the end result that really counted...finding hidden contraband and apprehending the people that had concealed it.

González started up the motor on the Zodiac once again and ferried the two divers back to Police Launch 8, where the other members of the scuba team were awaiting their turn to dive. He threw a rope to one of the men on the launch, climbed out of the raft and quickly went onto the deck of Launch 8.

Brodley and Rivedinera followed him on board. The two divers removed their scuba gear and placed the masks, regulators and other equipment into the empty lockers on the boat. Everything would be washed, thoroughly checked and put away in the storage rooms back at the scuba team's headquarters in Bay Ridge, Brooklyn.

While the divers were taking off their equipment, González started to don his own diving gear. He was going to be part of the next team of divers and was eager to get into the water. Tommy Burn and he were going to search the rear section of the Bright Eagle from the sea chest down to the rudder trunk.

González went into the cabin to get his mask and fins. Burn, who was already suited up, helped him don the harness and tank. They made sure that the release buckles on their weight belts operated smoothly and checked the sheaths attached to their harnesses to make sure that their knives were inside. They would need the knives to cut themselves loose if they got caught on anything. They carefully examined each other's equipment, knowing that the time checking all valves, hoses and regulators before a dive was time well spent once they were under the water. With their fins flopping noisily on the deck, they walked awkwardly through the covered cabin of Police Launch 8 and boarded the Zodiac that was tethered alongside. Mike Rivedinera climbed aboard the raft right behind them. On this dive he would act as the safety tender for the two men in the water.

The Zodiac's motor sputtered to life, and Rivedinera steered the craft towards the rear of the vessel. Once alongside the stern of the tanker, he stopped the engine and raised the red and white diving flag. González and Burn made a last-minute check of their masks and regulators, connected the buddy line to each other's harness, and made sure that the rope that joined them to the Zodiac was secure. Satisfied that everything was in order, they sat side by side on the raft's gunwale, simultaneously leaned over backwards and slipped into the icy water.

12 noon

In Captain Ho's quarters, Conti checked his watch again. He knew that if nothing had been found after two hours of searching by both the Customs agents and the scuba divers, there was probably no contraband on board.

The agents worked their way back to the bridge. They had examined every possible hiding place of the huge tanker and had not detected anything out of the ordinary or even suspicious.

Burn switched on the heavy-duty flashlight, but the normally powerful beam of light barely penetrated the murky water, the particles of debris and silt that were suspended in the water reflecting the beam of light and making it almost impossible for him to see anything. It reminded him of one night the previous year when he was driving through a fierce winter snowstorm and the beams of his headlights reflected by the swirling snow made the visibility worse instead of better.

González, attached to him, held his hands straight out in front of his body as he tried to feel his way towards the ship. He alternately flexed his ankles, and the broad fins propelled him closer to the hull. As soon as he felt the cold steel under his gloved hand, he gave one sharp tug on the line which signaled Burn to stop. Burn clipped the flashlight to his harness and then he and González, each with both hands remaining in contact with the hull, worked their way down the side of the ship. Although the flashlight was still switched on, they could have had their eyes closed for all the illumination it provided as they slowly continued investigating the hull with their hands.

12:05 P.M.

González gave two pulls on the buddy line and signaled to Burn that he was going down to the rudder trunk. He released his hold on the hull and, with Burn in tow, swam down to the massive rudder. Hand over hand, both divers felt along the hull, trying to find anything that had been clandestinely attached to the surface of the metal.

Suddenly, as they came around the outside edge of the rudder, the reverse current loosened their grip and they were swept away from the ship. Cummings had warned them about the rip tide that they would encounter, but they had not realized the strength of it until they were yanked away by its force. Both men literally swam for their lives. Because they were attached to each other, they knew that survival depended on coordinating their movements and regaining control of their direction. After a few frantic minutes, the strong stroking of their arms, aided by the vigorous kicking of their feet, enabled them to swim against the powerful current.

Their hearts were pounding in their chests when they finally reached the rudder again. They considered themselves lucky that they had found it at all, because although their flashlights clipped to their belts were switched on, it was impossible to see anything through all the silt and particles of garbage that were suspended in the water.

Not wishing to be swept away again, they clung to the rudder with one hand while they painstakingly searched its metallic surface with the other. Then, with Burn swimming alongside him, González grabbed the rudder shaft and with both of his gloved hands slipping on the slick metal, he inched his way upwards.

Nicolás realized with a sudden rush of alarm that the sound of a motor was again approaching the Bright Eagle.

He held his breath and prayed that it was just a boat passing alongside the ship. His heart pounded in his chest and in spite of the cold, a hot flush of fear washed over him as he heard the sound of the small boat stop and pull right next to him on the other side of the hull.

Nicolás could not believe his eyes when faint lights appeared in the water below. At first he thought that it was just his imagination, but as he continued to watch, the submerged lights became brighter and more distinct.

With mounting terror, he saw that they were moving from side to side as though in search of something. He uncrossed his arms and held onto the board with both hands as he hunched over and stared in disbelief and horror at the shifting lights. Because he had been living in almost total darkness for nearly a week, it took his eyes a while to focus, but they were functioning perfectly a few seconds later when he discerned the forms of the two scuba divers.

Terrified now, he looked first to the right and then to the left, searching for any small space in which he could conceal himself. But the cramped compartment in which he was entombed offered no such refuge.

Unable to find a way out of his desperate situation, he began to tremble as he stared with morbid fascination at the divers moving in the water below him. One of them was moving slowly alongside the bulkhead while the other was approaching the now motionless propeller, his light cutting a cloudy swath through the water.

Nicolás could hear the bubbles of the divers breaking the surface of the water. Suddenly a blinding light blazed in the rudder trunk. He instinctively squeezed his eyes shut against the intruding illumination, his widely dilated pupils contracting painfully.

When he managed to open his eyes a second later, he saw the two upturned hooded heads of the scuba divers. One of the men aimed the beam of the flashlight upwards and around the rudder trunk.

González held the flashlight at a forty-five degree angle and pointed it upwards to where the ceiling and the walls met. He had been instructed to take special care in searching this compartment because the location and its unique features were common knowledge to anyone who knew anything about ships.

Very slowly and methodically, he directed the light on the rusted walls. His examination of the wall on his left yielded nothing unusual, but a few seconds later, the beam of the flashlight revealed three large brown bags situated on a protruding platform with a smaller white bag placed on top of them. González grinned with satisfaction and turned to Burn to see if he had also seen the bags. Tommy nodded in agreement and gave him a "thumbs up" as he stared at the four bags they had just discovered. Then he turned the flashlight to scan the rest of the compartment.

Suddenly, the light washed over Nicolás, and as it stabbed painfully into his eyes, he realized that he had been spotted.

"Ya!" yelled the diver as soon as he saw the light reflected in Nicolás' eyes.

Nicolás sprang to his feet and quickly balanced himself on the wooden board. The diver had obviously seen him. The hoarse shout that he had heard told him that the diver had been shocked to find a person in the compartment. Even though the diver wore a mask which covered most of his face, Nicolás was near enough to see the expression of surprise mixed with fear in the man's eyes.

González hit the release valve on his suit and frantically tried to dump the air out. The extra buoyancy that the air provided, which had made his movements in the water less fatiguing, was now a hindrance that was preventing him from escaping as rapidly as possible.

González was terrified that the person whose eyes the flashlight had revealed might be pointing a gun at him even now as he prepared to dive under the surface of the water. He quickly inserted his mouthpiece and bit down hard. Then he extended his arms straight in front of him, rested his chin against his chest and tucked his head between his arms. He raised both legs simultaneously until they were resting on the surface of the water and kicked powerfully with both feet. With a noisy splash he dove under the water. He didn't know if the person that he had seen had any weapons, but he wasn't about to stick around to find out.

Tommy Burn dove down under the water right beside him. He was also trying to get away as quickly as possible. In the small space of the compartment he was an easy target, and he didn't want to stay there any longer than he had to.

As the terrified divers turned and kicked their feet to propel themselves downward as fast as they could, their fins splashed water over Nicolás and his already saturated clothing. Nicolás grunted with silent satisfaction as he saw one of the men bump into the rudder's axle in his desperate attempt to make a hasty exit. Then, the only thing he could see in the water was the spreading swirl of bubbles left in the wake of the departing divers.

Two seconds later even the air bubbles had disappeared from view as Nicolás crouched at the far edge of the plank, his back still against the wall in his futile attempt to conceal himself. He forced himself to take a deep breath of the dank air in order to slow down the rapid rhythm of his heart that was pounding in his chest. He couldn't believe that after nearly a week of being entombed in this cramped hole and after nearly a week of surviving on a daily ration of a few bites of food and a few sips of water, that it would end like this. He couldn't believe that after a week of suffering through the darkness and the noise and the constant threat of the deadly propeller and the heat of the tropics and the intense cold of the northern waters, that he would be discovered just when he was so close to the end of his ordeal, so close to the freedom and to the new life that he had been longing for all these years.

He rubbed his eyes and stared into the dark void of the compartment.

The young boy rubbed his eyes and gazed at the small boats arriving and sailing away. He sat cross-legged on the pier, watching the sailors and fishermen hurrying back and forth between the docks and the streets of Turbo. Barefoot, he ran after them, the laughter of their easy camaraderie ringing in his ears as they strode towards the cantinas in the low red-roofed, wooden buildings that lined the waterfront.

They were his heroes, these mysterious vagabonds who lived a life seemingly unfettered by the cares and concerns of day-to-day existence. They were his idols, these descendants of pirates and buccaneers and slaves who lived a life more at home on the ocean than on land. And young Nicolás wanted to be just like them when he grew up.

Born and living in Turbo, a small coastal town in the northwestern part of Colombia, had instilled in him a love of the sea for as long as he could remember.

Turbo, situated at the Gulf of Uraba, on the Caribbean
Sea, is very close to the border of Panama. Its population
exceeds 47,000 inhabitants, forty percent of whom are Black,
the descendants of slaves, and the rest are White or a combi-
nation of the Black, Indian and White races.

It is a rapidly growing municipality, famous nationally
and internationally as the birthplace of Perea and other soccer
heroes and for the production and exportation of bananas. It is
a free port where freighters from all parts of the world arrive
to fill their holds and where there is the constant movement of
small boats ferrying men and goods back and forth from the
shallow coastal waters to the ships anchored in the Gulf of
Uraba.

There is a great disparity of income. The small percentage
of the descendants of the Spanish conquistadors and colonists,
who own most of the factories and offices as well as run the
local government, live in relative luxury, while the descendants of the African slaves and the indigenous native population barely survive from day to day by fishing or farming.

Although education is free, it is not compulsory, and the
poverty-stricken members of the population are more concerned with filling their stomachs than their minds.

Nicolás was no exception.

As a young boy he went fishing with one of his uncles who
felt sorry for the fatherless boy and took Nicolás along whenever he could. Instead of a rod and a reel, he and his uncle
fished at night from a tiny boat, armed with a flashlight and a
spear. As the fish swam silently below the surface of the
water, Nicolás and his uncle would take turns spearing them
as they became motionless, transfixed by the beam of light.
Then they would take the fish to town and try to sell them. If
they were unable to find enough buyers, they would distribute
the fish to their many relatives for the next day's meal.

Nur, his mother, was two months short of her eighteenth
birthday when Nicolás was delivered by Jacinta, the local
midwife, one rainy day in September, 1966. Listening to his
first cries were Jessid and Yaned, Nicolás' brother and sister,
who were one- and three-years old.

The family lived in one of the poorest neighborhoods of
Turbo: the Barrio Obrero. As the name of the district signifies,
it was the home of the working-class people who barely eked
out their day-to-day existence. The unpaved streets, which

gave off clouds of dust in the dry seasons, were rivers of mud when it rained. Nur's house, like all the others in the barrio, was constructed of wide wooden boards and covered by a metal roof. It contained two rooms and a kitchen. Water for drinking and cooking was collected in large barrels outside the door because Turbo, like most of the small towns in the area, lacked potable water.

The early years of Nicolás' life were no different than those of the other children of the barrio. Surrounded by his brothers and sisters and cousins of all ages, he ran barefoot and half-naked through the unpaved streets, playing and getting into mischief. Store-bought toys were not a luxury; they were non-existent. He and his companions devised and constructed games and toys from pieces of wood, stones and discarded items that they found in the trash.

From an early age he was a born mimic who sent people into gales of laughter as he altered his voice and even transformed his face and physical appearance in realistic portrayals of family members and neighbors. No one was safe from his impersonations. This talent, combined with his wide grin and cheerful disposition, made him the favorite of the family.

This all changed with the arrival of his stepfather when he was six-years old.

Maybe it was because Nicolás was mischievous or because he was the comedian of the family, always pulling pranks and making people laugh. Or maybe it was just because his stepfather, a sullen, sadistic alcoholic, had no patience for his playful stepson.

Whatever the reason, life for Nicolás soon became a living nightmare. Nicolás found himself at the receiving end of occasional slaps which rapidly escalated into almost daily beatings. Nur, herself fearful of her husband's quick temper and even quicker fists, while at the same time in desperate need of the money he provided for her increasingly growing family, begged him repeatedly to leave the child alone, but to no avail.

Nicolás' only means of defense was to try to stay out of his stepfather's way. He would run out of the house and hide when he saw his tormentor approaching in the distance.

When her husband arrived home, Nur would nervously lie, assuring him that she had no idea of her son's whereabouts. Nicolás would return only when he was sure that his stepfather was sleeping or had left the house again.

Luckily the man was employed as a mechanic and was away most of the time, repairing the motors of the many boats lined up at the docks in Turbo. But he never came home at the same time every day, and sometimes Nicolás didn't get a chance to get out of the house before his stepfather spotted him. By the time his stepfather arrived home, already drunk from the countless bottles of beer that he had consumed while working in the blazing tropical sun, he was mad at his boss, mad at the broken engines, and mad at the world in general. And Nicolás, who was usually in the kitchen helping his mother prepare the evening meal, was the immediate and customary target of his stepfather's wrath.

His mother pleaded and argued and tried to protect her young son, often standing between the child and his attacker and receiving some of the blows herself, but this only seemed to make her husband angrier. The beatings became more sadistic, so she stopped trying to intervene. Instead, she kept a vigil at the open door, keeping watch on the street as the sky grew darker and her husband's arrival time grew near, so that she could warn Nicolás of the approach of his tormentor.

Nur continued this strategy for a few months and was occasionally successful in keeping Nicolás out of the clutches of his stepfather. But with four children younger than Nicolás and two older, his mother found it impossible to protect her six-year-old son.

Finally, after two weeks in which his stepfather didn't emerge from his drunken stupor except to stagger from room to room looking for something else to drink, after two weeks in which Nicolás' beatings were punctuated with punches and kicks, after two weeks in which her son's tortured screams filled the air and sent the younger children running terrified to her side, after two weeks in which she watched Nicolás stumble and trip, barely able to see through eyelids swollen from crying, she realized that she had to take him away from the claws of her sadistic husband.

Afraid that the next beating Nicolás received would kill him, she sent him to live with his grandmother, Ana Teheran.

Ana Teheran loved Nicolás more than her own children. She had begged her daughter to let Nicolás live with her, realizing that the longer her grandson stayed in the same house with his stepfather the greater were his chances of being beaten to death. But Nur had refused, insisting that she could take care of the situation. When she arrived at her daughter's house to take Nicolás home with her, she saw that her daughter had come to her senses and changed her mind not one minute too soon.

Standing in the doorway, holding on to his mother's skirt with one hand and sucking on the thumb of his other hand, was her grandson, weighing just over forty pounds but already tall for his age. His hair was dirty and matted and his bony elbows and knees were covered with crusted scabs. Dime-sized circular scars dotted his forearms where his stepfather had extinguished his smoldering cigars. Both eyes were black and blue and one eye was swollen completely shut with a ribbon of yellow pus oozing out of the corner, streaking his cheek.

After speaking to her daughter for a few minutes, Ana went into the house and checked to see if any of her other grandchildren were in a similar condition. She was relieved to find them unscathed. She hurriedly spoke a few last words to her daughter, who kept nervously looking towards the direction of the docks, afraid that her husband would come home at any minute and thwart the rescue attempt.

Nur realized that she would probably be the recipient of her husband's fury when he discovered she had sent Nicolás to live with her mother, but she hoped that his rage would be short-lived. She hoped that life would be more peaceful now that the object of his anger was no longer living at home.

Nur gave her son one last kiss and told him that she loved him and that he should obey his grandmother.

Ana Teheran stepped out of the house and stood in the street, giving a few final words of advice to her daughter. Then she laid aside the small sack of clothes that Nur had given her and crouched down on one knee on the dusty road. She was a tall woman, and her deep voice combined with her no-nonsense manner might have made her frightening and intimidating if it were not for the smile that creased her face and transformed her features when she was laughing or pleased with something.

She wasn't smiling now.

She opened her arms wide and said just one word: "Venga (come)."

Nicolás, sensing that the moment of his deliverance had finally arrived, leaped into her outstretched embrace and threw his arms around her neck.

Ana Teheran stood up and settled Nicolás on her hip. Then she picked up his small sack of belongings and said goodbye to her daughter. She knew that she needed to catch the last bus in order to get back to her house. She lived two hundred miles away, and the trip would take at least eight hours over the rough country roads, assuming the bus did not break down.

Nicolás wrapped his left arm even more tightly around his grandmother as she lifted him off the ground and he burrowed his head into the crook of her neck. He stuck his thumb in his mouth again. Years of scolding and applications of hot sauce on his fingers had not cured him of this habit, and he sucked on it furiously. He closed his eyes and never looked back as his grandmother started walking swiftly away from the only home he had ever known. Ana Teheran hoped that her daughter's husband would not pounce upon one of the other children for his sadistic ministrations now that Nicolás was gone, but she could not take all seven of the children home with her. She still had three of her own children and a few other grandchildren living with her, and just didn't have the room for his brothers and sisters.

And so Nicolás began to live with his grandmother, calling her "Mamá" and receiving from her the tenderness, love, affection and care that his mother, who he began to call "Tía" (aunt), had been afraid to show him since the arrival of his stepfather.

It was not a life of luxury or ease, but for this cowering, tortured child whose scrawny arms and legs protruded from his shorts and shirts, who hid behind his grandmother's skirts or ran into a back room at the approach of strangers, it was an oasis of peace compared with the life that he had lived with his stepfather. In his eyes, his grandmother was one of God's angels that was sent to earth. For the first time that he could remember, he felt loved, protected and safe. No longer living in fear, his appetite increased and he started to grow in width as well as in height.

His grandmother was anxious to take care of the outside of her young grandson as well as the inside, and every day after his bath she inspected him to make sure that he was clean. If the results were not to her liking, she would scrub his face and brush his fingernails until they were to her satisfaction. All too frequently she took his toothbrush and brushed his teeth again.

Every day he emerged more and more from the self-defensive barriers that he had built around himself, although he would never, ever again completely trust anybody. From all outward signs, he was soon a typical seven-year-old child, tall for his age, maybe a little more reticent than most, but one whose appearance gave no indication of the past.

His grandmother worked from before sunrise until long after nightfall every day, cooking meals and washing clothes for at least thirty men that worked in the fields and banana plantations that surrounded her small country farm. These men lived far from their families in order to find work, and sent almost all their money home. They could not pay her much, but they helped with the heavy chores and appreciated the clean clothes and the simple meals that she provided.

Nicolás followed his grandmother everywhere she went, helping her clean the house until it was spotless and assisting her in the washing and ironing of not only the family laundry but all the clothes of the men she cared for. He fed the animals, collected the hens' eggs and milked the goats and the two cows. Side by side, from sunup to sundown, Ana and her grandson labored together in the garden, in the field and in the house, talking and laughing and enjoying each other's company immensely.

The only time that his grandmother rested from her endless chores was during her daily morning and evening visits to church. She was a devout and ardent Catholic. Now that she had saved Nicolás' life, she was determined to save his soul as well.

Every morning after the floors were swept and the freshly-washed clothes were hung on the lines to dry, she took Nicolás by the hand and they walked to church. For the first few weeks, Nicolás sat when his grandmother sat, kneeled when she kneeled and stood when she stood. As she recited her prayers, Nicolás softly mumbled his own, occasionally parroting a word or two that he had just heard his grandmother say. Hearing him, his grandmother turned her head, looked at him and then shook her head in dismay. Although Nicolás tried to recite his prayers, he had trouble remembering them, and because he didn't know how to read, he could not study them from a book.

Strong in her determination to instill in her grandson the same unshakable faith and trust in God that she had, she devised a method for instruction. Every day as she cooked and cleaned and washed, she recited the prayers and the liturgy of the Mass. Nicolás, who was constantly at her side, repeated the words and the phrases over and over and over again until they were fixed in his mind. After several months of this tutoring, he was able to recite them automatically.

Nicolás accompanied his grandmother to church twice a day, and although he tried to concentrate, the droning of the priest, the buzzing of the flies in the torpid air, and the flickering of the votive candles had a soporific effect on him. All too often he found it impossible to keep his eyes open and he drifted off to sleep. As soon as his grandmother sensed the small body next to her starting to sway or slump over, she pinched his arm, not too painfully, remembering the abuse he had suffered, but hard enough to jerk him awake instantly. Then, with a severe countenance and a sibilant whisper, she reminded him of the unpleasant fate destined for those who fell asleep in church.

He forced himself to stay awake not only because he wanted to avoid the painful pinch but also because he wanted to please her. She was his "other mother" and he loved her more than anybody in the world.

Every evening, when at last the work was finished for the day, she would read the Bible to him. She spoke about the men and women of the Old and New Testaments as if they were neighbors living next door with problems and tribulations just like their own. His grandmother assured Nicolás that God was always with him and would always watch over and protect him. She told Nicolás that whenever he was in trouble or in danger, he could pray to the Virgin Mary and she would always come to his assistance.

Because he trusted his grandmother so completely, he took her words quite literally and felt in his heart that he was under the loving care of the Virgin Mother and that she would save him from all danger. In his eyes, his grandmother and the Blessed Mother were on nearly the same footing, and just as his grandmother had rescued him from an almost certain death, he felt that Mary's protection would deliver him from all danger and even death itself.

The steadfast faith that his grandmother instilled deep within his very soul gave him the inner strength and courage that enabled him to survive any and every obstacle or hardship in his path. When he was eleven-years old, this faith was put to its first and worst test when his grandmother suddenly died of a heart attack.

Nicolás had never even seen his grandmother sick. She was a strong woman with a sturdy build, and years of working on the farm and taking care of her large family had made her body hard and sinewy. She never complained of any aches and pains or spoke of any physical ailment. But one morning as she was carrying a basket of newly washed clothes outside, she stopped in her tracks and suddenly uttered a sharp cry. She dropped the basket and fell to the ground.

Nicolás, who was a few yards away removing the dry clothes from the line, raced over to her side.

"Mamá!

"Mamá! Mamá! Mamá!" he screamed over and over again.

His grandmother, her perspiration-soaked face contorted by the agony of her dying heart, was unable to speak. She gasped painfully, and with great effort raised her arm and pointed in the direction of Elsa and Juan's house.

Realizing that he could do nothing for her by himself, he leaped over the overturned basket and the damp clothes that were spilled on the ground and bolted over to the neighbors' house.

Juan and Elsa, hearing Nicolás calling out their names from the distance, stood in their open doorway with puzzled looks on their faces.

"What's the matter…what's happening?" they asked.

Nicolás, gasping from the frantic dash that he had just made, grabbed Juan by the hand and started pulling him in the direction of his grandmother's house. Elsa threw the door shut and ran after them.

"Hurry! Hurry!" Nicolás finally managed to sputter, as he ran stumbling and tripping over rocks and sticks.

As soon as they rounded the corner of the house, Juan could see immediately that they had arrived too late. Ana Teheran was laying on her back with one leg doubled up under her, the front of her blouse still clutched in her right hand.

Elsa, panting heavily, caught up to the pair and tried to catch Nicolás's arm, to lead him away from the sight of the dead woman, but he twisted free and ran over to his grandmother's lifeless body.

"Mamá! Mamá! Mamá!" he screamed as he roughly grabbed his grandmother by her shoulders and tried to shake the life back into her.

Juan crouched down on the ground next to Nicolás and tried unsuccessfully to pull him away. With tears streaming down his cheeks, brought on more by the wails of the anguished child than by the sight of his good friend and neighbor lying dead on the ground, he pried Nicolás' hands open, put his arm under the boy's kicking legs, lifted him up and took him into the house.

For the last five years Ana Teheran had been his "Mamá." Now she was gone.

Nur, his mother, whom he loved but saw only on the rare occasions when he visited her, was wrapped up in her own private world of grief. He sat beside her now in the filled church, surrounded by brothers and sisters and aunts and uncles and dozens of cousins. They were all sobbing and wailing aloud over the untimely death of Ana Teheran...all but Nicolás.

He sat motionless, as if in a trance. His dark eyes, wide with fear and apprehension, darted from left to right. Aunts and uncles came over to him, put their arms around his shoulders and told him how brave he was. But he wasn't brave. He was stunned into silence. His body was devoid of everything but a constricting pain in his heart that would not go away. His eyes were dry. The enormity and suddenness of his loss had drained him of all outward signs of emotion.

Sitting hunched over on the worn bench, he rocked his body back and forth with his arms folded protectively in front of him and his crossed knees touching his chest. He seemed to be shrinking physically on the outside at the same time that he was withdrawing on the inside. It felt as if his heart was shriveling within his chest and his bones and muscles were fusing into one small hard lump of flesh.

He was eleven-years old...too young to be a man...too old to be a child.

Nicolás went back to live in his mother's house.

Although he had hoped to stay there, the presence of his stepfather made life unbearable once again, and he left after a week. With only a few clothes in a cloth sack and a peso that his mother had secretly pressed into his hand as he said good-bye, he turned his back on Turbo and started walking, stopping at every shop he passed, asking if they had a job for him and a place to sleep.

Some of the shopkeepers were kind and gave him something to eat or drink. Others chased him away with curses. Nicolás was not the only one in search of a job, and with an abundance of able-bodied men to choose from, there was no need to hire a tall, scrawny eleven-year-old boy, even if he did look older and said he would do anything.

After a few weeks of walking, sleeping anywhere he could, eating anything he could, he finally found work in a bus factory in the city of Montería.

The noise and the heat were bad enough, but the filthy conditions were almost more than he could stand. His entire body was smeared with grease and dirt, which he unsuccessfully tried to scrub away every night after work. He had been glad to find the job in the bus factory, but a year later he left thinking that even no job was better than this one.

Ruefully, he quickly realized how wrong he was.

After working for a few days as an eager and very hungry apprentice to a local petty thief, Nicolás was thrown in jail for eight days by a magistrate who hoped to teach the twelve-year-old boy a lesson and turn him from a life of crime.

Unfortunately, the eight days in jail did nothing to convince Nicolás that going hungry was better than hustling.

After three unsuccessful weeks of looking for a job in Turbo, he hitched a ride to Cartagena. Cartagena was worse than Turbo.

He walked from shop to shop and from house to house looking for work, but could find nothing. He left and decided to try his luck in Medellín. Medellín was even worse than Cartagena.

For six days he knocked on doors, looking for any kind of work in exchange for food, but he was not the only hungry, homeless boy looking for work, and doors were either slammed in his face or never even opened. He would not be able to get his *cédula*, the official government work identification card, until he turned thirteen, and nobody would hire him without it.

Hanging around a clothing store after one such fruitless day, he stared at the racks of clothing and stacks of shoes with a sudden inspiration born of desperation. Quickly, while the owner was busy with a customer, he exchanged his torn slippers for a pair of leather moccasins. Keeping his eyes on the shopkeeper, he also put two pairs of trousers on over his shorts and three shirts over his own. Making sure that the owner of the shop had his back to him, he walked out of the store with a blank expression on his face, his calm gait betraying none of his fear.

He knew it was wrong. He knew it was a sin and that his grandmother would have been appalled if she had known what he had done. Automatically, he looked up as if she were actually watching him from heaven and said, "Grandma, if you were alive, I wouldn't have had to do this. I'd still be living with you...safe and sound with a roof over my head and food in my stomach. But I'm not blaming you...so please don't blame me."

Crossing himself guiltily for being disrespectful of his grandmother, he headed towards the barrios on the outskirts of the city. This was where the poorest of the poor lived in shacks made of boards and scraps of metal and where naked children and raw sewage ran side by side down the streets.

The people of the barrio could not pay much, but a few pesos were better than no pesos. In an hour, Nicolás sold the shirts, trousers and even the shoes on his feet. Barefoot, he trekked back to Medellín and bought something to eat. With a full belly for the first time in over two weeks, he headed for another clothing store.

It was only a matter of time until he got caught. The judge sentenced him to two months in prison. He was twelve-years old.

In the same room with him were forty boys his age. They took turns sleeping on the floor because there wasn't enough room for all of them to lie down at the same time. They shared the one toilet because that was the only one there. They ate the salty soup made from ducks' heads because that was the only food they were given.

He survived.

When he was released, he begged at back doors for odd jobs and food. For three months he slept in one public park after another, trying to avoid getting picked up by the police, usually sleeping on the ground or, sometimes if he was lucky, in a large carton he had stumbled upon during the day. Eventually he scrounged enough money together to buy some shoe wax and brushes, and he walked around the city with his precious box of supplies clutched tightly under his arm, offering to polish shoes.

He turned thirteen and still could not get a job and was not sure of how much more of this life he could stand, when one morning he woke up and discovered that his left shoe had been stolen off his foot while he had been sleeping. After hobbling down the road, he leaped onto the back of a bus as it stopped to pick up passengers and jumped off as it slowed down to discharge them. Transferring from bus to bus in this fashion and hitching rides from an occasional passing motorist, he arrived in Baranquilla four days later.

With no time to appreciate the beautiful coastal city, Nicolás set upon his immediate quest of securing another shoe. Appearing as if in answer to a prayer, he spotted a drunk sleeping off an alcoholic stupor on a park bench. Nicolás leaned over and started slipping the shoe off the man's foot, coordinating his movements with the drunk's exhalations, when suddenly the man woke up.

Nicolás grabbed the shoe and dashed down the street. All he wanted, he told himself, was a shoe for his left foot; he didn't care if it didn't match. But he had a perfect pair when the right shoe smacked him right between the shoulder blades. He scooped it up from the ground and continued running, ducking into alleys and spinning breathlessly around corners until he was sure there was no one in pursuit.

Figuring that it was better to go barefoot with money in his pockets than walk around penniless in a beautiful pair of shoes, he sold them the following day to a man on the street who did not ask any questions other than, "How much?"

Again he searched for a job and was able to paint houses occasionally and do other chores that nobody else was willing to do in the oppressive heat. Sometimes over a week would go by without any work at all.

Reluctantly, he returned to Turbo.

Nicolás could not live with his mother again. He sought out his godfather and asked if he could stay with him. His godfather, insisting that Nicolás needed an education in order to survive in this world, agreed to let him live with him on one condition... that Nicolás go to school. Nicolás protested that he could get by just fine without knowing how to read or write, but to no avail. After all the necessary documents had been filled out, his godfather left his reluctant godson at the threshold of the classroom.

Señor Celino looked up at his new pupil. At just under six feet in height, Nicolás would probably have been taller than most of his fellow students in any class. Here, in the first-grade class of six- and seven-year olds he was a giant, immediately dubbed "Juan Grande" ("Big John") by his fellow classmates.

Señor Celino was an ascetic-looking man whose stern appearance hid a kind heart. He reached up and put his arm around Nicolás' shoulders and ushered him into the room.

They were greeted by gales of laughter.

Señor Celino walked to the front of the room with his arm still around his new pupil's shoulders and, frowning at the class, demanded silence. In the expectant hush that followed he softly spoke.

"What we have here today is this young man," he said, pointing to Nicolás, "who I hope you will be like in the future. What courage to admit your weaknesses and disabilities and then to take drastic steps to take advantage of the opportunity to remedy them without fear of laughter or negative criticism!" Señor Celino continued, "This boy, I think, is more intelligent than all of us put together. For his action, that he has undertaken in our presence here today, I ask of you children a big round of applause of welcome!"

With no suitable place to sit other than the top of a first-grader's desk, Nicolás attended class every day. He was not concerned with spelling, grammar or writing, but just wanted to devour the words on paper. He struggled and labored over each page, placing his finger under each word as he read it aloud in his deep voice.

After a few months, although he was reading on a third-grade level, he decided to leave the school, still embarrassed about sitting in a class where he towered over not only his fellow classmates, but his teacher as well. Whenever he would hear the children laughing, he would turn his back to them and duck his head down in humiliation, incorrectly assuming that he was the object of their amusement.

Nicolás transferred to a higher grade in an Evangelical school in Turbo, worked in an ice cream factory after school, and went to live with his mother again. His stepfather still managed to strike him whenever he had the opportunity, but now that Nicolás was older, smarter and stronger, the opportunities were not as frequent or as violent as in the past.

He attended the Evangelical School for a few months, improving his reading and learning mathematics, and pored over geography books, especially fascinated by photographs of the United States.

"Someday I'll go there," he promised himself.

By the time he was eighteen years old, he was a licensed seaman earning 160 dollars a month. It was barely enough to live on.

He knew he could find a good job at a decent salary in the United States. He'd even be able to send money to his mother. Then, after a few years, he'd be able to return to Colombia and live well there for the rest of his life.

Whenever his ship docked at Turbo, Nicolás headed for the local discotheque to listen and dance to the music, drink a few beers, and hopefully meet a willing female. One evening as he entered the bar, he encountered some former companions that he hadn't seen for a few years. He walked right past them and would have continued on his way if one of the men had not yelled out his name above the din of the music. He turned around, about to ask this stranger how he happened to know him, when he got a closer look at the man's face. He stared at one and then at another of his old friends.

They were completely transformed after a brief stay in the United States. Not only did they have on brand-name blue jeans and leather-fringed shirts, but they were also wearing cowboy boots encrusted with medallions of silver. Nicolás had only seen boots like theirs worn by sheriffs in the movies.

Nicolás looked hungrily at the new clothes of his friends and then compared them with his own. Wearing clothes like theirs would not only make a man feel terrific, but would endow him with more prestige and respect. He could just imagine the effect his appearance would have on women.

As if reading his mind, one of his friends informed him, "A guy like you, with your good looks and fine clothes, will turn the eyes of any woman, believe me."

Nicolás didn't say a thing; he just stared at them, his imagination awakening his deepest longings. He had never been envious or jealous of anyone. But now in his innocent ignorance, he pictured himself returning as an almost god-like hero from a stay in the United States.

"You don't say!" he finally replied.

"I tell you there is abundant work which pays incredibly well," they went on. "In this land of opportunity you can arrive naked and, in less than one year, you can have a brand-new car, a luxury apartment and a designer wardrobe. You can have social security that pays you when you're unable to work...and the government even gives you free medical assistance and free education! The police watch over you; you don't have to watch out for them, and the judicial system protects you."

Nicolás swallowed hard and stared at his friends in open-mouthed incredulity. He couldn't believe that such a place actually existed.

Seeing the expression on Nicolás' face, his friend slapped him on the back and added, "Yes, believe me, it's true! And what's more, there are beautiful fair-haired blondes that abound like sand on the beach, who fall like flies before cunning and enchanting Latins like us."

The other men nodded their heads and grinned in agreement.

Nicolás had heard stories before about life in the United States. Sitting at the bars across from the docks, he had often heard seamen speak about life in the "promised land" or "the famous USA." Each time Nicolás had listened to their stories, a madness had inflamed his mind. His entire being was drawn as if by a powerful magnet to this land that the sailors called "El Dorado," where he was certain that he would find a better life. Now, after hearing his friends' stories and seeing their magnificent clothes, he was consumed with an irresistible desire to enter the United States at any cost.

"That's it!" he exclaimed. "I'll go there someday! I'll make a lot of money and come back to Turbo a huge success!"

Two years later, the dream that smoldered in Nicolás' heart re-ignited when first his older brother and then a younger brother were murdered.

Now he knew that he had to go the United States...his and his family's very survival depended on it.

Jessid, his older brother, had been attacked as he was on his way home from work. Robbed of his watch and the gold chain around his neck, he was left in the street with the handle of a nine-inch knife protruding from his stomach. He died, bleeding to death, before he could be taken to a hospital, leaving behind a wife and young daughter.

Nicolás, now the oldest male in the family, immediately assumed the paternal role, making sure that his sister-in-law and niece were protected and taken care of.

The family had scarcely recovered from mourning the death of Jessid when student riots broke out in Turbo, and Javier, Nicolás' sixteen-year-old brother, was accused of being a member of a rival gang. On October 21, 1989, while crossing a picket line during a strike, he was shot in the head.

Just at that moment, Nicolás happened to enter the street and came upon the crowd that had gathered around his younger brother, who was lying on the ground in a growing puddle of blood, his eyes already staring blankly at the sky.

Nicolás screamed and rushed over to his brother's almost lifeless body and held him in his arms. Calling his brother's name over and over again, Nicolás rocked back and forth, cradling what was left of Javier's head in his hands as his brother's blood coursed through his fingers and down his arms. When Javier exhaled his last breath, Nicolás gently laid him on the unpaved street and embraced him for the last time.

Never realizing the consequences of his next act, he reached into his dead brother's pocket and removed Javier's soccer-team identification card. As he heard the sirens of the approaching police, he impulsively put it into his wallet, wanting to keep it as a memento of his favorite brother.

Now, although he was more determined than ever to get into the United States, he knew that getting in illegally was a matter of luck and timing, and he waited patiently.

He hung around the docks for months, waiting for some sign, some feeling in his gut, that would tell him which was the right ship and the right time. Then one day in the middle of January, while taking his customary tour of the docks, Nicolás stopped dead in his tracks.

There it was.

He knew immediately that this was the ship that would take him to the United States. Anchored 2,000 feet offshore, towering high above the calm surface of the water was a giant oil tanker, the Bright Eagle.

Concealing his excitement and strolling along as nonchalantly as possible, Nicolás contemplated its size, already calculating what provisions he would have to purchase for the trip. He noticed a worker on the dock and asked the man if he knew the destination of the tanker that was resting at anchor at the end of the oil pipeline in the harbor.

"To the United States," the man replied, "and it leaves tomorrow."

12:20 P.M.

Mike Rivedinera, waiting in the Zodiac floating alongside the hull of the Bright Eagle, wondered what was taking González and Burn such a long time. He checked his watch again and leaned over the side to see if he could detect the divers' shadowy silhouettes in the gray water beneath him.

Suddenly, one head popped up ten feet away from the Zodiac. An instant later, another head broke the surface. González, the first one to reach the surface, released his grip on his mouthpiece and excitedly told Rivedinera about the four bags and the guy he had discovered in the rudder trunk.

Rivedinera's mouth gaped in astonishment as he heard the news. He hurriedly switched on his radio that linked him to Cummings, who was on Police Launch 8 waiting for word from the latest team of divers, and told him about the bags and the stowaway.

Cummings grinned and gave a "thumbs up" to the rest of the divers who had stopped drinking their coffee and hot chocolate as soon as they heard the crackle of the radio. They had been huddled inside the cabin, trying to keep warm while awaiting further developments, and they strained their ears to hear the message that was coming over the radio.

Cummings got back on his radio and instructed Rivedinera to get the divers back to Launch 8 so they could take off their scuba gear and change into dry clothes, and then to return to the stern to make sure no one would leave the rudder trunk via the water. As soon as he ended his conversation with Rivedinera, Cummings immediately called the captain's quarters on the ship. The phone was picked up even before the sound of the first ring died away.

Customs Agent Jack Conti jumped to his feet. Nodding his head, he listened as Cummings excitedly relayed the message. He slammed his fist into the palm of his hand and told himself that finally...finally they had found something. He had anticipated that they might find a torpedo-shaped device attached to the ship, but he had never in his wildest dreams expected them to find a person. He was surprised, even shocked, to hear that a stowaway had been discovered in the rudder trunk. Usually stowaways were found on planes or on boats that traveled a short distance for a short period of time.

Conti had been with the U.S. Customs Service for twenty-three years. Starting as a patrol officer searching vessels, he had also served as the tour commander at Kennedy Airport, where he was involved in the searching of aircraft. In fact, he had been involved in vessel searches all of his career and had searched all types of commercial cargo ships, including bulk carriers that carry sugar and raw materials, tankers, private boats and other kinds of crafts.

Conti was well aware that the Coast Guard and Customs agents had encountered and apprehended thousands of people in the past who were trying to enter the United States illegally. Many of these had set out to sea to escape tyranny, poverty and desperate conditions. The Vietnamese boat people and the thousands of refugees fleeing from Haiti and Cuba had all risked their lives utilizing the sea as their route to freedom, but Conti had never heard of anyone trying to survive for a week in a submerged air pocket like the rudder compartment.

Conti turned and relayed the news to Captain Ho, who had been keeping vigil with him in his quarters since before ten o'clock in the morning. Then they grabbed their jackets and rushed out the door. After several wrong turns, winding their way through several crew passageways and down several ladders, they finally reached the deck of the steering-gear room.

The steering-gear room housed the hydraulic mechanism that turned the rudder. Coils of pink, white and yellow rope were piled in the corners. The steel deck was covered with brown slats of wood which provided a relatively dry, non-slippery surface on which to stand. Set into and nearly flush with the deck were two manhole covers, also known as access or inspection plates. They provided access to the compartments below if the walls had to be painted or the rudder had to be repaired. One was more to the stern of the ship while the other was more towards the bow. The manhole covers were identical in appearance, each a 15" x 18" oval plate of steel with a handle on each side. Protruding from the twenty-four holes that were evenly spaced around the perimeter of the cover were steel bolts that were welded to the deck. Thick nuts, securely fastened on top of the bolts, secured the cover onto the deck.

A gasket between the steel plate of the access cover and the steel-deck surface ensured an impenetrable, water-tight seal which provided an air-tight atmosphere inside the rudder trunk and prevented the ocean water from rising to the top of the submerged compartment, much like an inverted glass held into a bowl of water.

If the seal was broken or the cover was opened while the ship was underway at sea, the water level inside the rudder trunk would rise to the level of the water outside and the ocean water would surge into the rudder trunk and, coming up through the manhole, inundate the deck. The only things that prevented this were the seal and the air inside the compartment, which was compressed slightly and replenished by the air bubbles generated by the churning propeller.

Sergeant Cummings spotted Customs Agent McCloud drinking coffee with the divers and told him to accompany him. McCloud jumped to his feet and walked over to the side of Police Launch 8. Ducking his head down as he passed under the doorway, he and Cummings climbed up the gangplank and boarded the Bright Eagle.

Cummings and McCloud rushed down the well-lit stairwell, reached the steering-gear room, roughly pulled the door open and stepped inside. Other police officers were already there, panting noisily from the exertion of running nearly the entire length of the ship, their breaths creating white puffs of vapor that quickly dissipated in the frigid air.

Agent Conti and Captain Ho stepped through the open doorway of the steering-gear room, followed by the rest of the Customs agents. Conversation ceased as Agent Conti stepped into the steering-gear room with Captain Ho. Everyone in the room looked expectantly at Conti, awaiting instructions. The normally vacant room was crowded with agents, police officers and members of the crew.

Agent Conti followed Captain Ho to the manhole cover at the foot of the stairwell, the one toward the bow of the ship. The captain spoke some words in Korean to a crewman who returned a minute later with a large wrench in one hand and a heavy sledgehammer in the other. The agents and officers positioned themselves around the cover, attempting to get the first peek at what was inside while at the same time trying to stay out of the way of the crewman who had just knelt on the deck.

The man placed his knee on the wooden flooring that surrounded the hole and held the wrench in his right hand. He placed the open end of the wrench on the nut closest to him and adjusted it until he could no longer tighten it. Then he positioned both hands on the handle of the wrench and grunted as he pushed his arms and his body forward, trying to loosen the grip of the nut.

It didn't budge.

There was no sound except for an almost inaudible crackle, as little chips of paint from the nut loosened and fell to the deck.

The crewman turned his head and looked at Captain Ho, who was standing in back of him to the left. The captain nodded, and the sailor picked up the sledgehammer. Bracing his knees further apart, he gripped the sledgehammer with both hands, swung it over his head until it was between his shoulder blades, and delivered a resounding blow to the first nut.

The abrupt clang of metal striking against metal coming from above caused Nicolás to jerk his head upwards toward the ceiling of the compartment. Again and again at a rapidly increasing rate the reports reverberated through the steel ceiling and walls, each one sending a jolt of terror through him.

Although he had never fully gotten used to the deafening grinding of the propeller, this noise was far worse. Maybe it was because he realized that the sounds signified that his horrible ordeal would not end in freedom but in imprisonment. Maybe it was because he had reached not only his physical but also his mental limit. He had endured the din of the propeller for a week by telling himself that each of its revolutions propelled the ship closer to his dream of a new and better life. But now each clang of metal only seemed to shatter that dream forever.

He covered his ears with his hands, trying to shield them against the piercing clamor that was coming from above. Each sharp blow entered his head like an explosion of gunfire and his body jerked involuntarily with each shot.

He frantically shook his head from side to side, trying to escape from the strident shrieks that were penetrating his ears and skull. Desperately, he realized that the only way to get away from them was to throw himself into the water and try to escape.

Just as he was about to lower himself into the water, the clanging ceased as abruptly as it had begun. He heard the rusty squealing of metal straining against metal and held his breath, anticipating the worst.

12:45 P.M.

The Customs agents, police officers and crewmen in the steering-gear room winced at the sharp clang and reverberation of steel striking steel as the steering-gear mechanism shook with resounding vibrations and the oxidized grip of each nut was released from each bolt. When all the nuts had been loosened by the sledgehammer's blows, Captain Ho motioned to a second seaman to replace the first, who was now mopping the sweat off his forehead as he stood up and walked away.

The second man leaned over and picked up the hammer. He set his feet a few feet apart, held the hammer in both hands and raised it above his shoulders. Then he swung his arms in a downward arc in front of his body and dealt the cover a mighty blow that echoed across the deck. He struck it three more times in three different places, grunting with the effort and then with satisfaction as he felt the steel plate yield ever so slightly with each impact.

Then he put the sledgehammer down and knelt on one knee. He started to remove the first of the twenty-four nuts that secured the cover to the deck.

Conti, Cummings and all the agents and police officers closed ranks and hovered over the crewman kneeling on the deck. A few of the men had already unbuttoned their jackets and unsnapped their holsters. They craned their necks and, with their eyes riveted on the steel plate, they placed their hands on the butts of their revolvers as they tried to get a closer look.

Sergeant Cummings picked up the shotgun that one of his men had brought over from Police Launch 8 and stood two feet away from the unbolted but still unopened manhole.

Another officer stood on the opposite side, a rifle in his hand. Everybody else stepped back a few feet to give them enough room to shoot if necessary.

Agent Conti signaled to two of his men. They walked over to the manhole and each one knelt down next to the steel cover. Then, with one man holding the handle on the right side of the cover and the other man holding the handle on the left side, they lifted the cover straight up in the air.

There was no sound emanating from the rudder trunk, so Conti silently and cautiously edged his way closer to the opening. The other customs agents eyed him nervously as he stepped right up to the rim of the open hole, crouched down and peered in. Silence and empty space greeted him.

There was nothing there.

Conti turned with a questioning glance to Captain Ho, who was standing to one side, talking to one of his crewmen. Captain Ho looked up and pointed towards the other manhole that was located right next to the steering gear mechanism. Then the Captain barked a command in Korean to one of his crewmen, who immediately rushed over to the newly-opened manhole and retrieved the wrench and the sledgehammer.

All the agents and police officers in the steering-gear room followed as the sailor hurried over to the second manhole, laid down the wrench, picked up the sledgehammer, gripped it with both hands and with a powerful swing of his arms cracked the seal on the first nut.

Nicolás heard voices shouting to one another in English and in another language that was foreign to his ears. The ceiling above him shook with the vibrations of running footsteps on the deck right over his head. As he cocked his head and looked up as if he could actually see what was happening above him, loose flakes of paint and drops of rusty water fell into his eyes and onto his upturned face.

The strident clang of metal striking metal directly overhead caused another shower of rusted paint and water. Nicolás realized with a growing sense of panic that all the efforts of the people on the deck were directed at the manhole cover right above him.

His heart pounded rapidly again in his chest as panic reached its climax. He gulped breaths of cold air and exhaled them noisily through his suddenly dry, open mouth. His eyes, wide with fear, searched first left and then right, looking for a solution. Waves of heat repeatedly and rapidly washed over him accompanied by inundations of perspiration. His heartbeat accelerated even more and he felt like he was going to faint or vomit or perhaps do both simultaneously.

Nicolás knew that all the shouting and clanging and hammering above him on deck only meant that someone was about to open the cover right on top of him. He covered his ears tightly with his palms, trying to shut out the clangor of the hammer that jarred his teeth and shook the entire compartment, and squeezed his eyes shut, not only to protect them from the water and flecks of paint that were raining down on him from the ceiling, but also to obliterate the four walls that suddenly seemed to be closing in on him.

With an alacrity generated by alarm, he stood up on the wooden board and darted over toward the corner of the rudder trunk, not trying so much to conceal himself in its shadows but to protect himself from any assault that might be forthcoming. In his mind he pictured a barrage of bullets showering down upon him, and he wanted to get as far away as possible from the center of the compartment. As he scurried along the plank, he kept glancing upwards toward the ceiling, which still vibrated with each sharp clang of metal.

He pressed himself close against the wall, hoping to present as small a target as possible if anyone should start shooting from above.

1:05 P.M.

Sergeant Cummings released the safety mechanism on his shotgun. The officer standing opposite him, holding the rifle, also released the safety catch on his weapon. Nine other officers stood in a close circle around the manhole, each with legs spread slightly apart, positioned in the classic firing stance, prepared for anybody and anything that would come out of the rudder trunk.

Agent Conti spoke a few inaudible words to Captain Ho and then motioned to his men to close ranks around the circle of police officers. The Customs Agents jockeyed for position between and behind the armed men.

Captain Ho barked a single word of command to the crewman with the sledgehammer. The man raised the tool high above his right shoulder and swung it forward and downward, striking the cover on its edge. Then, with the hammer still in his hand, he cautiously retreated, trying to avoid bumping into any of the men or their drawn weapons. The officers closest to his point of exit moved aside to let him pass, their gazes never wavering from the still sealed steel plate.

One of the Agents crouched down on the left side of the manhole cover and grabbed the left handle with both hands. Another knelt down on the right-hand side and held onto the opposite handle with a similar grip. They looked up expectantly at Conti, waiting for his signal.

The agent holding the left handle glanced at his counterpart gripping the other handle and nodded. Then with a grunt, they both pulled simultaneously, the tendons in their necks bulging with the strain of their efforts. The cover released its grip on the gasket directly under it, but wasn't lifted high enough to clear the tops of the bolts. Doubling their efforts, the agents tugged at the cover and finally freed it from the restraining bolts. Then they rested it on the deck, holding it like a shield at a forty-five degree angle in front of the hole.

Complete silence fell over the steering-gear room. Sergeant Cummings stepped forward a few feet, stood slightly behind the upturned manhole cover and waited for whomever was down in the rudder trunk to make the next move. He pointed the shotgun directly at the open hole. The officers positioned around the perimeter of the open manhole also held their guns pointed towards the oval opening, waiting for someone to come up from the compartment below.

Cautiously crouching next to the opening, one of the officers flicked on a flashlight and directed its powerful beam into the dark void below. He held the flashlight at arm's length, careful not to let his body near the opening. He didn't want to present himself as an easy target to whomever was in the compartment.

A second officer also switched on his flashlight and, kneeling at the other side of the opening, shone the light in. He
shouted an order to the unseen occupant to get out.

Fine dust and small chips of paint and rust rained down
on Nicolás as he stood trembling at the far end of the wooden
board, his back pressed tightly against the wall of the rudder
trunk. Unable to hold his breath any longer in the dust-filled
air, he started coughing, realizing that he was not only giving
away his presence but probably his position as well.

His bloodshot eyes had squeezed shut as the pupils contracted instantly at the sudden appearance of brilliant light.
He slowly forced his eyelids open and discovered the compartment illuminated by the beams of the flashlights. Seeing the
inflated raft floating in the water, a fresh wave of despair
washed over him as he realized that his chance for a new life
was gone forever.

"Get out...get out!" he heard someone shouting.

Paralyzed with fear and anticipating a hail of bullets to
rain down from the opening in the ceiling at any second, he
tried to force his body even closer to the wall. Although he
heard the voice of the man above him, he didn't understand
what he was saying. Tucking his head down, he tried to shield
it with his arms.

He heard a different voice yelling even louder to him in
Spanish.

"¡Salga!"

"¡Salga!"

This time Nicolás understood it perfectly, and with a
shudder of defeat he dropped his head to his chest.

Nicolás raised his streaked face and opened his eyes in
astonishment as he saw the barrels of the rifles and guns that
were extended into the compartment. He immediately threw
his hands up in the air in surrender.

One officer leaned slightly over the opening, trying to see
what was happening. The rest of the men who were standing
side by side around the open manhole kept their weapons
aimed toward the opening and braced themselves to fire if
necessary.

Nicolás staggered along the wooden plank and inched over to the opening. With one hand still upraised in surrender high above his head, he grabbed onto one of the steel rungs that were set into the wall and started to climb through the recently opened orifice. As soon as his head and shoulders emerged above the rim of the open manhole, he screwed up his face and squinted. Dazzled and instantly blinded by the intense glare of light, he hesitated for a second before resuming his ascent.

All at once he felt his wrists being roughly clasped while at the same time other hands grabbed him under his armpits and lifted him completely off the rungs of the ladder. Still unable to see, he screamed as he lost his balance, terrified of plunging into the water of the compartment with its awaiting propeller.

But the hands that gripped his wrists and seized him under his arms prevented him from breaking free or falling back into the rudder trunk.

When he was entirely free of the manhole, the officers, who had still not relinquished their grips on his arms and wrists, pressed him face down on the wooden deck. He could feel each groove and ridge of the rough wooden planks of the deck through the layers of his sweatshirt and thin jacket. His arms were still above his head in surrender, the last position that he had been ordered to assume.

As he tried to raise his head to get his bearings and to prevent his face from being thrust against the boards, an officer yelled something to him in English and then walked over with one swift stride and leaned over him. Placing his knee on Nicolás' back, he roughly pressed him down against the wooden deck and tried to clamp a pair of handcuffs on Nicolás' wrists, which were still raised high above his head because he hadn't understood the officer's command to lower them.

Nicolás screamed as he felt a sudden heavy pressure and an excruciating pain at the base of his spine. He groaned aloud and arched his back in a futile attempt to throw off the weight on his back. Twisting his body from side to side, he kicked out with both legs, trying to strike his unseen assailant. Suddenly, a violent kick in his right side took his breath away. He writhed back and forth, still pinned down on the deck by the force of the knee that was pressed against him. He was repeatedly punched and kicked in his ribs and sides by the men that surrounded him. Screaming and crying out with pain, he instinctively tried to protect himself by curling his body into a ball, but the incessant rain of blows made this impossible.

His arms flailed wildly as he shook off the grip of the hands on his wrists and arms and tried to protect himself from the frenzied attack of the men surrounding him. Still aiming their weapons at him, they kicked and punched his heaving body as he struggled to break free. Screaming in terror and shrieking with pain, he was finally grabbed by several officers who roughly twisted his arms behind his back and clamped his hands together with handcuffs. Then with one officer gripping his right arm and another holding onto his left arm, he was roughly lifted from the floor and set on his feet.

The barrage of blows finally stopped as Nicolás felt the cold steel of the handcuffs around his wrists. His arms were twisted painfully behind his back, and he flexed his fingers to try to restore some sensation to his hands. He rotated his head from side to side and from front to back, trying to alleviate the spasms of his aching neck. Each breath was torture to his bruised and battered ribs as he sucked in huge gulps of cold air.

Simultaneously pushed and dragged along the deck towards the stairwell that led to the steering-gear room, he was shoved into a sitting position onto one of the steps and shackled to the steel banister.

Nicolás' face was a reflection of the anguish he was feeling. His shoulders slumped forward and he stared down at the deck, oblivious to the frenetic activity around him. He didn't hear the sound of the men on the deck calling to one another. He didn't even notice the officers and Customs agents passing in front of him.

"If only...if only...if only," he thought morosely to himself. "If only there hadn't been any scuba divers, I wouldn't have been spotted. If only the water hadn't been so cold, I could have left the compartment as soon as the ship had stopped. If only the rudder trunk hadn't been the only place to conceal myself, I could have gotten out of there and found a different place to hide. If only there hadn't been bags of drugs tied to the ledge, I wouldn't be sitting here in handcuffs.

"If only... if only... if only. If only I had not decided...

"No!" he almost said aloud.

He still didn't regret the decision he had made back in Colombia in what now seemed a lifetime ago. He had realized that there might be a risk in trying to enter the United States illegally, but he had figured that he could slip in undetected in the middle of the night as soon as the ship reached the end of its voyage and docked.

He also knew that the rudder trunk was an extremely dangerous place to hide himself. One slip, one false step, and he could have been pitched directly into the vortex of the giant propeller and killed instantly as well as painfully.

He admitted to himself that he hadn't been prepared for the cold. He had thought that the ship would be terminating its voyage in Miami, a city that he knew was warm this time of year. It was the frigid temperature that had prevented him from leaving the rudder trunk.

He told himself ruefully, "If it wasn't for the cold weather, I wouldn't be sitting here right now, sitting on this cold steel step with my arms behind my back and handcuffs digging into my wrists."

Nicolás raised his head and a long sigh of despair parted his lips. He tried to shift his position on the metal step and winced at the stabbing pain in his side.

Customs Agents hurried back and forth in front of him, calling to one another. Several police officers, still wearing their dark-blue bullet-proof vests emblazoned with the word "POLICE" in yellow block letters, spoke into their radios and hung around the open manhole.

Sergeant Cummings unloaded the shotgun, handed it and the cartridges to one of his men and told him to take them back to Police Launch 8. Then he instructed all the other officers still holding their weapons to holster them. The rifle was handed to the man leaving with the shotgun, and it was also taken off the ship and placed in Police Launch 8.

Cummings approached the hole once again.

He directed the men with the flashlights to make one last visual inspection. After a few minutes, the men reported that nobody was left in the rudder trunk. Finally Cummings leaned over the open manhole, switched on a powerful lantern, and slowly aimed its beam of light from left to right and up and down as he directly saw with his own eyes the contents of the compartment.

His first impression was of a tangle of pink and yellow ropes, crossing and recrossing and joining each other at twisted angles, seemingly with no sense of purpose or order. As his eyes grew accustomed to the glare of the light that was reflected off the slimy walls, he saw the four large bags piled on the ledge.

Two officers crouched at his sides and peered into the hole. One whistled softly to himself as the light from the flashlight illuminated the bags.

Cummings stood up and turned to the officer behind him and told him to get the camera so that he could take pictures. He didn't want to remove any of the contents of the hole until he had photographs of everything exactly where it was when the cover had been removed. He asked another officer to grab the video camera and to start shooting with that also because he wanted a minute-by-minute account of the removal of all the objects in the rudder trunk.

Nicolás sat on the third step from the bottom, on the stairs leading to the steering-gear room. Spotting Sergeant González, he called to him in Spanish. González turned and asked him, also in Spanish, what he wanted. Nicolás replied that he wanted to get out of his wet clothes and change into something dry.

González asked one of the Customs agents who was standing close to the open manhole to see if there was any clothing in the personal bags in the compartment so that he could get Nicolás a change of clothes. The agent brought a bag over to González and took out a damp sweater. Showing it to Nicolás, González told him that there was nothing dry to change into.

One of the police officers walked over towards Nicolás carrying a yellow blanket. The man folded it in half and wrapped it around him, tucking the open ends behind his back. Although Nicolás was surprised at this unexpected gesture, he was grateful; for the first time in three days a sensation of warmth spread over him.

Sergeant Cummings stepped gingerly over the lip of the manhole and put his left foot on the first rung of the ladder leading down into the rudder trunk. Brodley, holding the flashlight, moved over slightly to give him room to swing his other leg into the hole. Cummings held onto the rim of the opening with both hands, swung his right leg around and placed his foot on the second rung. Turning his head and looking over his shoulder as he slowly descended, he carefully stepped onto one of the wooden boards that crisscrossed the compartment.

He placed one foot on the edge of the board and rested the other foot on the narrow railing that ran along the perimeter of the four walls as he backed up. Then, holding the camera with both hands, he began to take pictures of the interior of the rudder trunk. He methodically and slowly panned the compartment from side to side and up and down as he pressed the shutter release button every few seconds.

Although Cummings was taking pictures below the level of the deck, the flashes of his camera that illuminated the rudder trunk simultaneously flared through the opening of the manhole and reflected off the glossy walls of the steering-gear room. The officer with the camcorder approached the open manhole, focused his camera and started taking pictures of the area adjacent to the manhole and directly down into the opening.

After Cummings finished taking pictures, he took out his pocketknife and started to work on the ropes. He looked up through the opening to Detective Brodley and Officer Rivedinera, who had positioned themselves at the lip of the manhole in order to assist.

The objects closest to the opening were removed first to facilitate the removal of the items that they themselves were placed on. Each item was passed through the hole and then ceremoniously handed over from one officer to the next and carefully placed on the wooden planks covering the deck. First, the nearly empty plastic jug was cut loose and passed through the hole. Next came two small gym bags.

Cummings struggled with the knots that secured the white bag to the three bags beneath it. After a few minutes of unsuccessful attempts to untie the intertwined rigging, he slipped the blade of his knife under one of the ropes and very slowly severed it, being very careful not to nick the bag.

After spreading his feet a few feet apart in order to balance himself, he passed his hands over the surface of the bag to determine if there were any more ropes holding it to the ledge. Finding none, he placed one hand on each side and slightly under the bag and with one swift motion lifted it to his chest.

Brodley and Rivedinera stretched their arms as far as possible into the hole and grabbed the sides of the package. Then, as Cummings straightened his arms and pushed the bag above his head, they simultaneously pulled it until it cleared the rim of the opening. As soon as they placed it down, two other officers carried the bag over to the far side of the deck.

Sergeant Cummings bent over the three duffel bags. They appeared to be identical in size and weight, three-feet long, about eighteen-inches wide and at least twelve-inches high. The large brass grommets on the open end of each bag were tightly laced with rope. He pushed against one side of the bag to see if he could move it slightly, but it wouldn't budge. He looked up at Brodley and Rivedinera and, laughing, told them that they had "a fucking lot of weight down there."

The men bantered back and forth while Cummings took some of the ropes that were securing the bags to the ledge and fashioned them into a handle on the top of the first duffel bag. Then he pushed and shoved and pulled and finally maneuvered the bulky package until it was directly under the aperture of the open manhole.

Brodley and Rivedinera leaned into the opening. They extended their arms once again and, grabbing the makeshift handle with both hands, pulled as hard as they could. As soon as he could see a clear space, Cummings placed both hands, palms upraised, under the bag and pushed it upwards. Brodley and Rivedinera groaned as they carefully and slowly hauled it up and out of the hole. Two Customs agents who were watching the operation stepped closer, bent down and helped the officers position the bag on the deck near the steering-gear mechanism. The two remaining duffel bags were removed in a similar fashion and were also placed on the deck.

Cummings climbed out of the rudder trunk and Brodley took his place handing the rest of the items up to Agents Conti and McCloud, who were standing by to assist. The plastic bags of food, the two planks of wood, the hammock, the other water jug, the ear protectors and everything else were taken out of the compartment and placed on the deck.

Customs Agent Conti, satisfied that all the items were out of the rudder trunk, finally turned to the men in the corner who were crouched over the white nylon bag that had just been removed. One of the officers bent over and loosened the ropes that secured the top of the bag and pulled with both hands, making the opening wider. The officer holding the video camera moved closer to the corner where the men were opening the bag in order to get a good angle for his picture as the bag was being opened. Bursts of light from the still camera flashed every few seconds on the drama taking place in the corner of the steering-gear room. Extraneous movements stopped and idle chatter halted as everybody on deck watched the man kneeling over the white bag.

Nicolás, sitting at the bottom of the stairwell, could only guess at what was going on. His restricted movement and field of vision allowed him to see only what was directly in front and to the right of him. From his position on the stairwell, he could not see the group of police officers and agents who had been drawn to the corner of the steering-gear room as if by a magnet, where one of the officers was crouching over a white bag.

The man slowly opened the bag, inserted his gloved hand and extracted a brick-shaped package wrapped in plastic. The men who were gathered around watched him closely as he proceeded. With deliberate care, he took his penknife from his pocket. Still crouching, holding the package in his left hand and the knife in the other, he slowly inserted the tip of the knife under the protective plastic wrapping, worked it back and forth a few times, and carefully extricated it. A minute mound of white powder clung to the tip of the blade. He placed the package on the floor and withdrew a test tube from his field-testing kit. The test tube already contained the chloroform and concentrated hydrochloric acid needed to perform the Scott Reagent Test for cocaine.

He removed the cap, tipped the test tube at a forty-five degree angle and inserted the tip of the penknife. By tapping the edge of the blade with his forefinger, he dislodged the white powder and it settled at the bottom of the glass tube.

Then he put the knife down and replaced the cap. The video camera zoomed in for a close-up. All the men turned and watched as the clear liquid in the test tube suddenly turned a clear azure blue. They started to grin.

Nicolás did not see any of this. The police officers, Customs agents, and crewmen standing at the back of the group did not see these proceedings either. But no one there in the steering-gear room of the Bright Eagle at 1:33 on the afternoon of January 24, 1991, could escape the cry of satisfaction which greeted the appearance of the blue liquid as someone yelled, "BINGO!"

Nicolás swung his head to the right when he heard the cry and the babble of excited voices that followed. Although he did not understand the words that were spoken, he could see some of the members of the crew nudging each other and pointing to him. He realized with a sense of dread that he had been inexorably and permanently linked to the bags of cocaine.

"This must be what a captured animal feels like...to be absolutely helpless and at the mercy of its captors...to be gawked at and pointed at like some rare and dangerous specimen in a zoo," he thought.

Inspector Raffaele walked over to the stack of duffel bags. He pulled on the rope that sealed the open end of the top one and shook his head. Reaching into his pocket, he pulled out his penknife and quickly slit the rope. Immediately, eager hands were reaching past him, inserting their fingers into the narrow opening, trying to make it wider so that he could observe and remove its contents.

The top of the bag was quickly spread apart and now revealed a clear plastic inner wrapping. Carefully cutting the tape that sealed the corner, Raffaele managed to insert his fingers into the hole he had just made and extricated one of the packages. It was rectangular, ten-inches long, six-inches wide and two-inches high. The white powder it contained could easily be seen through its wrapping.

He held the package flat in one hand and worked his knife back and forth until he made a small hole. Then he slid his knife under the wrapping, keeping the side of the blade flat against the plastic, and moved the knife from side to side a few times. He withdrew the knife, making sure that he did not dislodge the white powder that was perched on top of the blade. Finally he inserted the blade into the test tube held by one of the agents and waited to see the results.

Barely a second after the cap had been put on the test tube, the indicative tell-tale blue color appeared.

"There it is!" one of the men exclaimed, probably for the benefit of the video camera which had been recording the proceedings.

"That's the blue!" proclaimed another.

2:24 P.M.

Nicolás shifted his position on the steps, looked up and saw one of the police officers approaching with a sandwich held in his hand. At first, Nicolás did not realize that the man was offering it to him and did not pay any attention to him. Remembering all too painfully the beating he had recently received at the hands and feet of these officers, he was reluctant to open his mouth and admit how hungry he was. He was afraid that the man might be playing a cruel joke on him and did not want to give him the satisfaction of seeing the hunger in his eyes and the disappointment on his face when the food was snatched away. But the officer continued to hold the partially unwrapped sandwich in front of Nicolás' mouth, so with a hesitant grimace of gratitude Nicolás leaned forward and took a large bite of food.

The officer quickly snatched his hand back. Perhaps he was afraid that he would be bitten. Perhaps he was just afraid of getting too close. He asked Nicolás in Spanish if he wanted something to drink. When Nicolás nodded affirmatively, he called over to one of the men to get some milk.

Nicolás closed his mouth as he chewed the food hungrily. As he started to swallow what remained in his mouth, the officer approached with the rest of the sandwich. Nicolás leaned forward once again and the officer inserted the sandwich into his open mouth. As soon as Nicolás had the sandwich between his teeth, the officer recoiled and jerked his hand away, leaving his hapless captive with the remaining half still in his mouth.

Nicolás' eyes widened in incredulity as he realized his dilemma at once. With his wrists in handcuffs behind his back, he was unable to use his hands to assist himself. He knew that he had only two choices. He could either bite off the portion of the sandwich that was inside his mouth and let the rest of it fall onto his lap or he could tilt his head back and try to manipulate it with his lips and tongue so that the entire half would slowly fall into his mouth without choking him.

With a sigh of resignation and dejection he slumped over, chewed the part of the sandwich that was in his mouth and let the remainder fall to the deck at his feet. He had too much self-respect to permit his hunger to overcome his pride.

"I'm a man, not an animal!" he told himself.

Unwilling to look at the curious stares of the sailors who were amusing themselves by watching to see what he would do, he lowered his gaze to the floor. He could already hear the laughter of some of them who were observing his predicament. He tried to block them and his present situation out of his mind by reciting from memory the prayers that he carried in his wallet. These small plastic cards with their prayers and pictures of saints had comforted him during the voyage, and although he could not see them because of the darkness of the compartment, he had held them in his hands while he prayed and pleaded for deliverance from his perilous journey. He knew that they were mere pieces of paper, with no magic powers, but they brought back memories of his grandmother, who had first given him one.

Now all the religious cards and the rest of his papers were in the hands of U.S. Customs. His wallet had been removed from his pants as soon as his hands had been cuffed behind his back and all the contents had been carefully examined.

Not bothering to throw out the assorted pieces of paper in his wallet before leaving Colombia, he had hurriedly stuffed in some money. He made sure that he had his *cédula*, the Colombian photo-identification card that was carried by all citizens, and his seaman's photo-ID card from Panama. He had not realized that his wallet contained so many odds and ends until he saw the agents going through its contents. They found his brother's soccer card, a copy of his friend's prescription for skin cream, a clinic appointment card, his religious cards and some scraps of paper with telephone numbers of friends and relatives. It was obvious to the agents that Nicolás was trying to get into the United States illegally, because he had neither a passport nor a visa.

He looked to his right and saw the Customs agents and police officers still milling about. It was starting to get late, and the blanket that was wrapped around his body had long lost its warmth. Nicolás wanted to get the whole legal process over with so he could find out what was going to happen to him and so he could change into some warm dry clothes and go to sleep. His body and mind were crying out for relief.

However, the police and the Customs agents did not seem to be in any hurry to take him off the ship. In fact, they seemed to be in a jovial mood. The packages of cocaine and the test tube of blue liquid were passed from hand to hand as Cummings, Brodley, Burn and Rivedinera, the heroes of the day, were congratulated and slapped on the back. The divers, officers and agents took turns holding the packages and the test tube while the video camera recorded their smiling faces. For more than fifteen minutes, in groups of two and three and even six, they stood next to the duffel bags and posed with the packages and the test tube, grinning at each other and at the camera.

Captain Ho stood by himself watching the testing of the bags' contents and hubbub of activity in the steering-gear room. Customs Inspector Raffaele walked over to him. They spoke for a few seconds and Raffaele assured him that he had nothing to worry about. The captain gave an inward sigh of relief and relaxed. Apparently the answers he had given during the questioning that morning had been satisfactory. As captain of the Bright Eagle, he knew that he would ultimately be held responsible for any hint of involvement, and he knew that his seventeen-year career was at stake.

Both Raffaele and Captain Ho knew that U.S. Customs imposed high fines on ships in which cocaine was found, and that those fines could be imposed even if the ship owner, captain and crew were innocent. With fines set at one thousand dollars per each ounce of cocaine that was found, or in other words, at sixteen thousand dollars per pound, the ship owners faced a fine of over five million dollars. The Customs Service could even seize the ship, which could ultimately be forfeited if proved directly involved.

For this very reason, most shipping companies signed the Sea Carrier Initiative Agreement, in which ship owners agreed to comply with certain measures to protect their ships. In return for this compliance, Customs would regard them favorably with respect to fines and penalties should drugs be found. These measures included a search checklist procedure that was prescribed by the United States Customs Sea Carrier's Security Manual, the authoritative text on smuggling techniques which required random and unannounced searches of all tanks and void spaces in order to look for stowaways as well as drugs.

Instructional video tapes were provided and produced by the Customs Service. These tapes insisted that searchers should never work alone and showed smugglers' behavior on vessel searches. The tapes also demonstrated the techniques of using mirrors and evidence-preservation bags. In short, the instructional video tapes showed the many ways that carriers could assist U.S. Customs in stopping the flow of drugs into the United States.

Captain Ho had been questioned that morning by two men, Special Agent Jack Conti, a member of the Freighter Intelligence Surveillance Team (FIST), and Jack Lane, the supervisor of CET, the Customs Enforcement Team. They had asked him many questions. But they had not asked him if he had tried to assure that the random searches he conducted would take the crew by surprise. They did not ask him if he had used the checklist or if he had used mirrors and evidence-preservation bags or even if he and the officers and the crew had searched alone or in pairs.

That morning, after the captain had been questioned, each crew member was searched by a team of Customs inspectors, after which their personal belongings and quarters were searched. Although a computer check of their names and data was run, the men were not fingerprinted. In addition, they were not interviewed, because they only spoke Korean and the Customs agents had not brought along an interpreter.

Captain Ho and Raffaele stood together and spoke for a few more minutes. It was almost three o'clock in the afternoon and the leaden sky over Manhattan mirrored the gray-green water of New York Harbor beneath it. Whatever sunshine that had managed to emerge that January day was now com-

pletely obscured by the thick cover of clouds that threatened
to lay more snow on the city.

Nicolás sat and watched the crew members performing
their various tasks and wondered what was going to happen
next. Soon two blue-clad men approached him and barked
some words in English. He gazed at them with a blank expression on his face. Then one of the men, remembering that communication in English was pointless, reached over and
grabbed Nicolás under his armpits and pulled him up into a
standing position.

Nicolás' knees buckled immediately and he would have
collapsed onto the deck if the second officer had not steadied
him. Like an astronaut after a long stint in a weightless state
or an invalid after an extended time in bed, Nicolás' legs were
reluctant to obey the commands of his brain. In the cramped
confines of the rudder trunk, where he had lain suspended
over the water in his hammock for nearly twenty-four hours
each day, he had hardly used his legs for a week. They trembled spasmodically beneath him now as he tried to steady
himself on his feet without assistance.

An officer brought over a bright orange life jacket and
handed it to the Customs agent. The agent placed the opening
over Nicolás' head, pressed the captive's arms firmly against
his bruised ribs, and laced each side up tightly. The vest
restricted his movements even more than before, and Nicolás
realized with dismay that whereas before, even though his
wrists were in handcuffs behind his back, he could still move
his shoulders and arms slightly, but now he could only wiggle
his fingers. Not wishing to be overly optimistic, he nevertheless wondered if his donning of the life vest signified that he
was going to be taken off the Bright Eagle.

The yellow blanket that had been wrapped around him
had fallen to the floor around his ankles. One of the agents
bent down and tossed it out of the way. As he did so, a convul-
sive chill coursed through Nicolás' body and his teeth started
to chatter audibly again.

The police officer held Nicolás in an upright position
while the Customs agent tied a pink nylon rope around Nico-

lás' chest, twisted it around his handcuffed wrists several times, wrapped it around his waist and then knotted it tightly. The agent made a loop with the long end of the rope and held it in his hand. Then the officer held the other end of the rope and the three men started walking, sometimes in single file, sometimes three-abreast, up the stairwells and through the ship towards the upper deck.

2:53 P.M.

The flanks of Police Launch 1 and Police Launch 8 bumped each other as they lay side by side in the choppy water alongside the tanker. Their engines rumbled dully and their bows occasionally nudged the towering hull on the port side of the ship.

Police Launch 8 was the larger and the closer of the two boats, and the bottom of the gangplank led directly to its deck. It measured fifty feet in length and fifteen feet in width. A red flag slashed by a white diagonal stripe was painted next to the door, signifying that it was an official boat of the scuba team. The word "POLICE" was emblazoned across its bright blue side and a broad band of gray separated the white of the cabin. There was ample room on the open deck toward the stern to accommodate the Zodiac and the rest of the equipment required by the divers.

Police Launch 1, at anchor directly next to it, was slightly smaller. Its hull was of a darker shade of blue and the words "NYC POLICE" were emblazoned on its side towards the bow. Painted on the white cabin next to the door was "No. 1." The cabin was about twenty-feet long and had large rectangular windows along both sides.

The towering superstructure aft on the deck of the Bright Eagle did little to mitigate the force of the biting wind that whipped across the open space. The massive pipes and valves that ran the length of the huge tanker glistened dully under the sunless winter sky as Agent Conti walked over to the gangplank, looked down and checked the two police launches waiting below.

In his tan pile-lined hooded jacket, Conti seemed oblivious to the cold. The only parts of him that were exposed to the elements were his gray-bearded face and his eyes, which peered out from under the visor of his bright orange cap. Anxious to bring today's business to a close, he had been awake since before dawn and was starting to feel it. He knew that many days and weeks of investigation lay ahead of him and he wanted to get this phase of the operation over with.

The four bags that had been removed from the rudder trunk had to be transported to the Big Apple Launch in Staten Island. From there they would have to be delivered to the Field Office of U.S. Customs in Newark, New Jersey. There in the Office of Enforcement on the fourth floor, they and their contents would be tested, weighed, measured and photographed.

Conti had known that loading the four bags off the ship and onto the police boats would be no easy matter, and he wanted it to go without a hitch. He looked up as he saw the men coming from the stern of the ship, hauling the contents of the rudder trunk.

Finally, a young officer wearing an orange life vest hoisted the white bag onto his shoulder and started walking toward the gangplank. He walked slowly and cautiously, adjusting his body to counterbalance the unaccustomed weight on his shoulder.

"If you drop that fuckin' dope into the water, you can go with it," Conti warned him as another officer rushed over to help the first man reposition the bag as it started to slip. Then, realizing that the video camera that had been recording the proceedings for the past few hours was now recording the loading of the evidence into the police launches, he started to apologize for his language. "I'm sorry. I keep forgetting about the camera. I'm not used to the camera."

Conti leaned over the railing and watched the officer as he slowly descended the gangplank. Once the man reached the deck of Police Launch 8, he turned his attention to Customs Inspector Raffaele, who was getting ready to singlehandedly carry one of the brown duffel bags down to the police launch.

Raffaele had dressed for the occasion. A heavy vest over his partially opened jacket and the dark-blue trousers that matched the rest of his uniform kept him warm in spite of the bitter cold. His short steel-gray hair that matched his mustache was all but hidden under his blue cap. Thick white gloves covered his hands. He squatted down on the deck as two agents lifted the duffel bag onto his back.

One of the Customs agents, a tall heavyset man with a black mustache and a dark receding hairline, grasped the bulky package with both of his white-gloved hands while his counterpart raised the other side. The other man, also warmly dressed in a vest over his jacket, dark gloves and a pile-lined hat with earflaps folded up, held his side of the duffel bag as Raffaele put his arms through its straps and hoisted it onto his back.

Raffaele started to walk towards the gangplank and reached across his chest to tug at the strap under his right armpit. As he approached the railing where Conti was waiting near the top of the gangplank, he turned to him and asked, "Do I have to do any jumping down there?"

Conti laughed and replied, "You know, you're the only guy strong enough to do that kind of stuff."

Raffaele's smile spread across his face as he grinned in acknowledgement of the compliment. "Yeah," he replied, "but I don't want to do no jumping. I don't want to fall in the fucking water."

Then he swung onto the open steps of the steel gangplank that hugged the ship's flank and slowly descended with his cumbersome package. As soon as reached the deck of Launch 8, he crossed over the bow and stepped aboard Launch 1, where two men relieved him of his burden.

While Raffaele was unloading his duffel bag, two members of the scuba team were awkwardly struggling with the second bag. Half-lifting it by its straps and half-dragging it, they managed to get the bag as close to the gangplank as possible without carrying it. One of the divers had changed into his street clothes and was dressed like the other officers, with a cap on his head, dark-blue pants and an open jacket over his blue sweat shirt. The other officer was still wearing his bright-orange scuba suit, which seemed out of place on the deck of the Bright Eagle. The hood of his diving suit hung limply on his chest like a deflated orange balloon, and the gaping zipper of the suit that spread across his chest and shoulders only added to his alien appearance.

The first officer bent down and placed the flashlight that he had been carrying on the deck and hoisted the duffel bag onto his companion's back. With his arms through the straps, the second officer, leaning forward to support the weight of the bag, started to walk down the gangplank. Meanwhile, behind him, his partner grabbed the duffel bag's strap. Then, gripping the railing with his hand while at the same time tucking it under his armpit, he followed him down the steep steps. They walked slowly, making sure that they would not accidentally drop their water-soluble evidence into the turgid depths of New York Harbor.

As soon as their feet touched the deck of Launch 8, the officers and agents on board took the duffel bag from them and placed it into Launch 1. Right behind them two other officers, carrying dark-blue bags containing the rest of the evidence removed from the rudder trunk, boarded the police launch and passed the bags over to the swarm of men waiting with outstretched arms to assist them.

Up on the deck of the Bright Eagle, the last remaining brown duffel bag was being dragged over to the gangplank by two of the agents. With one man holding the strap on one side and the other holding the strap on the opposite side, it too was carried down the gangplank and placed into Police Launch 1.

A small Coast Guard boat approached as the agents and police officers milled about on the decks of the police launches. Although it was only the middle of the afternoon, it had been a long day and they were all eager to leave.

3:03 P.M.

Nicolás, walking between the two men holding the rope that was tied around him, rounded the corner of the stern, emerged on the deck, and began to walk toward the bow of the ship. His head was down as he cautiously placed one foot in front of the other, determined not to stumble on his still unsteady legs. His mind was so filled with the pain of his present situation that he scarcely realized that he was outdoors, breathing fresh air for the first time in nearly a week.

Suddenly, a sharp gust of wind whipped across the open expanse of the Bright Eagle and stung him in the face. He inhaled sharply, ducked his head down even further, and squeezed his eyes closed to avoid getting more dust into them.

He continued walking. Blinking the grit out of his eyes, he slowly raised his head and opened his eyes to look at the skyline of Manhattan for the first time. Suddenly he stopped short and turned his head towards the horizon, his gaze remaining fixed on a point in the distance. His body refused to obey the orders of the two men holding the rope as he stood motionless between them, contemplating as if in a trance the colossal pale-green statue that was sitting on a small island in the bay. A sudden constriction clutched his heart as he beheld the Statue of Liberty for the first time. "I'm in the United States at last," he thought to himself, realizing the irony of that statement.

The police officer on his left started to push Nicolás to get him to start walking again, but the man on his other side silently signaled to his companion to let him stand there for a minute as he informed Nicolás in Spanish that this was New York, the capital of the world.

Nicolás' eyes widened with amazement as he gazed upon the skyline of Manhattan. The height and size of the massive buildings that soared above the streets were taller and more magnificent than he had imagined they would be. Although he had seen photographs of this very scene in books, they were no comparison to reality, and he stared in awe. Almost everything he knew about the United States he had learned from movies or from his friends. Now he realized that his first view of the United States would probably be his last.

He took a deep breath of the cold air and stared transfixed at the Statue of Liberty for one last time. Now the country and the new life that he had dreamed of for so many years was lost to him forever. Nicolás reluctantly turned his head and slowly began walking toward the bow of the Bright Eagle. The men on each side of him quickened their pace and pulled at the rope on their captive.

"What am I? A dog on a leash?" he asked himself. "Some wild animal? Some beast that has to be chained?"

In all his life, though he had never enjoyed the respect accorded to the wealthy, at least he had been treated like a human being. Now, he clearly was not. He walked more briskly now, trying to keep up with his captors. He was anxious to get the humiliating ordeal over with.

A bitter wind gusted across the ship and a few scattered flakes of snow swirled in the air.

The men on deck turned and watched the trio approach the gangplank. The Customs agents and police officers had been awake since four o'clock that morning and they were anxious to get underway. It had been a long cold day and they were hoping to have enough time to get some decent hot food and some sleep before they would have to be back on the job. Their adrenaline-induced energy and euphoria had dissipated, and the day's activities had sapped their strength and drained their enthusiasm almost completely. With the loading of the contents of the rudder trunk onto the police launch, most of the men knew that their participation in the first stage of the operation was almost complete.

The choppy waters of the bay were dotted with boats while two armed police helicopters hovered in the air, slowly circling the Bright Eagle.

The officer with the video camera noticed the stowaway and his escorts coming towards him and he breathed a sigh of relief. He had been standing on the windy deck for a half-hour recording the loading of the evidence onto the police launch and he was glad that his assignment was nearly over. Although he was warm inside his heavy parka, his hands were getting stiff from the cold. He jammed his left hand deep into his pocket and, grasping the camera with his right hand, continued to shoot.

Nicolás mechanically put one foot in front of the other and strode the length of the ship, keeping pace with the two men at his sides. He tried to ignore the stares of the men on deck and, although he did not understand their comments, he knew they were talking about him, especially when one of the officers told another, "He looks like fuckin' Eddie Murphy"—that was the same name his friends used to call him.

When the trio reached the gap in the ship's rail that opened onto the gangplank platform, everybody stopped and moved in closer to assist if necessary.

Grasping the rope around Nicolás tightly in his hand, the Customs agent stepped around him and stood on the metal platform of the gangplank. The officer on his other side gripped the other end of the rope as Nicolás crossed one foot over the other and sidestepped into position on the platform.

He kept his eyes cast downward and concentrated on placing his feet squarely in position.

When he had first arrived at the top of the steep gang-plank, he had glanced down at the water and the police boats that awaited below and, although he had been on boats and ships for almost his entire life, he was suddenly overcome with a wave of nausea and vertigo. Whether it was caused by the height of the ship or his debilitated condition he didn't know, but he had to force himself to swallow several times to fight the bile that was rising in his throat as he cautiously stepped onto the platform. Without the use of his hands to steady himself or to hold onto the railing, only the grip of his sneakers on the metal surface of the platform and the rope that was wrapped around his body prevented him from top-pling over and pitching into the water.

The first officer steadied Nicolás with one hand while the other untied the rope that had been twisted around his cap-tive's wrists. Nicolás flexed his fingers a few times as the removal of the restraining rope restored the circulation in his hands. With one man holding the rope walking in front of him and the other holding the rope walking in back of him, Nicolás slowly descended the steps, his eyes lowered.

"This is it," he thought to himself. "It's almost over. Now I'll be able to sleep."

He reached the bottom step of the gangplank and looked at his captors. There were two boats and he did not know which one he was supposed to board. The officer guided him across the bow of Police Launch 8 onto the deck of Police Launch 1. Still attached to the rope, Nicolás followed him towards the door and ducked his head down as he stepped over the threshold. The Customs agent motioned for him to sit down on the bench next to the doorway, and Nicolás settled down on the hard wooden seat with a sigh.

In spite of the open doorway, it was relatively warm inside the cabin and Nicolás had to struggle to keep his eyes open. Although his body cried out for the sweet release of sleep, his mind kept telling him to stay awake and not let his guard down for an instant. But the vibrations of the boat's engines that he felt through the wooden bench had a lulling effect on him, and he was unaware that his head had slumped forward in sleep until his eyes snapped open as the engines increased their revolutions and the boat started to move.

Slowly, ever so slowly, Police Launch 1 backed away from the side of the Bright Eagle, turned around and headed for the pier.

Nicolás looked around at the faces of the men in the boat. They were congregated in small groups of two and three. From their animated conversations that were accompanied by glances in his direction, he guessed that they were still talking about him. Uncomfortable at being scrutinized at such close quarters, he tried to ignore their stares by looking through the windows directly across from him to see where the boat was headed. It was difficult see anything because his view was obstructed by the movements of the men as they walked about the cabin.

The bench that he was sitting on ran parallel to the side of the boat and there was a row of windows running at shoulder level. Nicolás twisted around and craned his neck upward, looking through the window above and behind him as he tried to get one last glimpse of the pale-green statue of the lady in the harbor. His eyes searched right and left and scanned the near and far horizons, but Liberty was nowhere to be seen.

Police Launch 1 slowed down and approached the piers of Hoboken. As soon as the bow nudged the wood pilings, the men on each side of Nicolás grabbed the rope at his waist and wordlessly motioned for him to stand up. He rocked unsteadily on his feet as the boat bumped into the pier. Automatically ducking his head down as he passed through the portal of the cabin, he followed the Customs agents and police officers across the deck, up the steps alongside the boat, and onto the pier.

Like two white lights that had just been switched on, his eyes widened in astonishment at the congregation of photographers, TV cameramen and reporters from the national and international media assembled there. As soon as they spotted Nicolás, still trussed with the pink nylon rope between two customs agents, they surged forward with their cameras flashing and their microphones stabbing at the air in front of them. They hurled questions at him both in English and in Spanish, each one louder and more insistent.

Nicolás recoiled from their verbal barrage and retreated a few steps towards the boat he had just exited. His escorts, sensing that their captive was about to be swamped, formed a protective shield around him with their bodies and, carving a path through the still-clamoring members of the press, escorted him to one of the black sedans that was waiting for them with its motor running. One of the officers darted ahead of the phalanx surrounding Nicolás and opened the door of the unmarked car. Turning back to the others, the officer beckoned for them to proceed.

Glancing backwards with relief, Nicolás resolutely strode towards the car and placed one foot inside the open door. The officer standing there held Nicolás' shoulder with one hand and placed his other hand on the top of Nicolás' head so he wouldn't bump into the door frame as he got into the car. He held the door open long enough for a Customs agent to slide in next to Nicolás and then slammed it shut. Another agent opened the opposite door and made himself comfortable on Nicolás' left while a third seated himself next to the driver. Six more agents divided themselves among the other two cars lined up at the curb behind them, and the entourage slowly headed off the pier and towards the street.

With much muttering about the amount of hours they had each waited on the windy pier only to receive no responses to their questions, the crowd of reporters and cameramen packed up their equipment, grumbled their goodbyes to each other and left. They had been eager for an interview with the stowaway who, it was rumored, had survived for a week in an unprecedented voyage in the rudder compartment of an oil tanker. Now, unless they could intercept him again, they would have to be satisfied with the skimpy information they had managed to glean from their observations and anonymous sources as well as the few pictures they had been able to take before their subject was completely surrounded and whisked away by his escorts.

Relieved to have escaped the assault of reporters, Nicolás sat back in the luxurious warmth of the car and wondered what other surprises this day had in store for him. Through hooded eyelids that threatened to close at any minute from sheer exhaustion, he morosely gazed through the windows at the slushy streets. Because he couldn't see the tops of the buildings from his position in the middle of the rear seat, he angled his head and stared at their glass facades mirroring the sooty clouds that hung over the city.

Oblivious to the face of the prisoner staring at them through the window as the car paused at a traffic light, the bundled-up pedestrians rushed past with their heads tucked down on their chests and their bodies bent into the wind.

After three-quarters of an hour, the procession of cars finally reached its destination and pulled up in front of the U.S. Customs Service at Hemisphere Center in Newark, New Jersey. Nicolás looked up at the main entrance of the building in front of him. Scores of reporters and cameramen were already waiting for them on the scene. The flashes of their cameras combined with the glare from the banks of lights mounted on the television vans to create a deceptive aura of extended daylight in the early dusk of the winter afternoon.

As soon as he exited the car, Nicolás was immediately surrounded again by the agents who were both surprised and annoyed to find the press so well-informed of their movements. The agents swept past the press, ignoring the persistent questions, and rapidly escorted their prisoner into the building.

As he walked down one of the corridors, with his arms still behind him in handcuffs, Nicolás suddenly lost his balance and tripped. He was saved from falling flat on his face only by the fast reflexes of one of the agents beside him who instinctively grabbed him as he pitched towards the floor. Nicolás looked at the man gratefully, and from then on kept his eyes on his feet as they passed through several sets of doors.

Finally they reached a hallway containing two rows of steel-barred cells. An officer opened one of the doors and the two agents led Nicolás inside. Turning him around, they removed his handcuffs and motioned for him to sit down. Then they left the cell and the officer locked the heavy-barred door.

Nicolás walked the few feet over to the cement bench that was set into the wall and sat down. He held his hands in his lap and leaned over to assess the damage the handcuffs had inflicted on his wrists. He had been wearing them for hours and the sharp steel had left deep red grooves in his skin. He rubbed the impressions with his fingers as if he were trying to erase them. He thought to himself that he would not only be mentally marked by this ordeal, but he would also carry the physical stigmata of his arrest forever. He stood up and linked his fingers together high above his head, then brought his hands down in back of him as he attempted to loosen up the muscles in his back and shoulders. His arms had been pinioned behind him for such a long time that his bones creaked as he twisted and stretched his arms and torso from side to side. He eyed the cement bench sleepily, figuring that he was so tired he could sleep anywhere. Laying down on his back, he folded his arms beneath his head as a pillow just as the door to his cell opened.

Outside with a key in his hand was a tall, well-dressed man in a dark suit and blue tie. He beckoned to Nicolás to follow him and, with a guard accompanying them, led him to one of the small rooms down the hall. After opening the door, the guard closed the door behind them and sat down in a chair just outside.

Seated behind a narrow table was a young man in a maroon ski jacket. Nicolás stared at him curiously, wondering if he was also a Customs agent or perhaps a plainclothes detective, when the man introduced himself in Spanish and explained to Nicolás that he was an interpreter assigned to translate both the questions of the Customs agent and Nicolás' answers. Nicolás nodded that he understood and sat down in the single wooden chair opposite the two men.

"State your full name."

"Nicolás Córdoba-Zapata."

"What is your date of birth?"

"September 27, 1966."

"Where are you from?"

"Turbo, Colombia"

"Are you married?"

"No."

"Do you have any children?"

"Yes."

"Well...what are they? Boys? Girls? How old are they? Who do they live with?"

"They're both girls...one's four and the other's six...they live with my mother."

"Who do you work for?"

"Some guy on the beach...I just rent stuff...beach chairs, umbrellas...you know...to the tourists."

"No, that's not what I mean! Don't get smart with me. Tell me who you work for...who's the owner of those drugs we found in the compartment? How did you get them in there? Who gave them to you? How much did they pay you to do this?"

"I don't know anything. I already told you guys that the bags were already there when I entered the ship, all tied up the way you found them. I didn't put them there...I didn't even know they were in there."

"All right, let's try to approach this from another angle. Who are your accomplices here? Who's waiting for you? Who were you supposed to deliver the drugs to? You can help us you know.... It'll be better for you if you cooperate and help us make a controlled delivery of the drugs. You can make believe you still have the stuff and deliver it to the guys that are waiting for you in Roseton...then we can grab them and the government will go easy on you."

"No sé nada...no sé nada...I don't know anything...I don't know anything," he kept on repeating in a deep monotone.

Shaking his head slowly from side to side, Nicolás thought to himself, "This guy obviously doesn't believe me...he keeps on asking me the same questions over and over and over again."

The Customs agent tipped his chair back and placed his pen and pad on the table. He opened the top button of his shirt and loosened the knot in his tie.

"All right," he said, "tell me how you came to be on that ship...what you did...when you did it...and how you did it. Tell me everything, and I mean everything you know about the drugs that were in that compartment with you. Take your time and tell me precisely what happened. Take a break every once in a while so that he," pointing to the interpreter with his thumb, "can translate your exact words, so there won't be any misinterpretations or misunderstandings. Okay?"

Nicolás gazed across the scarred table at the two men. His head kept threatening to fall onto his chest, and he had to force his eyes to stay in focus. He just wanted to get the interrogation over with so he could go back to his cell and get some sleep.

He raised his head and, directing his answers to the interpreter, explained precisely why and how he had stowed away on the Bright Eagle…repeating time and time again, "Soy un polizón…soy un polizón." (I'm a stowaway…I'm a stowaway.)

The Customs agent set his chair back again on all four legs, leaned forward and picked up his pen. "Okay, let's just go over a few more details."

Again he asked Nicolás what time of day he had entered the tanker, what distance the ship was from the shore, how he had gotten into the rudder trunk and what was the appearance of the compartment when he had first seen it. He entered Nicolás' replies in his pad and then, seemingly satisfied, stood up.

As if on cue, there was a knock on the door.

"Come in," replied the Customs agent.

Carefully balancing a large flat box in one hand, the guard opened the door with the other and, then keeping the door open with his foot so it wouldn't slam shut, he handed the carton over. The interpreter smacked his hands together in eager anticipation and opened the box, revealing a still steaming pizza. He separated one of the triangular slices and handed it to Nicolás, who hungrily reached over the table to grab it. Chewing it slowly, it seemed to Nicolás that the warm cheese and the spicy pepperoni were the most delicious foods that he had eaten in years. In fact, it was the first warm food he had eaten in over a week.

The guard returned with three cans of soda, and Nicolás, the interpreter and the Customs agent each took one. For fifteen minutes the trio ate in silence until Nicolás, after devouring three slices of pizza, indicated that he had had enough.

The Customs agent opened the door and told the guard that he was finished with the interrogation. The guard took Nicolás by the arm and led him back to the cell. A gray woolen blanket now lay folded at the foot of the bench. Nicolás relieved himself at the toilet in the corner and then wearily unfolded the rough blanket and lay down. With a shuddering sigh of relief mixed with exhaustion, he turned on his side, cradled his head in the crook of his elbow, and was fast asleep in less than a minute.

Feeling that he had just shut his eyes a few seconds earlier, Nicolás was loudly awakened after a few hours. He sat up and rubbed the sleep from his eyes with his fists. Then he stood shakily on his feet and tried to regain his equilibrium.

His body still rocked internally, echoing the rolling of the waves, and it was only his eyes that told him he was on land.

Two guards escorted him out of his cell and down the corridor to a room awash in the blue-white glare of fluorescent lights. Directed to stand with his back against the wall, Nicolás sullenly stared at the camera taking his picture. All the frustration and helplessness he was feeling, all the exhaustion and physical pain he was suffering, and all the fear and anxiety he had experienced the past seven days were reflected in his haunted eyes and desolate expression.

After the obligatory photographs were taken, Nicolás was led over to a formica counter where an officer grabbed his left wrist. "Just relax," he advised him in Spanish.

Then taking Nicolás' fingers one at a time in his own, he rolled each one on an ink pad and then pressed the finger onto a sheet of paper, carefully rolling it again to ensure that a perfect impression was made in each designated square on the official document. Nicolás looked down in horror at the accusing black marks, realizing that he had been branded a criminal for life. Although the branding iron was cold ink, it seared him just as much as if it had been burned into his flesh.

"What am I? What have I become? What will become of me?" he asked himself. "There's got to be some kind of mistake…I can't be here…this can't be real…this can't be happening to me.

But it was.

Nicolás was led back to his cell. This time the sleep he sought so desperately eluded him, as he tossed from side to side, kept awake by tormented memories of the past and tortured visions of the future.

"What should I have done differently?" he asked himself. "What could I have done differently?" He had endured so much to end up here, like an animal in a cage, branded as a criminal for the rest of his life, not knowing when or even if he would ever return to Colombia and see his mother and two daughters again. They were so young. They would probably forget him in a few years. It would be as if he had never even existed.

"At least I'm alive," he reminded himself. "I wasn't so sure of that a week ago. A week ago I didn't think I was going to last another hour."

As he lay there on the cement bench, he was surprised to find his eyelids growing heavy. Sheer exhaustion had defeated his fears and he found himself at the brink of sleep.

"I'm going to make it!" he assured himself. "It can't get any worse than this."

But it did.

At five o'clock in the morning a guard entered and told Nicolás to get out of bed and stand up. The guard placed Nicolás' hands behind his back, snapped a pair of handcuffs on his wrists and led him out of the cell. They retraced the route taken only a few hours before and left the building. A cold gray dawn as grim as his mood was just breaking as the guard escorted Nicolás to a side parking lot and into one of the two cars waiting there. It was identical to the one that had brought him there yesterday. The agents accompanying him took their former positions on each side of him.

The silence of the car was broken only by the crackling of the police radio. The heat that permeated the vehicle immediately induced a state of drowsiness which Nicolás tried in vain to resist. He leaned his head against the soft cushion behind him and closed his eyes.

He had no idea if he had been sleeping for an hour or just a few minutes when he woke up as the car came to an abrupt halt. He leaned over and then looked out of the window and saw a tall building looming in front of him. At the entrance he noticed several armed guards, three of whom stood to one side as the heavy iron door automatically swung open. The driver of the car got out, opened the rear door of the vehicle, and gestured for Nicolás to exit.

Nicolás needed no inducement to walk quickly as an icy gust of wind whipped around his legs and struck him in the face. He tucked his chin down and, with an agent right beside him, rushed through the open door and into the building.

He swiveled his head in surprise when the door shut as soon as they crossed the threshold and another door opened in front of him. The agent led Nicolás through the door, down a short corridor, through another door and down a passageway until they arrived at an elevator. They entered the elevator and stood side by side in silence as it ascended to the third floor and stopped. The agent placed a hand on Nicolás' shoulder and led him down another long corridor punctuated with rooms every few feet until they finally entered the last one on the right.

Inside the brightly-lit room, one female and two male corrections officers were seated at large steel desks; at a chest-high counter opposite them another officer was sorting papers. They were all dressed alike in gray slacks, navy blazers, white shirts, maroon ties and black thick-soled oxfords. Motioning to Nicolás to sit down, the agent walked over to an officer bent over forms at his desk and handed him a large manila envelope.

"He's all yours," he remarked, turned to the door and, without so much as a backward glance at his prisoner, left the room. His responsibilities had terminated with the delivery of Nicolás, who was now under the jurisdiction of the Federal Bureau of Prisons, an arm of the Department of Justice.

The officer at the desk withdrew the papers from the sealed envelope, rifled through them for a few seconds, and then called out, "Córdoba!"

Nicolás' knees protested noisily as he stood up and walked over to the desk. Wondering what was in store for him, he was relieved when the officer released him from his handcuffs and led him over to a white counter. He noticed the ink pad on the desk and realized that he was about to be fingerprinted again. He marvelled to himself how something so demoralizing just a few hours ago could now seem so familiar. After obtaining his fingerprints, the officer made sure that Nicolás signed the bottom of each page as mandated by law. The fingerprints would be permanently kept on file with the FBI and could be used to identify Nicolás at any time in the future.

He then directed Nicolás to stand with his back flat against the wall. Positioning him first to the right, then to the left and finally towards the front again, the officer snapped pictures of each of the poses. After he extracted the photographs from the camera, he examined them to make sure that he didn't have to retake any. His Polaroid camera was fitted with four lenses that quadruplicated each photograph; this assured that enough copies were immediately available for the various forms and documents that were required.

Two officers got up and led Nicolás down a corridor to a small cell and ordered him to remove all of his clothes. Not knowing what to expect, Nicolás reluctantly stripped off his sweat shirt and tee-shirt with one motion and then, hands visibly shaking, slid his sweat pants off his legs and climbed out of his underpants.

Seeing that Nicolás was finally naked, one of the officers ordered him to stand in the middle of the room with his arms and legs spread apart. After closely examining every inch of Nicolás' anatomy to make sure that he had no weapons or drugs attached to his body, he ordered him to spread his legs wider and bend over.

Shaking with rage and humiliation, Nicolás stared down at the floor. One of the officers left the room and returned a few seconds later and handed Nicolás a large empty plastic bag, sheets, a blanket, a toothbrush and bundle of clothes. He told Nicolás to get dressed and put his old clothes into the bag. Nicolás quickly donned the underwear and snapped up the brown short-sleeved jumpsuit he was issued. Then he put on green socks and slipped his feet into blue canvas slippers.

Pinching the corners of his soiled clothing, and holding them at arm's length, he dropped them one by one into the plastic bag. He was glad to be rid of them.

He looked at the eight numbers marked on the bag. It was his inmate registration number and would identify him and all his property and monitor all his movements and activities as long as he remained under the jurisdiction of the Bureau of Prisons. He repeated the numbers aloud and tried to memorize them. Noticing him reciting the numbers in Spanish, one of the officers told him he had to know them in English, and Nicolás struggled to repeat the unfamiliar words.

After taking the bag from Nicolás' outstretched hand, the officer informed him that he was taking him to a temporary holding cell where he would remain until they had finished processing his papers. Nicolás nervously looked around for a stick or something that he could use to defend himself in case he was assaulted by other inmates, but he couldn't find anything. Resigning himself to using his bare hands if necessary, he followed the officer down the hall to the cell. The officer unlocked the cell's heavy metal door and unceremoniously deposited Nicolás inside.

Permeating the large room was the stale odor of cigarette smoke mixed with sour exhalations of alcohol. Seated against the walls at the long concrete benches that ran the length of the room were men with hair in all styles of disarray and faces grimly set with frightened eyes that darted nervously at the newcomer. After furtively scrutinizing them, Nicolás was relieved to find that no one presented an apparent or immediate danger.

"Do you speak Spanish?" he asked the man sitting next to him as he settled down in a vacant spot.

"Of course," the man replied. "All of us here are Colombians, except that white guy in the corner who jumped bail, something that we can never do because they don't give us bail." He laughed softly to himself, amused at his ironic humor. "Oh, and that guy with all the tattoos," he added, indicating in the typical Colombian manner with pursed lips and an upthrust chin a tall man with a mustache who had just gotten up from his seat. "He's here for violating parole."

"What's that?" asked Nicolás curiously.

"Parole," his countryman patiently explained, pleased to educate this novice in the ways of the United States judicial system, "is the part of your prison sentence that you can serve on the street in freedom, although carefully monitored by the government. You have to report to a parole officer who asks you where you went, who you talked to, what you did. Don't worry about it," he assured Nicolás, seeing his raised eyebrows, "we never get paroled because we're deported automatically after we finish serving our time."

"Are there usually so many Colombians here?" Nicolás asked incredulously.

"Okay, let me explain," continued the man. "After Avianca arrives from Colombia on Sundays...by Tuesday and Wednesday this place is usually filled with men from the Bolaños Cartel."

"Bolaños Cartel? I never heard of it," interrupted Nicolás.

"The Bolaños are the ingenious men who exchange balls for years; that is to say, they agree to swallow condoms filled with cocaine in exchange for tickets, hotel accommodations, and three thousand dollars. When they arrive in the United States and hand over the drugs, they are supposed to receive three thousand dollars more. But this never happens because the deal is concluded with these incautious souls handing themselves over to the public prosecutors in order to reduce the amount of time served by inmates already sentenced, inmates who have paid them well for this service. Approximately one year is taken off the sentence for each traveller that has been deceived into giving himself up. In this manner the flow of narcotics is inexhaustible, because each person who has a sick child, or who has been thrown out of work, or who has been seized by debt, is a potential candidate to feed the American legal system in its satanic game called 'The War Against Drugs,' which functions like a pyramid: one guy brings two, two guys bring four, four guys bring eight and so on."

Nicolás sat in stunned silence at these revelations. He knew that people lived in desperate conditions in Colombia. He knew only too well, first-hand, that life often seemed hopeless and sometimes the illegal way was the only way one could survive. But he could not comprehend anyone knowingly and willingly giving up his freedom, his most precious possession, for any amount of money in the world. Even the thought of it depressed him. He massaged his temples with the tips of his fingers. The dull headache that he had awakened with now throbbed beneath his hands, and he wished he could ask someone for something to relieve it or maybe for a cup of coffee, which sometimes helped. He walked over to the bathroom at the back of the room and splashed some cold water on his face. Then cupping both hands under the faucet, he leaned over and drank deeply.

The pain in his head abated somewhat and he sat down again next to his now laconic companion and stared blankly at the opposite wall. With a protracted sigh, he forced himself to think of the brighter side of his situation. Maybe it was merely rationalization, or perhaps it was his personal defense mechanism for coping with adversity, but it was something he had always done in the face of every setback he had ever encountered.

"I still have my life and I still have my health," he reminded himself. "I'm young. Even if I get sent to prison for a year or two I'll be...what?...twenty-six or maybe twenty-seven when I get out. Still young. Still with my whole life ahead of me. God works in mysterious ways," he told himself, recalling with a pang of nostalgia his grandmother's words.

"Maybe," he mused, "something good will come out of even *this* disaster. Maybe something good will happen after all."

Suddenly, appearing as a genie summoned to grant the first of Nicolás' three wishes, an officer materialized at the door of the cell and called out his name and number.

Nicolás and nine other inmates whose names were also called walked in single file down a corridor and into an elevator. The officer unsnapped a black case attached to the side of his wide belt and extracted a bulky two-way radio. "Calling Control," as the Control Room that monitored and controlled the access to all doors was referred to, he told it to send the elevator to the ninth floor. The radio crackled with Control's affirmative reply, and the elevator ascended rapidly to the ninth floor. They exited into a corridor that divided the ninth floor into two sections. To one side was the section known as 9 South. This was an area used for the segregation of inmates who could not be mixed with the general population... either for their own safety or the safety of others. Their meals were brought to them and they were only permitted out of their cells for visits from their lawyers or for court appearances.

Nicolás and the nine other inmates halted at the door on the other side of the corridor that led to 9 North while the officer spoke into his radio and the door automatically opened. He escorted the ten men to an Hispanic female officer seated inside a glassed-in office and handed her the fresh ID cards emblazoned with the photographs taken just an hour ago. She picked up Nicolás' card, looked at him to confirm his identification, and then stood up from her desk. Nicolás followed her down the corridor, clutching his linens in his arms and looking around curiously at his new home.

He was now officially at MCC.

The Metropolitan Correctional Center, a facility of the Federal Bureau of Prisons, was located in downtown Manhattan and housed inmates of all ages, sizes, ethnic backgrounds, races, religions and nationalities. Here, men arrested just a few hours previously and prison-wise inmates with years of incarceration behind them were thrown together while they appeared at trials or waited to be parceled out to other facilities. Here, leaders of organized crime families, bank embezzlers, income tax evaders, arms dealers and street-corner drug pushers ate the same food, wore the same clothes and shared the same showers. The very rich and the never rich, the famous and the infamous slept in identical two-man cells on identical bunk beds covered by identical blankets; they washed their faces in identical sinks and dried them with identical towels.

If the United States was the "melting pot" of the world, MCC was a miniature replica of that conglomeration of nations. And like its counterpart, MCC held the aspirations and expectations of men who wanted to be free...not from the shackles of a political or a religious despot, but from the chains of poverty. Here were desperate men, representing nearly every country on the globe, who had tried anything, legal and illegal, to alleviate the dire situation of their families back home. Here, too, were the hopes and dreams for a better life.

But this was where the dream ended instead of began.

Nicolás followed the female officer through a small kitchen that contained a double sink, a refrigerator, an ice maker and a machine that dispensed both hot and cold water. Two microwave ovens rested on the counter opposite the sink; they were utilized by the inmates to heat up their food, which was delivered lukewarm in individual plastic trays from the institution's kitchen on the second floor. Next to this kitchen and adjacent to the doorway was a tiny laundry room with a single washing machine and dryer, where the inmates could wash their own clothes instead of exchanging them for clean clothes once a week when they received their fresh linen. Piled against one of the corners in the laundry room was a mountain of mops and brooms. The floors were *very* clean in MCC.

As they entered a large common area known as the multi-purpose room, Nicolás was surprised to see a ping-pong table and two billiard tables. He couldn't imagine how anyone could be so complacent about his situation and so oblivious to his surroundings to be able to enjoy himself. Neatly arranged in one corner were a few sets of barbells and several pairs of dumbbells. In the other corner were four public telephones, now quiet and unused this early in the morning when all the inmates were still locked in their cells.

Through the four large windows Nicolás could see the tall gray buildings of lower Manhattan emerge from the shroud of dawn. It was his second day in the United States.

Nicolás followed the officer across the multi-purpose room and down one of the cell-lined corridors. There was a row of six cells on each side of the passageway with another set of identical cells above them connected by a short metal staircase. A shower capable of accommodating six men at a time was on the lower level and was for the sole use of the inmates of this "tier," as this arrangement of cells was known.

Just as Nicolás was marching up the steps and wondering if he would be following this woman all morning, the officer abruptly stopped in front of the third cell and unlocked it. After handing him a small bar of soap, a tube of toothpaste, a razor and a plastic hair pick, she ordered him to enter. Then she shut the door behind her, locked it, and returned to her office downstairs.

Nicolás looked out a small window set into the heavy metal door, but could only see the corridor directly ahead. He placed the items he had been carrying in his arms on a small metal table that was bolted to the floor and surveyed the contents of his cell. It didn't take very long.

Inside the room were a pair of bunk beds, a toilet, two small lockers, one chair and a sink with a metallic mirror hanging on the wall above it. Nicolás eyed his reflection with a mixture of disbelief and disdain. He rubbed his hand over his cheeks and felt the crisp bristles of his unshaven face; the mustache that he had always kept carefully trimmed hung unevenly over his upper lip. Disgusted with his image in the mirror, he stepped over to the wall opposite the door and looked out the small, barred window.

From his cell on the ninth floor, Nicolás looked down onto Park Row and the other streets that bordered MCC. A few taxis sped by, their doors splattered with a week's accumulation of slush. Near the corner, a sanitation truck stopped to pick up the frozen plastic-bagged garbage that had been deposited on the curb during the night. The sun, just barely over the horizon, pierced the gray canyons below him with frosty slivers of light, and the mercury street lamps splashed amber puddles on the nearly deserted sidewalks. From every angle, he saw tall buildings extending upwards toward the leaden clouds above.

"New York...the capital of the world," he sighed, remembering the police officer's words to him as he was being taken off the Bright Eagle.

"I should be glad," he chided himself, "I should be glad I didn't fall into the water...I should be glad I wasn't sucked into the propeller...I should be glad I didn't bleed to death or starve to death or freeze to death." But he didn't feel very glad. All he could think of was his mother and daughters back in Colombia.

Nicolás walked over to the bottom bunk and sat down with his head between his knees. Then with a start he jumped up as if he were physically trying to throw off the cloak of depression that was threatening to smother him. He rapidly made up the bed and lied down on the thin mattress, cradling his head on one arm in order to prevent it from touching the clean linens. His hair was uneven and matted and exuded the same briny redolence as his unwashed body.

He had just closed his eyes in his latest attempt to get some sleep that morning when his door was suddenly opened and the officer that had locked it barely a half an hour ago shouted, "Chow time, breakfast!"

She walked up and down the rows of cells, unlocking and opening their doors as she passed them, repeating over and over again, "Chow time...chow time, breakfast."

As she retraced her steps and passed by Nicolás' cell, she poked her head in and told him in Spanish that it was time for breakfast and that he could get up and get it if he wanted to.

Nicolás not only hadn't understood what she had been shouting, but he also didn't realize that he was free to move about and associate with the other inmates. The audible grumbling in his stomach propelled him out the door. Nervously surveying his new surroundings again, he walked down the stairs and entered the multi-purpose room. A small group of dishevelled inmates stood in line next to the kitchen, and he walked over and got behind them.

A few of the men grunted greetings to one another, but for the most part everyone was silent, either too sleepy, too anti-social or too enveloped in a dream that had just been interrupted. Nicolás looked into the faces of the men as they returned to the small square tables near the TV room to eat their breakfast. "What did they do? Why are they here?" he wondered to himself.

It was impossible to tell by looking at them what they had been on the street. A few of the men had neatly ironed and sharply creased jumpsuits; some of them had already shaved and were obviously concerned with their appearance. These fastidious few openly stared at him, some even unconsciously wrinkling up their noses as they passed by, not saying a word.

Taking his cue from the man in front of him, Nicolás grabbed a plastic knife, fork, spoon and a brown plastic mug. Then he picked up one of the identically-filled plastic trays and sat alone at one of the tables. Breakfast consisted of two fried eggs, some boiled potatoes and two slices of bread, but after subsisting on little more than cheese, crackers and water while he was in the rudder trunk, it tasted pretty good, and he ate it all, washing everything down with cold milk.

With his belly full and warm at last, Nicolás was looking forward to a long, long nap. He sat on the edge of his bed and took off his shoes. He was just about to lay down when an officer stuck his head in the doorway and told him that he had five minutes to get ready to appear in court. Nicolás hurriedly scrubbed and shaved his face, brushed his teeth, and broke off two teeth of his plastic pick while trying to fix his hair.

Exactly five minutes later, the officer reappeared and told Nicolás to accompany him. They walked down the hall, across the multi-purpose room and down another corridor until they stopped in front of the elevator. The doors opened and an officer inside the elevator beckoned Nicolás to enter. The elevator stopped on the third floor. Nicolás followed the officer into a large room, known as the "Bull Pen," in which a group of about thirty men was already assembled.

Nicolás found it hard to believe that these men were actually inmates. They were all dressed in the clothes that they had been wearing at the time of their arrest. He was the only one wearing the brown institutional jumpsuit. He gazed with silent admiration at their fine garments, for not only were these men wearing street clothes, but most were wearing hand-tailored silk suits that cost at least two thousand dollars, along with five-hundred-dollar alligator shoes or snakeskin boots and monogrammed silk shirts that cost more than Nicolás had ever earned in one month.

He had seen wealthy people before wearing the finest of clothes, but never so many at one time in so small a space. He was to find out later that most of these inmates were millionaires many times over, arrested for organized crime activities or for income tax evasion. Some of the others had been arrested on suspicion of conspiracy and drug trafficking.

Nicolás looked up as an officer opened the door and entered the room carrying a large plastic bag. He called out the number written on the bag, but received no response. Although Nicolás had been instructed to remember his inmate registration number, he knew it in Spanish but had not had sufficient time to memorize it in English. He finally concluded, however, that since he was the only one in the room wearing a jumpsuit, the bag must be his. Nicolás walked over to the officer and retrieved it. Inside were the clothes that *he* had been arrested in, the ones that he had been wearing inside the rudder trunk. The essence of seawater was imbedded in their fibers and that, together with a week's accumulation of grime and sweat, had combined to create a unique and altogether disgusting odor. They had been slightly damp when he had deposited them into the plastic bag yesterday and their confinement there had done nothing to enhance their aroma.

He changed in the bathroom, stepped out and looked around. For the ever-meticulous Nicolás, it was doubly embarrassing to be wearing clothes that were not only soiled and wrinkled but which stunk as well.

The door opened and a group of U.S. marshals walked in carrying handcuffs and chains, which they deposited noisily on a table. Then, one by one, each inmate was summoned over, where one marshal handcuffed his wrists and another snapped a pair of leg irons onto his ankles. The leg irons were each joined by a twelve-inch piece of chain, which was itself connected to a longer chain attached to the handcuffs.

When it was Nicolás' turn to be fettered, he stoically walked over and thrust his hands in front of him, repeating over and over again to himself the words his grandmother had drummed into his head...drummed into his very being so many years ago, "I may be poor, I may be black, but I am *not* a slave."

He returned to his seat as the next man walked up to the table to be shackled. One hour...two hours...almost three hours passed until finally everyone was ordered to leave the room. Taking as large a stride as the chain between his ankles would permit, he walked behind the other inmates in a single file into one of the waiting vans.

The ride from lower Manhattan to downtown Brooklyn was a short one, and a few minutes after exiting the Brooklyn Battery Tunnel, the vans pulled up in front of the United States District Court for the Eastern District of New York. The inmates entered a side door of the building, their chains clinking rhythmically in time with their steps as they marched, again in single file, into the building where they were locked into another bull pen.

The easy camaraderie of the brief excursion evaporated as the men filed into the room and sat down. Only a few engaged in whispered conversations. Most were solemnly contemplating what the next few hours would have in store for them. Although they knew that this arraignment was just a formality and that the time spent in front of the judge would amount to only about fifteen minutes, it was here that they would formally hear their charges read against them and, well-versed in the law as they were, they would immediately know how much time they would have to spend behind bars if they were found guilty.

Nicolás leaned his head against the wall in back of him. "What are they going to do to me?" he worried. "Where are they going to send me? What's going to happen to my daughters? I have nothing...I can't afford a fancy lawyer. I have nobody that can help me. What's going to happen to me?"

He had never felt so alone and so lost in his life. Even when he was a teen-ager scrabbling for his very existence in the barrios of Colombia, he had not felt this alone, this vulnerable. Right now he felt as if he had been dropped onto a distant planet millions of miles from his home, a world in which he couldn't understand or read or speak the language, a world in which the customs, the scenery and even the food was alien to him.

He closed his eyes and tried to pray, hoping for some indication, some sign that would give him hope, that would tell him that all wasn't lost. So many times during his childhood he had sat in church next to his grandmother and had fervently prayed that Christ Himself would appear before him to tell him that everything would be all right. In his mind, he had always tried to picture Him saying, "Listen to Me, from today

on you don't have to worry about a thing...I'm your friend."
But today, as desperately as he tried to conjure that image, all
he could see was a vision of Father Pérez, the local priest of
his childhood, materializing from the pulpit to condemn his
sinful soul to be seared forever in the fires of Hell. Nicolás
snapped his eyes open to expunge the picture from his mind,
but found that reality was just as horrible.

He sat and stared down at his feet, not speaking, wishing
this day would end. Finally, the marshals arrived two hours
later and he was taken up a long flight of stairs to the courtroom.

The armed guard opened the side door and Nicolás and
the marshal entered and joined the interpreter at a table on
the left. The judge glanced at the U.S. Attorney and then nodded to the marshal who took Nicolás by the elbow and raised
him to a standing position.

"Nicolás Córdoba-Zapata, you are charged with count one,
that on or about January 24, 1991, within the Eastern District
of New York and elsewhere, you did knowingly and intentionally conspire to import into the United States from a place
outside thereof in excess of five kilograms of a substance containing cocaine, a Schedule II narcotic drug controlled substance, in violation of Title 21, United States Code, Sections
952(A), and Title 21, United States Code, Sections 963 and
960(B), and Title 18, United States Code, Section 3551.

"You are charged with count two, that on or about January 24, 1991, within the Eastern District of New York, that
you did knowingly and intentionally import into the United
States from a place outside thereof in excess of five kilograms
of a substance containing cocaine, a Schedule II narcotic drug
controlled substance in violation of Title 21, United States
Code, Sections 952(A), 960(A) and 960(B), and Title 18, United
States Code, Sections 2 and 3551.

"You are charged with count three, that on or about January 24, 1991, within the Eastern District of New York, you did
knowingly and intentionally possess with intent to distribute
in excess of five kilograms of a substance containing cocaine, a
Schedule II narcotic drug controlled substance in violation of
Title 21, United States Code, Sections 841(A) and 841(B) and
Title 18, United States Code, Sections 2 and 3551.

"Do you understand the charges against you, sir?"

Nicolás, who had been concentrating on listening to the interpreter, slowly nodded his head in acknowledgement and in his deep voice replied, "Sí."

"Are you ready to enter your plea at this time?"

"Sí."

"How do you plead to count one? Guilty or not guilty?"

"Not guilty."

"How do you plead to count two? Guilty or not guilty?"

"Not guilty."

"How do you plead to count three? Guilty or not guilty."

"Not guilty."

"Thank you. You may be seated."

The judge checked his court calendar and informed Nicolás of the date of his next appearance and then turned to the marshal and indicated that he could remove the prisoner. The marshal gathered up his papers and escorted Nicolás back to the bull pen.

"What did they say...what did they tell you up there?" one of the inmates asked curiously as Nicolás was about to sit down.

Listlessly he repeated what his charges were. He was bewildered by the whole process and still surprised that he'd been in front of the judge for what had seemed like less than ten minutes.

"And how much cocaine actually was there?" the man pressed, hungry for details and more than eager to offer his legal expertise.

"About one hundred and eighty-five kilos," Nicolás stammered softly.

"A hundred and eighty-five kilos!" the man shouted, jumping up from the bench.

"Do you realize how much time you're going to get? Don't you know that for each kilogram of cocaine you get two years in prison?"

"Look at my case," he urged, shoving his papers under Nicolás' nose. "Look!" he repeated as he translated the pertinent parts into Spanish for Nicolás. "For the amount of cocaine they say you brought in...for one hundred and eighty-five kilos, at...ummmm...two years a kilo...you'll get two hundred and seventy years in prison."

Nicolás collapsed onto the bench. He couldn't believe it. Panic clutched at him and a wave of cold sweat soaked his clothes. "Two hundred and seventy years...they might as well kill me now and get it over with. I'll never see my daughters again, I'll never see my mother again...I'll never see Colombia again...two hundred and seventy years."

Seeing the young man sitting opposite him so obviously distraught, one of the older men sauntered over and asked Nicolás' bearer of bad tidings what was going on. He repeated the information that he had just given Nicolás, and the other man clucked his tongue sympathetically. Patting Nicolás encouragingly on the shoulder, he suggested, "Don't worry kid, you'll be all right. Hey, why don't you write to Eddie Murphy...maybe he'll help you? You look just like him...maybe he'll help."

Nicolás' companion translated the advice, and Nicolás looked up and smiled weakly in appreciation of the man's concern. He felt slightly less abandoned in the light of this obviously very wealthy man's attention, but he still despaired of anyone being able to help him in this situation.

A little while later, a few of the marshals returned with sandwiches and sodas for everyone. The men separated themselves into small groups, eating and drinking and discussing their cases. Nicolás didn't even look up, but continued staring morosely at the floor.

"Come on...eat a sandwich. You'll feel better," his mentor urged.

Nicolás shook his head. He knew that anything he'd put in his mouth now would just get stuck in his throat, and he didn't want to add to his misery by throwing up all over the place. Sighing to himself, he walked over and took a can of soda, hoping that at least this would stay down.

The endless afternoon did little to improve Nicolás' mood, and he was almost glad to see the marshals reappear with the handcuffs and chains. The inmates filed out silently to the waiting vans, each one ruminating over what had transpired that day, each one contemplating his own chances for possible acquittal and freedom. As they exited the building, a swarm of reporters and photographers descended upon them, trying to get close enough for a picture or a few words.

Nicolás didn't know whether the reporters had been waiting there for him or for the reputed Mafia chief who had also appeared in court that day. He didn't care. He just wanted to go back to his cell and go to sleep. Dark circles smudged deep grooves under his eyes that were barely visible under hooded eyelids. Always able to hide his emotions behind a bland mask of indifference, his face now reflected all the fear and turmoil of the week spent in the rudder trunk as well as the anguish of the last two days. He had hardly slept and barely eaten for almost ten days, and he stumbled as he got into the van.

Looking out of the window but seeing nothing except his dark reflection and the possibility of being sentenced to two hundred and seventy years in prison, Nicolás was oblivious to the lights and sounds of the city passing by. It was almost rush hour. Traffic was heavy and the return trip took twice as long as the one in the morning.

Finally they arrived back at MCC, entering the underground garage to elude the reporters gathered outside. The marshals escorted their charges back to the third floor where they handed them over to the corrections officers and then left. Checking the number on the tag to make sure it was his, Nicolás retrieved his plastic bag and changed back into his jumpsuit and slippers.

A hubbub of activity greeted Nicolás as he passed through the door into 9 North again. He had left right after breakfast when most of the men, so actively occupied now, usually opted to sleep instead of eat.

Two inmates were shooting pool while others stood around waiting their turns. There were inmates sitting on the floor with their backs leaning against the wall and transistor radios plugged into their ears. Scattered about the room at the small bridge tables and on the floor were men playing cards and dominoes. A small group of men watched a spirited ping-pong match while a dozen more in the corner of the room took turns spotting each other while they lifted weights.

All the telephones were occupied and there was even a line of men patiently and not so patiently waiting their turns. Next to the office, in the TV room, almost every chair was occupied with inmates, hungry for any news of the world outside.

As unobtrusively as possible, Nicolás entered the room and took a seat in the back. Trying to connect the English words he was hearing and the pictures he was seeing, he heard the officer announce the evening meal. Frustrated by having to struggle to watch a simple television show, Nicolás left the room to get something to eat.

Although it was dark outside, it was only five-thirty in the afternoon and he had eaten nothing since breakfast. He knew that he ought to at least try to eat something, because it would be a long time until the next meal. Then after dinner he'd take a shower and go right to bed.

Wondering why there weren't more men on the meal line, he looked down at the food on his tray and found out. A few brave chunks of ground meat floated in a thin tomato sauce topping a glutinous mound of spaghetti; on the side was a slice of bread and a container of juice. He was to discover that this meal, which alternated occasionally with mashed potatoes and meat, was the specialty of the house. Most of the inmates, at least those that could afford to, subsisted on whatever delicacies the vending machines offered each day.

Nicolás ate the bread and drank the juice, but pushed the spaghetti around on his plate for a while and then dumped the contents of his tray into the trash can. While he knew that he wasn't going to be served the *sancocho con pescado* or *arroz con coco* and other Colombian dishes that he was fond of, he didn't think that the food would be this alien to his palate.

He returned to the TV room and once again sat in the back. He was glad to see that someone had changed the station and that there was a Spanish-language news program in progress. His view of the television screen was obstructed by men seated in front of him; instead of craning his neck to see around them or changing his seat, he stayed where he was, content to hear the audio portion of the broadcast. He was half-listening to the show, half-listening to the conversations around him as the announcer continued his feature story about a stowaway that had been arrested with over one hundred and eighty-five kilos of cocaine after having survived a week-long voyage hidden in the rudder compartment of an oil tanker.

The voices of the men in front of him rose in a heated discussion about the impossibility of anyone surviving for a day or two, let alone a week, in the rudder trunk of a ship. While the reporter related the details of this unprecedented odyssey, the television screen was filled with footage of Nicolás arriving on the pier and leaving from the courthouse.

Suddenly one of the men in the front of the room turned around and, pointing his finger at Nicolás, shouted, "Look! There he is!"

As if they were connected by strings, all heads in the room simultaneously spun around to see who he was pointing at. Some of the men jumped up, overturning their chairs in their eagerness to discover who this new celebrity was. They encircled the former pariah, firing questions at him, each trying to be heard above the other, asking him how he got into the ship, how he slept, how he ate, how come he didn't drown, how come he didn't suffocate, in short...how he had survived.

Yelling into his two-way radio as he ran, a heavy set officer raced to the TV room, expecting a brawl to be in progress. Seeing him running, the rest of the inmates, who had been placidly playing cards and relaxing, also rushed across the multi-purpose room to the TV room, curious to find out what all the shouting and commotion was about. When the panting officer arrived, one of the inmates who had been speaking to Nicolás explained to him what was going on.

Relieved that there hadn't been a fight, while at the same time annoyed that he had rushed over there on a wild-goose chase, he snapped the dial of the television to an English station. To his chagrin, this station was also relating the unbelievable news about the stowaway discovered on an oil tanker. On the screen it showed Nicolás walking on the pier with his escort of Customs agents and policemen.

Most of the Colombian inmates huddled around Nicolás to ask for the most minute details about his voyage. A few went back to their cells and returned a few minutes later, their arms laden with gifts for him, items that they had purchased with their own money from the MCC commissary. Onto Nicolás' lap they piled t-shirts, sweat pants, shower shoes, sweat shirts, bars of soap, plastic bottles of shampoo and containers of deodorant. Others, following their example, disappeared for a few seconds and came back to give him bags of chips, candy bars and cans of juice. Each inmate seemed to be trying to outdo the other in generosity, determined to make Nicolás' stay in MCC as pleasant as possible.

Pleased, yet at the same time embarrassed, to be the recipient of this largesse, Nicolás thanked everybody profusely and, pleading exhaustion, returned to his cell. He had never been the beneficiary of such generosity. Sitting on the edge of his bed, he shook his head in bewilderment and gratitude as he gazed at the gifts he had piled onto his bed. He had never in his life been given a birthday party, been showered with presents or been surrounded by well-wishers. His entire life had been a struggle just to stay alive.

He laughed bitterly to himself at the irony of the whole situation. "Here I am, locked up, about to be sentenced to spend the rest of my life in prison, and I have more now than I have ever had in my life."

He jumped up from the bed as he suddenly realized that he had been daydreaming and it had gotten late. One of his new-found benefactors had gone over the daily schedule at MCC with Nicolás so that he could avoid any problems or confrontations with the staff. He remembered the guy telling him that they were locked inside their cells at nine P.M. sharp, so the officers could walk up and down the corridors counting inmates.

Quickly stripping off his clothes and slipping his feet into the newly-donated shower shoes, he grabbed his soap, shampoo and a towel and headed for the shower room down the hall. He emerged ten minutes later, rubbing his hair briskly with his damp towel. After donning fresh underwear and red sweat pants and sweat shirt, he managed to squeeze his gifts into the small locker by carefully arranging them like a Chinese jigsaw puzzle.

Later, munching a Snickers bar, he sat at the edge of his bed to contemplate his situation. In the space of less than an hour he had been transformed from a person who was not only ignored but also deliberately shunned to a person who everyone not only wanted to speak to but also to befriend. He had never had a real friend before; he had never trusted anyone enough. He certainly had no intention of making friends with anyone here, but it felt good to have people accept him and, even more important, look up to him.

His ordeal on the Bright Eagle had transformed him into a celebrity, a hero to these men. Indeed it had changed him and the course of his life forever, for better and for worse, and in ways he could not even dream of. Even now he realized that things would never be the same again.

There were no nightmares, or if there were any, thankful-
ly he didn't remember them.

Nicolás stretched and, as his knuckles scraped the wall
behind him, woke up. The glare of daylight streamed through
the barred window, and he realized that he hadn't even heard
the officer unlocking the cells and announcing breakfast.
Returning the friendly salutations of the other inmates with a
silent smile, he walked down the hall to the shower. When he
emerged fifteen minutes later, he felt that he had finally
scoured the stench of the ship from his body. He returned to
his cell and brushed his teeth vigorously until they gleamed
with their former brilliance. Then he dressed himself with
care, putting on one of the sweat suits that had been given to
him the night before. He inspected himself in the small mirror
and was shocked to see how thin he had gotten.

Just as he opened his locker to see what he could eat in
place of the breakfast he missed, he heard his name and registration number being called out. His name sounded strange,
uttered in the officer's accent, but he guessed that was just
one more thing he was going to have to get used to. He walked
over to the officer's desk and was informed that he had a visitor on the third floor. Nicolás was surprised at this news
because as far as he knew he didn't have a lawyer, but then he
remembered that one was going to be assigned to him. He was
escorted down the elevator to the third floor, where the officer
in charge led him to a small windowless room.

Already seated at a table were a tall man with glasses in
a navy three-piece suit and a woman in a simple but obviously
expensive red jersey dress. Also seated at the table was a
mustached young man wearing slacks and a heavy cable-knit
sweater. They all stood up as soon as Nicolás entered the
room. After shaking his hand, they introduced themselves as
reporters from the *New York Times* and their interpreter.
They explained to Nicolás that they wanted to interview him
about his experience on the Bright Eagle.

Abruptly standing up and scraping his chair against the
floor as he pushed it back, Nicolás walked over to the door. He
had been answering questions about the voyage almost con-

stantly for the last two days, and he told the interpreter in no
uncertain terms what they could do with their questions.

The reporters didn't need a dictionary to understand what
Nicolás was saying. They explained to him that this wasn't
just for a newspaper article, but they were interested in writing a book and making a movie about him and his experience.
Ignoring their repeated requests, he opened the door and
yelled to the officer that he wanted to go back to his cell.

"What am I," he asked himself, "some kind of specimen
under a microscope that everyone wants to probe and stick
pins into and examine? Everybody wants to know all about
the voyage, and all about what the compartment looked like,
and all about how I got into the ship, and all about what I ate,
and all about how I slept...every single detail."

But no one, not one person had asked him about himself...about *what* he felt or about *how* he felt. To everyone he
was a thing, like an animal in a cage, like an alien from
another planet that they wanted to study but couldn't con-
ceive of having feelings and emotions like their own.

Disgusted with the unwanted notoriety, he returned to
the ninth floor. He noticed a group of men stacking their
empty trays on the counter and realized that he had missed
his second meal that day. Although the food was still literally
foreign to him, at least it was a hot meal; he had been actually
looking forward to it. Resigning himself to a cold lunch of
potato chips, candy and soda from his locker, he was more
than pleased when one of his Colombian benefactors of the
previous evening tapped him on the shoulder and handed him
a tray of steaming meat, mashed potatoes, and vegetables.

"Here, take this," the man urged with a smile on his face.
"I saved it for you when you didn't come back by lunchtime.
Take it, take it...I just warmed it up."

Nicolás blinked rapidly to dispel the tears of gratitude
that had suddenly appeared in his eyes, and thanked the man
profusely for his unexpected kindness.

After he finished eating he walked across the multi-purpose room, nodding his head in greeting to those he remembered from the night before, and headed towards his cell to
take a nap. He sat down heavily on the edge of the bed and
had just taken off his shoes when he heard his name and
number announced again. Muttering under his breath about

the reporters that he had just left, he put his shoes back on again and stormed out of his cell.

Once again the officer led him into one of the small private visiting rooms. Nicolás shook the outstretched hand of the large, bearded man already seated at the table next to a middle-aged woman. The man introduced himself as Lawrence Stern and informed Nicolás, through the woman, his interpreter, that he had been appointed by the Court to serve as his attorney.

"He sure doesn't look like a lawyer," Nicolás thought to himself, scrutinizing the man warily. "If he *is* a lawyer, he's not a very rich one...look at that suit...not too clean and not very well-pressed. And look at the size of those hands...they look like they belong to a construction worker or a butcher...not a lawyer. But at least this guy's on my side." He had never held a lofty opinion of lawyers, thinking of them as individuals licensed to rob people, but destitute as he was, there was nothing for this guy to steal.

Setting a yellow legal pad on the table and extracting a gold-tone Cross pen from the breast pocket of his shirt, his attorney explained that although he had been told what the charges were, he was here today to find out all the details directly from Nicolás in order to begin preparing his defense.

"Here we go again," Nicolás thought to himself. But he realized that his defense and indeed his very life were in this man's hands, so he slowly and painstakingly related every detail of the voyage and everything he knew about the drugs, making sure that the interpreter understood exactly what he was saying.

After an hour, Stern took off his glasses, set them on top of his head and rubbed his eyes. Then he looked through the voluminous notes he had taken to see if he had forgotten anything. Nearly the entire pad was filled with his large scrawling handwriting.

Nicolás breathed a sigh of relief.

"Is there anything else you remember? Anything else I need to know?" asked the lawyer as he stood up to leave.

"Oh...yeah," answered Nicolás, suddenly remembering and telling him about the two reporters who had wanted to interview him that morning.

His lawyer looked up from the briefcase that he was stuffing his notes into and said, "Don't give any interviews...don't talk about your case to anybody...anybody except me...do you understand?"

Nicolás nodded affirmatively.

Stern, about to leave, stood in the doorway with the interpreter and handed Nicolás one of his business cards. "Here, take this, here's my number. Call me if you think of anything else or if you have any questions. I'll either see you or call you in a couple of days." Then he and the woman left the room.

An infinitesimal spark of hope ignited in Nicolás' heart for the first time since he had been pulled out of the rudder compartment.

"Maybe...just maybe...," he thought to himself, "maybe they'll only send me to prison for a few years. Maybe...maybe they'll just deport me...and...and I'll be able to see my mother and my daughters in a few weeks."

He tried to control the flicker of hope that was fluttering in his heart like a butterfly trapped in a glass jar that sees the world outside and struggles to be a part of it once again.

Nicolás had no sooner returned to his cell, when for the third time that day he was summoned to the visiting room. Thinking that his lawyer had forgotten to tell him something, he eagerly returned to the officer's desk and in a few minutes was back downstairs. Disappointed that it wasn't his lawyer, he was doubly annoyed to see three men sitting at the table. They looked up at him with such eager anticipation that Nicolás assumed, correctly, that they were probably reporters, not the same ones as before, but reporters nevertheless.

Nicolás reached for the doorknob and as he turned it and was just about to leave, the oldest of the three spoke directly and quickly to him in Spanish, hoping to change his mind by informing him that they represented *El Mundo*, the Colombian newspaper with readers in many countries.

Nicolás had heard of *El Mundo*. He had read it himself back home in Colombia and was surprised and more than a little flattered that reporters from this prestigious newspaper actually wanted to interview him. But he remembered the instructions that his lawyer had given him not more than fifteen minutes earlier. He politely explained that his lawyer had told him that he was not to grant any interviews.

"But your country needs to know where you are," they insisted. "You don't have to tell us anything that would jeopardize your case...but you have to tell us something...

anything...so that the people in your country know what has happened to you."

Conceding that they definitely had a point, Nicolás acquiesced and answered their questions, little realizing the far-reaching consequences. Little did he know that in two days his mother would buy the newspaper and run, screaming hysterically, into her sister's house, shrieking that Nicolás had been arrested in the United States, just before she collapsed, prostrate on the floor.

Less than a half an hour later, the reporters stood up and shook hands with Nicolás. They thanked him for his time and told him everything would be okay.

But things were about as far from okay that they could possibly be. The wheel of justice had started to roll and Nicolás was lashed to it. He could only hang on helplessly as it carried him to its final destination.

On January 31, one week after his arrest, the indictment was formally filed and his case was assigned to U.S. District Court Judge Reena Raggi, and Jonathan S. Sack was added to the case as the prosecutor. The legal process that Nicolás had wanted to "get over with" had finally begun.

By the end of the week he had settled into the routine at MCC. He was getting used to standing in line, getting used to being counted at least three times a day, getting used to being locked into his cell at night, even getting used to the food. Most of the time he watched Spanish TV programs or conversed with the other men, who never seemed to tire of speaking about their own cases or hearing about his.

New inmates were always arriving and old ones were always leaving. He realized that the only constant factor at MCC was change. You would strike up a friendly conversation with someone, and the next day, when you wanted to continue it, you'd find out that he had been transferred somewhere during the night and you'd never see him again, unless your paths happened to cross on one of your own transfers.

Most of the time Nicolás never made it to breakfast... although not because he didn't want to. When chow time was called at six o'clock in the morning and the officer went noisily up and down the tiers unlocking the cells, he had usually just fallen asleep.

Cells were locked at nine o'clock at night. And it was a long night with nothing to do except think about the present, which was bad enough, reminisce about the past, which was painful to recall, or to speculate about the future, which was even more frightening to contemplate. He looked at magazines and tried to sleep, read the Bible, ate a candy bar and drank some juice, made another attempt at sleep, then got out of bed and did pushups until he was covered with sweat. Then he washed and dried himself and lay down on his bed and tried again...but he couldn't sleep.

By Sunday night it became clear that one of the reasons for his insomnia was physical, not mental, when the pain in his bladder that had been gradually increasing over the last twenty-four hours culminated in tiny clots of blood that he noticed when he urinated. "I bet it's from when those guys were hitting me," he reminded himself angrily, remembering being thrown onto the deck of the Bright Eagle and hit with a rain of blows. "Yeah, that cop on my back and the others that were kicking me...they probably messed up something inside, that's what probably did it."

Nothing like this had ever happened to him before. He had never been really sick, and except for the time that he had been nearly delirious with pain and fever for a week after being stung by a stingray, he had always been in excellent health. Now, the thought of being seriously ill and incarcerated at the same time made him doubly frightened, frightened enough to go to sick call early Monday morning.

Nicolás had always viewed doctors with an air of apprehension mixed with awe; most of the doctoring he had ever experienced had been at the hands of his mother and grandmother. He dreaded going to doctors, but had great respect for their knowledge and expertise. In fact, he had always told himself that had he been born rich, he would have liked to have become a doctor himself.

Sick call was between 6:30 and 7:00 in the morning... you had to be really sick to be willing to get dressed and get over there that early. Nicolás was and he did.

The officer wrote down his name and made an appointment for him to see the doctor. Later that day when Nicolás returned, the doctor examined him but found nothing abnormal. But after noting microscopic amounts of blood in his urine, the doctor ordered blood and urine tests and told him to come back the next day. Nicolás returned on Tuesday, Wednesday and Thursday and was checked by the dentist, inoculated against tetanus and diphtheria, x-rayed, tested for tuberculosis and examined again by the physician, who placed him on antibiotics.

He still couldn't sleep, at least not at night. When he finally managed to fall into a light and restless slumber between six and seven o'clock in the morning, it was disrupted by the announcements over the public address system, the conversations of the inmates as they went to breakfast and the showers, and the jingling of the officers' keys as they passed by his cell.

"I"m going to remember that sound forever," he had often told himself. Like the other inmates, he was already conditioned to the sound of jingling keys, knowing that it heralded the approach of an officer, and he had better be doing the right thing at the right time and in the right place.

Nicolás finally had his first decent night's sleep since the night he had been seen on television. Sick and tired of feeling sick and tired, he had staggered red-eyed to sick call that morning and had received an appointment with Dr. Matthew Quiñones, the psychiatrist at MCC. Nicolás told him about his inability to sleep more than an hour or two each night and about his poor appetite, which he realized was not entirely the fault of the kitchen staff.

Dr. Quiñones, after noting that his patient was sad and rather depressed, no doubt an adjustment reaction to his recent incarceration, prescribed seventy-five milligrams of Elavil to be taken once a day. He patiently explained to Nicolás what it was and how it would help him, telling him that he would have to go to the "pill line," which was called at 7 and 11 A.M. and again at 5 and 9 P.M. to receive his medication. At first, Nicolás was reluctant to take the tranquilizer because he didn't want any drugs that would "mess up his mind," but he finally agreed and signed the consent form after the doctor told him that he would just be taking the medication temporarily, until he could get used to his situation...something that wouldn't and couldn't happen if he wasn't eating and wasn't sleeping. The doctor gave him his first dose of the medication and Nicolás returned to his cell.

And slept.
And ate.
And slept some more.

Valentine's Day arrived—not a day for hearts and flowers, but a day in court for Nicolás. Wearing the long-sleeved
khaki shirt and trousers issued by the Bureau of Prisons, he
appeared this time with his lawyer, Lawrence Stern. All he
could think about was how many years he might have to
spend in prison and his mother and daughters back home in
Colombia. He prayed that he would be deported so that he
could be with them soon.

Before the judge appeared, the prosecutor asked Nicolás'
attorney if he could have a private conference with his client.
The interpreter translated the message and Nicolás agreed. In
a small room off to the side of the courtroom with a guard
standing outside the door, Nicolás and the interpreter sat at a
table while the prosecuting attorney for the United States pro-
posed a deal.

"You know that you could get life imprisonment if you're
convicted," he reminded Nicolás, who nodded his head in
agreement. "I tell you what. If you plead guilty to the charges,
I'll see that you only get fifteen years. Will you agree to that?"

"I'll tell you what," Nicolás replied by means of the interpreter, "I'll agree to it if you let me do it out there, in court, in
front of the judge, not here."

Satisfied with this answer, the prosecutor agreed, and
they returned to the courtroom where the judge was just taking her seat.

Judge Raggi read the charges against him and asked
Nicolás if he was ready to enter a plea. Nicolás and his lawyer
stood up, side by side.

"Yes, Your Honor," Nicolás respectfully replied through
the interpreter, "I will agree to the offer of the prosecutor,
plead guilty and accept a sentence of fifteen years...if you,
Your Honor, will do five, the prosecutor will take nine, and I'll
do one."

The judge banged her gavel as the courtroom exploded in
laughter.

"Mr. Córdoba," she said, as the laughter immediately dissipated under her stern expression of disapproval, "have you discussed the charges against you with your attorney and are you ready to enter a plea?"

"Yes, Your Honor," he answered, "I plead not guilty to all charges." And he sat down, barely able to contain his rage and frustration.

When the judge asked him if he had anything else to say, he was so wrapped up in his thoughts that he didn't realize she had been addressing him until his lawyer touched his shoulder and the interpreter repeated the question. Nicolás told her that he was experiencing loss of hearing and that he still had bladder pain and blood in his urine. After asking Mr. Stern what treatment his client had received for his conditions, she ordered a subpoena of Nicolás' medical records. It became evident to her that his attorney had no idea of the treatment that had been administered so far. Setting February 21 for a pre-trial conference, she called court adjourned, and Nicolás was escorted back to MCC.

The next day, an officer called him three times for his follow-up appointment with Dr. Quiñones, but Nicolás slept right through it. Nicolás was finally seen on March 12 at the Beekman Downtown Surgical Center by Dr. Karl-Eric Johanson, a urologist, at the request of the Health Services Unit at MCC. The doctor examined him and set an appointment for an intravenous pyelogram (IVP) and a cystoscopy for March 21.

With no court appearances on the calendar in the immediate future and his medical tests scheduled for the following week, Nicolás was told to pack up the contents of his locker and the rest of his property in a carton and to be prepared to leave that night. He was not told where or when or how he would be going.

Nicolás carefully packed the sweat suits, tee-shirts and other articles of clothing that he had been given into the bottom of the carton. He smiled to himself, remembering the night he had received them and how he had appreciated everybody's generosity. The chips and candy and juice had been consumed a long time ago, and with no money at all in his commissary account, he had never replaced them. After placing his toilet articles in the carton, he closed it up, stripped his bed, folded his sheets and blanket and set them in a neat pile at the head of the bed.

Already locked into his cell for the night, he had nothing to do but wait until they came to get him. He placed his head on the stack of linens and looked up at the bunk above him; he didn't think he could sleep, but at least he could rest. He hadn't taken his medication because it made him groggy and he wanted to be awake on the trip. Planes and cars had always made him nervous, especially after an accident in which a car filled with some of his friends and two cousins had gone off the road between Turbo and Cartagena and burst into flames, killing all the passengers. The only mode of transportation Nicolás felt safe in was a boat or a ship, and he didn't think he was going to be sailing anywhere by ship...at least anytime soon.

"Córdoba!"

Nicolás snapped out of his reverie as the officer barked out his name.

"Come on, Córdoba, get your stuff, let's go."

Nicolás glanced at the clock as he and the other inmates who were also being transferred filed sleepily through the multi-purpose room. It was one o'clock in the morning.

"All right, guys, take off your clothes," ordered one of the officers in R&D, where the inmates were processed in and out of MCC. After searching each man for contraband and handmade weapons, he then handed him a bright-orange jumpsuit. Meanwhile, another officer opened a closet and took out an armful of restraints. One by one he called out each inmate's name and number, and as the inmate stood in front of him, checked his ID card against his paperwork and placed him in handcuffs, leg irons and chains.

The inmates sat on the bench while the officer made sure their paperwork was in order. A few of the men sat with their eyes closed and their arms folded across their chests. One snored softly. The others just stared into space; they had been transferred before and knew they were going to sit here for a few hours.

Nicolás tried to raise the collar of his jacket as a gust of wind smacked him in the face when he walked toward the bus, but the chain that connected his handcuffs to his leg irons didn't permit that luxury. Tucking his head down into his chest, he kept his eyes on his feet; it was a tricky maneuver to ascend the steps into the bus, and he didn't want to fall. He settled down in a seat next to the window and another similarly attired inmate slid in next to him. The other inmate was housed on a different floor at MCC and Nicolás didn't recognize him.

The officer counted the inmates, checked his list one more time, nodded to the driver, and the bus pulled away and headed for Otisville, New York, a small town in rural Orange County about two hours northwest of New York City.

If it weren't for the two parallel rows of twenty-foot-high chain-link fences topped with tightly coiled razor wire that completely encircled it, or the watchtowers that rose sixty feet above the recreation area, or the white pickup truck equipped with loaded rifles that drove around the perimeter of the compound twenty-four hours a day, you would think that FCI Otisville was a local community college. With its low brick buildings set on a gently sloping lawn planted with trees and flowers, it had a distinctly academic, not penal, atmosphere. Technically not a prison but rather a Federal Correctional Institution, it was originally designed as a facility where inmates who were already sentenced and designated could complete their sentences. A few short years after it was built, it became much more. Now, in order to relieve the overcrowding at MCC, it housed "pre-trial" inmates and "holdovers," inmates who for one reason or another had not been assigned to their more or less permanent institutions.

A gray dawn was just breaking as the driver switched into a lower gear and the bus climbed the winding two-mile entrance road towards the institution. At the crest of the mountain, FCI Otisville lay bathed in the surreal orange glow of the powerful mercury lamps that illuminated the nearly empty parking lot in front of the main entrance. Clearly visible from the parking lot were the tennis/basketball courts and the dirt track that circled the "rec yard" inside the fence. The rest of the institution was hidden from view.

Nicolás and the other inmates staggered off the bus, walked into a low building and entered R&D. There they sat and waited while their paperwork was processed, and then they were escorted to the Health Services section where they sat and waited while each inmate received a physical. After that they were taken across the compound to the laundry, where they waited to be issued linens and clothing.

The inmates designated to remain at Otisville received three sets of khaki shirts and trousers; the holdovers and pre-trial inmates were given three dark-green jumpsuits. Each man was then issued four sets of underwear, four pairs of socks, a flannel-lined brown winter jacket and a pair of black oxfords. In Otisville, an inmate wore an orange jumpsuit only when he was being transported between institutions or when he was placed in segregation, "the hole," as it was dubbed by its tenants, for an infraction of one of the rules or for his or others' safety.

Together with a group of other new arrivals, Nicolás was escorted to Housing Unit 3A and led to his cell. The officer told him to put his linens and extra clothes on the bed and then go directly to the dining hall to join his unit, which had already been called. Catching up to a small group of men who had obviously been there before, he entered the dining hall and stood at the back of the long line of men waiting for lunch.

As he mechanically followed the man in front of him, he surveyed his new surroundings. The dining hall was easily one-hundred-feet long by fifty-feet wide and two-stories high. Long Formica-topped tables ran the length of the room, parallel to the floor-to-ceiling windows that overlooked the compound with its administration building and the housing units. Along the right-hand wall where Nicolás was standing in line were stacks of trays, racks of plastic glasses and cups, utensil holders filled with plastic knives, forks, teaspoons and soup spoons. There was nothing made of glass or metal.

The line angled to the left and Nicolás found himself in front of a counter behind which white-uniformed inmates, with their hair and beards tucked into hair nets, stood over steaming metal trays of food. They dished out whatever meat, potatoes, rice, pasta and vegetables were on the menu. Nicolás didn't understand what they were saying, but he nodded his head as each one poised the serving spoon over his plate until it was filled. He walked over to the center of the room and was pleased to see trays filled with all kinds of salad ingredients. His bowl was soon overflowing as he helped himself to all the fresh vegetables that he had not eaten in almost two months.

After filling his cup with fruit punch from the dispenser, he looked around for an empty chair.

Nicolás found one and self-consciously walked over and sat down. The other men at the table were all speaking animatedly in English and completely ignored him. Pausing only for an occasional sip of punch, he wolfed down his food, not stopping until both his plate and salad bowl were empty. He didn't know where he was supposed to go next, but he followed the men at his table towards the left of the dining hall. Taking his cue from the man in front of him, Nicolás deposited his tray, dishes and utensils into the proper hoppers.

An officer at the doorway was "patting down" the inmates as they exited, making sure that they hadn't taken any utensils or extra food. They were permitted to take only one piece of fruit back to their cells, but that was all...taking two pieces or anything else from the dining hall was strictly forbidden and could earn them a visit to Segregation.

A plastic utensil could be fashioned into a "shank," a handmade knife, and almost anything edible could be transformed into an alcoholic brew, given enough time and imagination. It was the Bureau of Prisons' policy to provide a safe environment not only for its staff but also for the inmates, and these continual and vigilant examinations of their persons, clothing and cells assured the inmates that they had little to fear from each other.

Nicolás automatically spread his legs and held his arms outstretched as the officer quickly patted him down. He still resented the procedure, but he had gotten used to it. Snapping his brown jacket closed and picking up the collar so it covered his ears, he strode quickly across the windy compound and entered his unit. Running was not permitted.

Unlike MCC, the housing units at FCI Otisville, which had been built less than ten years before Nicolás arrived, reflected the latest innovations in penal efficiency and inmate management. Each square building was diagonally bisected into two triangular shaped units back to back. At FCI Otisville, the units were referred to by a number and letter, 3A and 3B and so on; at other, perhaps more creative or innovative facilities, the units had names like Navaho A and Apache B.

The rows of two-man cells ran three tiers high on each side of the triangle and encircled the common area that contained tables, chairs and six telephones. There were two TV rooms off to the side, one for the Spanish-speaking inmates and the other for the rest of the men. The officer's station was near the entrance and the microwaves and ice machine were across the common area at the far corner. A shower room with eight individual stalls was also located here, and adjacent to it was the laundry room containing a pair of washing machines, two dryers and four irons and ironing boards.

At FCI Otisville, the cells themselves were almost identical to the ones at MCC: small rooms with windows set into the electronically operated doors. The only difference was a small window outside the bars, which could be opened to let in fresh air. The March air was a little too fresh for Nicolás' taste, and he left the window closed as he made up his bed. Although he preferred the lower bunk, he was forced to use the upper, because he could see that his first choice was already taken.

Just as he was wondering with whom he was sharing his cell, a stocky gray-haired man entered. He shook his new roommate's outstretched hand as the man introduced himself, in English, as Mr. Shah from Pakistan. Nicolás introduced himself haltingly in English, realizing that he and his roommate, or "cellie," were not going to be engaging in any long midnight discussions. Mr. Shah spoke only Urdu and English, while Nicolás spoke only Spanish.

Nicolás put his newly-issued clothing into his locker, jumped up onto the upper bunk and lay down. The box with the rest of his property that he had packed the night before at MCC had not arrived yet. It could take anywhere from a few days to a few weeks until he received it, and he would have to make do without his extra clothes and shampoo and other toilet articles because he had no money to buy new ones. Although word would quickly spread about his daring odyssey, he had not yet achieved the celebrity status that he enjoyed at MCC, where he had depended on the good nature and generosity of others to fill in for what was not supplied by the Bureau of Prisons.

Folding his arms under his head, he looked up at the ceiling. He had been awake since 7:30 the previous morning, but he didn't want to take a nap now because that might prevent him from falling asleep at night, even with the medication he was still taking.

"It's better here than MCC," he thought to himself. "Here I can go outside where there's trees and grass. I saw a decent-size yard outside where I can walk and exercise, and the food is a lot better. Maybe they'll let me stay here until my trial...that should be in a few weeks or so. Maybe I'll be able to stay here."

He was wrong on both counts.

Exactly one week later, on March 20, Nicolás was awakened at one o'clock in the morning. Soon in handcuffs, leg irons, chains and an orange jumpsuit, he was transported back to MCC, where he arrived at seven o'clock in the morning. The next day he was escorted to the Beekman Downtown Hospital of the New York Infirmary where, in an attempt to find the cause of the blood that still persisted to appear in his urine, he was given the examinations and x-rays that the urologist had ordered the previous week.

That night, he was awakened at one o'clock in the morning and placed in handcuffs, leg irons, chains and dressed in an orange jump suit and transported back to FCI Otisville, where he arrived at seven o'clock in the morning. Four days later, he was again awakened at one o'clock in the morning and placed in handcuffs, leg irons, chains and dressed in an orange jumpsuit and transported back to MCC where he finally arrived at seven o'clock in the morning. This time, even though he had no scheduled medical tests or court appearances, he stayed at MCC for three weeks.

On April 10, Judge Rice ordered another extension until April 16 in order to give the government additional time to respond to the motions filed by Nicolás' attorney.

On April 17, Nicolás left MCC and arrived at FCI Otisville.

On April 19, he left FCI Otisville and arrived at MCC.

On April 23, he left MCC and arrived at FCI Otisville.

On April 26, he left FCI Otisville and arrived at MCC.

On April 30, his one hundredth day of incarceration, he left MCC and arrived at FCI Otisville.

The medieval ages had been over for hundreds of years and with them the racks and the thumbscrews, but for the inmates going back and forth between one facility and another, being awakened and kept awake for twenty-four, thirty-six or sometimes forty-eight hours in handcuffs, chains and leg irons, for no discernable reason that made any sense to them, the transfers were "torture by bus." Some of the inmates swore that the prisons received an extra one hundred dollars for each inmate that was put on a bus; others insisted that the government was transferring them from one institution to another until they would reveal the names of their confederates; others argued that the government was doing it to force them to plead guilty, so that it wouldn't have to spend any money on their trials.

Nicolás headed right for the rec yard after depositing his clothes in his locker and making his bed. It was the last day of April and it seemed like the warm spring weather was finally here to stay... at least during the day. Up there on the mountain, the nights were still quite chilly and there was usually frost covering the brown grass that was just starting to turn green again.

"Hi... how are you doing, Turbo?"

Nicolás turned around to see who was greeting him. He had been christened "Turbo," which was the name of the town where he was born, by the Colombian inmates who had known him at MCC. He was again a minor celebrity who was treated both deferentially and affectionately by most of the other inmates.

He fell in step with the other man and they walked briskly around the track a few times, not talking much but just enjoying the fresh air and the beautiful weather. There were very few things to brighten one's day when one was incarcerated, but sun and gentle breezes and birds in the trees were there to be enjoyed. After a few more laps, the two men sat on one of the benches, where they were soon joined by three of Nicolás' countrymen. They all leaned back on the benches and opened their jackets, trying to soak up the warmth of the sun.

"Oh, to be on the beach at Bocagrande in Colombia on a day like today," one of them remarked to no one in particular.

"As for me," announced another, "right now I'd like to be back in Cartagena, sitting at a table by the window at the Pedro de Heredia restaurant, digging into a steaming dish of *sancocho con pescado*, with fish and shrimp and chunks of lobster floating around in that delicious broth. I'm tired of this food here…I swear that if I eat one more plate of spaghetti, I'm going to start speaking Italian instead of Spanish."

Nicolás and the other men joined in laughter at his joke…understanding exactly what he meant because they all had voiced similar opinions of the prison menu at one time or another.

"Not me," sighed the third man nostalgically, "I'd like to be sitting at the bar at the Hotel Caribe, sipping a Cristal and gazing into the brown eyes of my beautiful Teresa, knowing that by the end of the evening we'll be wrapped in each other's arms."

They stopped laughing. That was one subject that was constantly on their minds, but rarely on their tongues. Unlike state prisons, conjugal visits with spouses were not permitted in federal institutions, and each man dealt with the lack of female companionship in his own way: some sweating it out of their minds and bodies with hours of strenuous exercise or weight lifting, others burying it in books and magazines in the prison library, some praying it away in the prison chapel, others smothering it to death in excesses of food, and others relieving their bodies' insistent urges in the dark privacy of their cells at night or in the showers, washing it away in torrents of water. There were also those men who sought and received their sexual gratification from other men.

All the men wistfully remembered the wives and girlfriends they had left behind and the love they had made in what seemed a lifetime ago.

From the rec yard, the men heard the voice over the loudspeakers announce that all inmates were to return to their units. As they walked down the hill of the compound, they could see the dense fog rapidly rolling in. The impenetrable fog at the top of the mountain where FCI Otisville was situated was a common occurrence that the inmates dreaded because they were confined to their units until it lifted, hours or sometimes days later. The only times they could leave were when they were escorted to the dining hall or to sick call.

Nicolás looked up at the gray mist already obscuring the sun, which had been blazing so brilliantly just fifteen minutes earlier, and noticed how closely the weather reflected the transformation of his mood.

Two weeks later, on May 13, he was transferred back to MCC, arriving there at 3:45 in the morning.

Fifteen days later, he was transferred back to FCI Otisville where he stayed for eight days.

On June 4, Nicolás was transferred back to MCC, where the next morning he was unexpectedly taken by van to the airport and flown to FCI El Reno, Oklahoma, where he arrived during a violent thunderstorm. He was locked in a one-man cell in Segregation for a week and allowed one hour of solitary exercise outdoors each day. All his meals were brought to him, because he was not permitted to use the dining hall or other facilities of the institution.

On June 11, his one hundred and forty-second day of incarceration, he was put on a bus and transferred to the United States Medical Center for Prisoners at Springfield, Missouri, where he arrived the next day. Conceived and operated by the Bureau of Prisons, it was a central facility where all federal inmates too sick to be treated or unable to be diagnosed at other institutions came to be treated and diagnosed. It also served as an evaluation center for inmates having emotional, psychological and psychiatric problems. Inmates referred to it as the "nut house."

Once an inmate had spent time there, for any reason—medical, physical or psychological—he was forever labeled by fellow inmates and staff alike as a "nut case," and he carried that stigma stamped in black and white on his medical records that followed him with every subsequent transfer, no matter what his diagnosis or treatment had been.

Nicolás had been transferred to Springfield for two reasons: to discover the reason for the blood in his urine and to evaluate him psychologically, that is, to check him for mental stability to see if he was fit to stand trial. Many believed that if he had not been crazy in the first place for stowing away in the rudder compartment, then surely after a week there he certainly would be.

After his initial physical examination and assessment, he was placed in segregation, not for any infraction but because it was customary to put all inmates undergoing psychological and psychiatric evaluations there until it could be determined if they were a danger to themselves or to others.

At his initial interview with the psychiatric staff, Nicolás complained, through the interpreter, about being on locked status, denying any past mental hospitalizations or having been prescribed any psychotropic or mind-altering medications. Remembering the pills that the doctor in MCC had prescribed for him, he explained that he had been taking medication for his "nervousness," relating how he had stowed away and that he thought his hearing loss was due to the loud noise in the rudder compartment. He told the group of doctors that he had become extremely nervous when he saw all the guns pointing at him, because he had once been tied up and locked up for four days in a room with six people who had been killed. Watching the psychologist out of the corner of his eye, Nicolás admitted that he was feeling bad because he was locked up, but he did not have any suicidal intentions. He was afraid, though, that he was going to contract some horrible disease that would kill him.

The psychologist noted in the report that Nicolás' hygiene was immaculate, but that he appeared sullen and withdrawn throughout most of the interview. The psychologist explained to him that he would have to remain in segregation until they obtained enough information. The doctor said they would see him again in a few days.

Nicolás sat on his cot and looked morosely at the floor. "Sure," he thought, "they tell me that they're not putting me here to punish me...but the effect is just the same. I can't get my own meals, I have absolutely no one to talk to, I can't watch TV or listen to the radio, I have to do pushups in my cell because I can't go to the rec yard or to the gym.... Here it is a beautiful spring day and they just let me go outside for one hour, by myself in a tiny fenced-in yard about twice as big as my cell...and they tell me they're not punishing me?"

"What is this a picture of?"

"A lion."

"What is *this* a picture of?"

"An elephant."

"Who is the president of the United States?"

"And who is the president of Colombia?" snapped Nicolás.

It was his sixth session with the psychiatric staff, and he was tired of their questions and of being locked in segregation.

"When am I going back to New York?" he asked. "My lawyer told me that I was going to be examined somewhere else."

"We don't know anything about that," they replied.

"Tell me," one of the doctors said, deftly changing the subject, "how are you sleeping lately?"

Nicolás proceeded to describe the nightmares he had been experiencing over the past week about the week in the rudder compartment and about plunging into the water and into the path of the propeller. Again they questioned him about the voyage, asking him if he had drugged himself into oblivion while he was in the compartment so that he wouldn't be aware of the danger, wanting to know how he had survived for a week without going crazy in the dark, with the noise and the water below him, and questioning him repeatedly how he had endured that day in the storm when the water had been up to his chest for over twenty-four hours. It seemed to Nicolás that he was having a difficult time convincing the team of doctors and nurses that he wasn't crazy.

Finally, after a court order signed by Judge Raggi that Nicolás be transferred to a New York institution for an examination to be conducted by Dr. Carmen Vázquez, Nicolás was put on a bus on July 2 and transferred to FCI El Reno, Oklahoma. He remained there, still in segregation, until July 8, when he was put on another bus and transferred back to MCC, arriving just past midnight on July 10.

On July 19 and August 1, Nicolás was escorted to the third-floor attorney conference room where he was examined and tested by Dr. Vázquez at the request of his lawyer. She administered both intelligence and psychological tests and reported her findings to his attorney and to the court, noting that although Nicolás was "somewhat guarded," he was "cooperative and pleasant." She went on to say that Nicolás appeared "depressed and distracted" and that his responses to certain tests indicated "vulnerability and fears of being hurt," a "high level of long-standing anxiety," and a "significant level of depression". She reported that Nicolás "claimed innocence and appeared very frustrated, stating that he wanted to get the legal process over with...a manifestation of the psychological pain he has been enduring as a result of feeling victimized." The doctor concluded that "The impairments evidenced by Mr. Córdoba-Zapata's responses, in addition to his poor planning and difficulties in reproducing simple designs... paired up with poor visual motor coordination, poor perceptual organization and poor spatial visualization, are consistent with his having wondered [sic] into the boat venture without

much planning and/or anticipation, and with possibly no criminal intent."

Nicolás' lawyer hoped that her findings would prove his
client's innocence.

After a little more than five weeks at MCC, Nicolás was
transferred back to FCI Otisville on August 16. The man who
"wandered into the boat venture…with possibly no criminal
intent" had now been incarcerated for two hundred and one
days.

The summer was sultry and the housing units weren't
air-conditioned, but for Nicolás the weather was perfect. He
spent all his free time, when he wasn't working in Food Service or required to be in his unit, outside in the rec yard, running around the track and playing soccer. His appetite
returned and he consumed huge quantities of fresh vegetables
and salad in addition to the hot meals that were served. He
was sleeping better now too; he had told Dr. Quiñones at MCC
that he wanted to discontinue taking his medication, and he
hadn't taken it for a week.

After the four-o'clock count, when all the inmates had to
stay in their units while they waited to be called for the
evening meal, Nicolás played dominoes or spades with the
other inmates or watched Spanish programs on TV. He was
learning a little English, picking it up by himself just by hearing it all the time, but he still preferred to watch television in
his native language. After dinner, he went to the gym or the
rec room, where he could shoot pool or watch a ping-pong
game. But he preferred the gym because the rec room was full
of cigarette smoke and shouts from high-spirited card and
mah-jong games.

He kept his cell scrupulously clean. Although as the occupant of the upper bunk, it was his responsibility to clean only
the sink and the windows, he also cleaned the walls and
scrubbed and buffed the floor, telling his cellmate that he
didn't mind doing it. Indeed, he didn't mind at all; he was
used to cleaning his mother's house and had often mopped the
floor again right after she had finished.

Wake-up call was at 6:30 in the morning, and by the time work call was announced at 7:30, all the cells had to be clean and all personal property had to be stowed in the lockers. Inspection was at ten in the morning and units lost points if anything was dirty or out of place in the cells, common area, toilets or showers. The unit with the most points received the privilege of being called first to all the meals for the week; the unit with the next highest points went second and so on. It wasn't the greatest incentive in the world, but it was better than nothing; at least the cleanest units got first crack at the good meals like chicken and roast beef, as well as the bad ones like beef stew, which the inmates insisted was made from buffalo meat.

With so many men to manage, everything had to be on a schedule to run efficiently; there were rules and regulations that ensured this. Lights were shut off at 11 P.M. and the TV at 11:30, and all inmates had to be in their beds by 11:35. On Friday and Saturday nights and on nights preceding a holiday, the lights were shut off at the same time, but the men could watch television until 3 A.M. During regular workdays, no one was permitted to watch television between 7:30 in the morning until after the four-o'clock count, when every inmate in the institution was accounted for. Even use of the showers was restricted to the hours between 6:30 and 7:30 A.M. and 3:30 and 11 P.M. on weekdays, and between 6:30 A.M. and 11 P.M. on weekends.

Inmates were counted several times a day, not only to make sure that none of them had escaped, but also to make sure that they were exactly where they were supposed to be. There were weekday counts at six o'clock in the morning and ten o'clock at night. Every day at four o'clock in the afternoon, the inmates had to stand up in their locked cells while they were counted. At night they were not permitted to place pillows or a blankets over their heads, just in case they were counted while they slept.

All activity came to a halt when a count was in progress and did not resume until it was called in and verified for the entire institution. When there was a "bad count," meaning that an inmate was missing or most likely in a different location other than the one to which he was assigned, everyone was recounted and recounted until the tallies were finally correct. Luckily, that didn't happen too often.

All the inmates, except those with medical disabilities, were given work assignments for which they received an hourly stipend. When Nicolás started working in Food Service, the rate was twelve cents an hour. For inmates of means, with families that sent them hundreds of dollars monthly, or even weekly, the money earned was less than inconsequential. For men like Nicolás, the six dollars or so that they earned each month allowed them to buy shampoo, deodorant and other items from the commissary.

The inmates worked in all areas of the institution. Under staff supervision they prepared, cooked and served all the food for both inmates and staff, and washed mountains of sheets, towels and clothing in the laundry. They ran the commissary, maintained the sewage treatment plant, mowed the grass, washed windows, dusted the warden's desk and filled his carafe with ice water. Wherever possible, wherever there was no security risk, all work was performed by inmates. It was the Bureau of Prisons' goal not to have a cheap labor force, but to rehabilitate the inmates by giving them meaningful employment while at the same time instilling in them a work ethic and work habits that hopefully would be continued after their release.

At the prevailing rate of twelve cents an hour, inmates considered it slave labor.

Five weeks after arriving in FCI Otisville, Nicolás was again transferred to MCC.

At 9:30 in the morning of the following day, September 19, Nicolás, dressed in sharply creased khaki institution trousers and shirt, appeared with Mr. Stern, his attorney, in front of Judge Sterling Johnson, Jr., who had been assigned to the case two weeks before.

Although his entire future depended on the outcome of his case, there was very little that Nicolás could do except listen to the arguments and comments of his lawyer and Prosecutor Jonathan Sack during this pretrial conference. Anna Silverio, the interpreter, sat between Nicolás and Mr. Stern, and whenever Nicolás wanted clarification along with the translation,

he would ask her a question which she would relay to his
lawyer.

When the conference was concluded, Judge Johnson
scheduled the suppression hearing requested by Mr. Stern for
December 17. Court was adjourned and Nicolás was escorted
back to MCC.

It was September 27, Nicolás' 242nd day of incarceration.
It was also his twenty-fifth birthday. He tried not to think
about it.

Although he had no court appearance scheduled until the
end of December, Nicolás continued to be transferred back
and forth between MCC and FCI Otisville four more times
during the next three months.

On December 23 and 24, Nicolás appeared in court as his
lawyer presented his arguments for motions to suppress the
physical evidence seized from the Bright Eagle as well as
Nicolás' post-arrest statements. He also made motions for sev-
erance and for certain discovery.

The next day was Christmas. Nicolás spent it in MCC.

He again appeared in court as the suppression hearings
continued on December 27 and 30.

On New Year's Day, Nicolás checked last year's calendar
and calculated that he had been incarcerated for three hundred and thirty-nine days.

In the early morning hours of January 8, Nicolás was
again transferred back to FCI Otisville.

At Otisville, Nicolás noticed the inmates shoveling the
previous night's accumulation of snow from the sidewalks as
he walked downhill to his housing unit. He was glad he didn't
have "extra duty," a punishment meted out for minor infractions that didn't require time in segregation. Most of the time
it consisted of going around the compound with a plastic bag,
wearing rubber gloves, picking up cigarette butts and papers
that had been thrown on the ground. In the winter, it meant
being awakened at four o'clock in the morning to shovel snow.
Inmates were better behaved during the winter.

On Monday morning, February 10, the wind peppered
Nicolás' jacket with ice crystals as he headed towards the
Education Building, his gloved hands shoved deep into his
pockets and his green knit cap pulled way down over his eyebrows. He was familiar with the building that housed the

Education Department; he passed it every day on his way to the rec yard.

"I can't believe they put me in school," he muttered to himself as he passed through the double doors and walked through the library. Gathered around the officer at the door was a large group of inmates, new students who were trying to find out where their classroom was. Nicolás, realizing that refusing to attend school would mean attending segregation, resolutely trudged downstairs to his English as a Second Language, or ESL, class. His friend Wilfredo, who was attending classes himself trying to get his GED diploma in English and in Spanish while he worked in Education as a teacher's aide, had pointed it out to him the week before, laughing at Nicolás' obvious and vociferous displeasure at being placed in there.

"You know how much I hate school," he had complained. "These other guys in the class...maybe they don't know English, but they're not like me...they went to school for more than a year. Most of them have high school diplomas and some of them even have college degrees."

Wilfredo, who knew about his friend's self-consciousness due to his lack of education, sympathized with him, but he fervently told Nicolás that being put into a class was the best thing that ever could have happened to him, because an education could change his entire life.

Nicolás removed his hat, and with his jacket still closed and his collar turned up, took a seat in the back of the classroom and tried to disappear. The student were noisily settling in their seats, bantering back and forth about being back in school after so many years, when the new teacher, Mrs. Ziegler, entered. She had taught ESL for many years, but this was her first week teaching at FCI Otisville.

The lesson was going well until she came to Nicolás, who didn't answer her question.

One of the men called out, "Turbo!" and then another yelled, "Turbo!" and a few more echoed, "Turbo!" "Turbo!" "Turbo!" "Turbo!" until Nicolás jumped out of his seat and stood in front of the instigator, telling him, in Spanish, that if he had a problem, they could go outside and settle it.

Another inmate jumped up and stood toe to toe with Nicolás. Mrs. Ziegler jumped up and called for an officer who immediately removed Nicolás from the classroom.

The next day, Mrs. Ziegler, realizing that Nicolás had been provoked into his actions, nevertheless did not want him to return to her class. She asked the other ESL teacher if she would take Nicolás into her class instead. The other teacher, figuring that Nicolás was a troublemaker, refused.

On Wednesday, February 12, Nicolás' friend Wilfredo had a brainstorm. He would ask Miss Carol, the teacher that he assisted, if she could help his friend. She had been working at FCI Otisville for two years, teaching inmates who had the lowest reading scores, inmates with learning disabilities and inmates who had never gone to school and couldn't even write their names. She worked with them individually, sitting down with them at her desk while she patiently tried to teach them the skills that they lacked.

Her immediate supervisor, Suzanne Brown, a corrections officer holding the position of Education Program Specialist, had labeled her "the true champion of the underachiever," and indeed she was, because she would take under her wing men whose lack of ability resulted in embarrassment and low self-esteem, which in turn prevented them from achieving any kind of success in their other classes. They would stay in her class for a few months or up to a year, and then with a solid foundation in reading and speaking English, they would transfer into more advanced classes to get their GED diplomas.

Wilfredo knew that if there was anybody in the world that could help Nicolás, it was Miss Carol.

PART TWO

I threw my red down-filled coat over my nightgown and rushed down the steps to start my car. It was February 12, 1992, and with a temperature of thirteen degrees at 6:45 that Wednesday morning, both the car and I needed time to warm up before we headed off to work.

After pulling on corduroy pants and packing myself into two thick sweaters, I poured myself another cup of coffee and headed back to the bathroom to put on my face.

"Not bad for an old broad," I complimented myself as I peered at my reflection in the medicine-cabinet mirror above the sink. I remembered Zsa Zsa Gabor's words of wisdom I had heard on a talk show two years earlier advising women that after the age of fifty, they had to choose between their face and their fanny...meaning that if you wanted your face to look better as you got older, you couldn't be too thin.

Too thin, an oxymoron if I've ever heard one, was certainly not how you could describe me. With one hundred and eighty-seven pounds packed onto my five-foot three-inch frame, I was more than pleasantly plump or even "zoftig." But people told me that I looked like I was thirty-seven or maybe thirty-eight-years old...not the fifty-one that I would be in May, so I guess that meant I had chosen my face.

I took the now cold hot rollers out and brushed my hair, admiring the frosting and haircut Vicky had given me that past Saturday. With my long blonde hair layered and styled like Farah Fawcett, I thought I looked really glamorous. I never looked at myself or even saw myself from the neck down. I didn't even have a full-length mirror in the house.

Putting my coat back on, I walked around to Mackie's side of the bed and kissed him on the cheek as I woke him up to say goodbye.

"Have a nice day, Shorty," he mumbled as he buried himself even deeper under the two comforters and immediately fell asleep.

"It must be nice not to have to work," I muttered to myself as I marched down the steps and out of the house, exhaling little white puffs into the frigid air with each breath.

The car was nice and toasty as I pulled out of the driveway and onto Old Ridge Road. Although it had snowed steadily Saturday night and most of Sunday, the snowplows had heaped the heavy accumulation in high drifts that lined both sides of the road. Mackie, my boyfriend of nine and a half years, had shoveled out the unpaved driveway. I figured that it was the least he could do.

With the radio tuned to WQXR, my favorite station, classical music reverberated through the Cadillac's four speakers. I had purchased the 1979 white Sedan de Ville two years earlier for four thousand dollars, and I still enjoyed its luxuriousness. I settled back for the half-hour trip from Warwick to Otisville where I worked. As I drove past cows huddled together on the snow-covered fields, I wished that it was already spring. Seed catalogs arrived almost daily and I pored over them, planning an even bigger garden than ever, with asparagus and strawberries and a special area for herbs, just like I had seen in a magazine.

I made a left and pulled onto Two Mile Drive, the entrance road that spiraled up the mountain to FCI Otisville. I marvelled at the fact that I had been working there at the prison for exactly two years.

After parking and getting out, I tightened the strings of my hood around my neck, raised the collar of my coat so that only my eyes were visible and walked briskly across the windswept parking lot, never knowing, never dreaming, never even imagining that on this day, February 12, 1992, my life would be changed forever. That was the day I met Nicolás Córdoba.

There were no fanfares, no mysterious lights, no auras surrounding him, no curious tingling in our fingertips as we shook hands when we met that morning. Nothing. In fact, if anyone would have told me that in one year and two months from that day I would be married to him, I would have laughed out loud.

"Me?" I would have asked incredulously.

"Me?...short...overweight...fifty-one years old... divorced...Jewish...mother of three sons in their twenties...Me?"

Yes, me.

How did I become the wife of someone seemingly so completely different from me that he might just as well have stepped off a spaceship from another planet? How did I come to teach in a prison in the first place?

That's easy. I was desperate. I needed a job.

It seemed ironic, after deciding to return to the teaching profession after a hiatus of twenty-two years and struggling to secure my Masters' Degree in a year and a half while working full-time that I found myself unemployed. But after teaching one year in a private school and another year in a public elementary school, I had been looking for another teaching job since the end of June, 1989.

Optimistically, I had assumed I would have no problem in securing a position by the time school started in September. Hah! I couldn't have been more wrong. After applying to all the school districts in Orange County, where I lived, without receiving one affirmative reply, I mailed resumes and applications to school districts in Rockland, Sullivan and Westchester counties, each an hour's drive from my home. By the time school had started and Halloween had passed, I was discouraged but not disheartened. I felt that it would just be a matter of weeks until I found something.

But after Thanksgiving passed and Christmas rapidly approached, I was becoming desperate. I applied at schools in nearby New Jersey and searched the Sunday *New York Times* every week for a teaching job in New York City, where I had taught for three years after graduating from college.

My rapidly dwindling savings account took care of the bills. Rent was only $350 a month and luckily I didn't have any car payments to worry about. The biggest expense was the fuel oil that was purchased each month to heat the house, plus the propane gas for the hot water heater, stove and clothes dryer.

Mackie, my boyfriend, didn't have a job; in fact, I didn't remember when he had last looked for one or even thought about looking for one. His solution was to eat cheap turkey hot dogs and to redeem, for five cents each, the soda and beer cans that he picked up at the side of the road while he took the two dogs out for a walk each day.

I didn't want just any job...I wanted to teach.

I was getting more than desperate but then I saw it at last, in the local newspaper: an advertisement for a teaching position at the Orange-Ulster Board of Cooperative Educational Services.

BOCES, as it was called, was a large educational complex encompassing vocational and technical educational buildings as well as a special education facility that serviced two counties.

"This is perfect!" I said to myself, and immediately sent off my resume along with a carefully worded cover letter. BOCES is only four or five miles away, this was really a job worth waiting for.

So I waited. I waited one week. Then I waited another week.

After two weeks, wearing my best "teacher dress," I was finally interviewed both by Randy Brown, the Coordinator of Adult Education and his immediate superior, Bob Michel.

A week and a half later, Randy called and told me that I had gotten the job and that I should come to his office on Monday to discuss the particulars.

"You realize that this position is teaching in a prison, don't you?" he started out that morning.

I gulped. "Uh...no," I responded, probably sounding like the village idiot. "The advertisement had just said 'teacher' and I assumed that the job was right here teaching at BOCES."

"No," he went on smoothly, as if it were just some minor detail that he had forgotten to mention, "it's teaching Adult Basic Education at the Federal Correctional Institution in Otisville. With your experience as a first- and second-grade teacher, we thought you'd be ideal for teaching inmates who don't know how to read."

"Oh," I said, trying to sound flattered.

"Of course, we want you to visit the prison first...walk around the Education Department...get a feel of the place before you decide to take the position. How does that sound? Do you want to go up this morning?"

"Sure!" I replied, with more enthusiasm than I felt.

"Do I have a choice?" I asked myself. "This is the first job offer I've had in the last seven months...does he think I'm actually going to say no?"

I left my car in the parking lot and we got into Randy's and drove up to FCI Otisville. It was a good thing that he was driving, because not only was I unaware of the fact that there was a prison in Otisville, I didn't even know where Otisville was.

Randy kept up both ends of the conversation on the twenty-minute trip, explaining to me that the Bureau of Prisons, a branch of the Justice Department, contracted with BOCES, which furnished teachers to work in the prison, and that although I would be working in a federal institution, I was nevertheless employed by New York State. My salary would start at $25,000 a year and I'd be covered by all the medical and dental insurance available and would be eligible for the New York State Teachers' Retirement benefits. It sounded like it would be a terrific job, if it weren't for the location.

"No wonder nobody knows this place is here," I thought to myself as we climbed higher and higher up the mountain and finally arrived at the summit, where FCI Otisville sprawled before us.

The coiled razor wire festooning the top of the fence that surrounded the prison glittered in the crisp February air as Randy and I walked toward the entrance.

I don't know what I expected to see. Maybe grim uniformed guards armed with nightsticks, herding columns of unshaven men who shuffled along in silence, clad in their black- and white-striped prison garb. Or perhaps hardened criminals with beady eyes who licked their lips and stared lasciviously at any female from behind the tiers of barred cells.

I wasn't sure what it would be like, but...hey...I was knowledgeable...I was sophisticated...I was intelligent...I had seen *Birdman of Alcatraz*. Probably the last thing I expected to see was the unarmed corrections officer in gray pants and navy blazer behind the counter in the lobby who politely instructed me to place my pocketbook and coat on the counter. While I passed back and forth through the open archway of the metal detector, he opened my purse and removed and inspected its contents, then examined the sleeves, lining, and all the pockets of my coat. After checking the photographs on our driver's licenses, the officer directed me to sign my name under Randy's in the "Official Visitors' Log," then phoned the Education Department to send someone to escort us inside.

Waiting nervously, I hoped that I wouldn't be too frightened by what I might see once we were past the lobby. I needed this job badly and hoped that my trepidation wasn't visible as we followed a different officer through three sets of electronically operated doors and entered the prison compound.

Dorothy, opening the front door of her house that had just landed in Oz, could not have been more surprised than I was. I stared at the rolling expanse of snow-covered lawn and the two-story brick buildings that flanked it on each side. In spite of a monochromatic landscape, I recognized the bare branches of weeping cherry trees and clumps of white birches. Seeing the tips of tulips and daffodils protruding from the snow, I could imagine how beautiful everything would look in the spring.

The officer led us down the recently shoveled and spotless sidewalk to the Education Department, the first building on the right. Unclipping from his belt a heavy key ring containing an assortment of at least fifteen keys, he deftly selected one and opened the steel door.

I was right at Randy's heels as he led me through the library and into the Plexiglas-enclosed office of Don Griffin, the Supervisor of Education at FCI Otisville. Standing up behind his desk, Mr. Griffin extended his left hand, which I shook in greeting. It was awkward, despite Randy having forewarned me that Don, as I later came to call him, wore a prosthesis instead of his right hand, which he had lost in an accident.

Don welcomed me, assuming that I had already decided to work there, and told me about the GED classes, where the inmates studied to earn their high school diplomas, and the ESL classes, where non-English speaking inmates learned English. There was even a class where the inmates learned typing.

"Inmates...inmates..." I kept repeating to myself. "I have to stop calling them 'prisoners.'"

"Come on, let's look around," urged Randy, standing up and guiding me out of the office after Don finished his mini-orientation. He seemed either anxious for me to make a decision or to demonstrate how comfortable he felt in these surroundings.

Stepping into the doorway of one of the classrooms, I saw a gray-bearded man in a shirt and tie writing at the black-

board in front of three rows of desks. Seated at the desks, with
books open in front of them and taking notes, were about two
dozen men of various ages clad in dark-green jumpsuits or in
khaki work clothes.

"I guess those are the prisoners...I mean inmates," I said
to myself.

Other than the fact that there were no women in the
room and that the men were all dressed alike, it would have
looked like a typical college class.

They all turned and stared. I gripped the strap of my
purse more for support than in fear that someone would take
it...I think.

"This is Mr. Thomas and one of our GED classes," Randy
murmured to me in *sotto voce* as I self-consciously surveyed
the scene in front of me.

"Mmmn," I replied, nodding my head and trying to appear
as nonchalant and matter-of-fact as he was.

"Let's go look at the Typing Class," suggested Randy,
guiding me out of the room by my elbow and leading me past
the large open area that held the prison library.

We entered a large room in which almost thirty inmates
sat at four long rows of tables intently typing at their key-
boards.

"This is Olympia, our Typing instructor," Randy said as
he introduced me to the matronly woman seated behind the
desk.

I breathed a sigh of relief upon seeing another female in
the vicinity.

"Why don't you talk to her for a while," continued Randy,
oblivious to my relief. "She can give you an idea of what it's
like to work here."

With that, he turned and left the room. And left me alone
inside the classroom...with only Olympia to protect me.

"Come on, let's get out of here for a while," she said,
standing up and coming toward me from around her desk.

I was only too willing. "What about them?" I asked, gesturing towards her students from our position in the hallway
outside her door.

There was no guard, no officer in the room to watch over
her class. I had taught in two of the most dangerous neighborhoods in New York City where you couldn't leave your class

unsupervised for a minute, let alone turn your back towards your students. I was shocked at her complacency.

"Oh, they're okay," she said, dismissing my misgivings with a wave of her hand. "Everybody wants to get into my Typing class and they know that if they give me a hard time, I'll take them off my roster and there will be ten other guys waiting to take their place."

"You seem so relaxed, so calm," I remarked. "Doesn't it make you uncomfortable being the only woman in the room. Aren't you nervous being alone with all these men...these prisoners?"

"Maybe I felt a little nervous for the first few days," she replied with a laugh as she reminisced, but I've been teaching here for seven years and I've never..."

"*Seven* years?" I interrupted incredulously.

"Yes, seven years," she said, nodding her head. "And it's the easiest job I've ever had."

That was all I had to hear. If she could work here at FCI Otisville for that long it couldn't be all that bad. Right then and there, I decided to accept the job.

"It's easy," she repeated, trying to convince me, not realizing that I had already made up my mind.

"It's easy...you'll like it."

She was right in the first case, but wrong in the second. True, it was easy. In fact, it was the easiest teaching job that I ever had. I didn't have to write lesson plans or report cards and there certainly weren't any parent-teacher conferences to worry about.

But she was wrong...very wrong in her second prediction. I didn't like it. I loved it. Anybody could teach. Anybody could just explain the basic rules about sounds of letters and sight words and vowels and consonants. But I wasn't just teaching...I was turning the inmates' lives around.

Convinced that most of these men had turned to crime due to a lack of opportunity to obtain an education, I believed that by teaching them how to read and write, I would enable them to have a crime-free future upon their release.

I loved my job. And to think, I had never even wanted to become a teacher.

"Miss Carol, this is the guy I told you about," declared Wilfredo as he sat at one of the large tables in the library as he introduced me to his friend.

I extended my hand and Nicolás shook it wordlessly.

It was a few minutes after nine o'clock in the morning, and both the inmates and the teachers were free to leave the classroom for a short break. Most of the students were downstairs smoking a fast cigarette while others milled about the library in small groups.

Wilfredo had been the assistant in my classroom for the past few months and knew that I was a sucker for a challenge. So far, my greatest success had been teaching English to an inmate from Turkey whose native language was and still is impossible for me to understand or speak. Now I was ready to take on another student that nobody could or would teach.

He told me about what had happened in Mrs. Zeigler's class while Nicolás intently watched both of us.

"There's only one problem," I said after agreeing to help him. "I have fifteen students already in my morning class and fourteen in the afternoon class. Not only is there physically no room for him, I wouldn't be able to spend enough time with him, even if they would put him into my class."

Wilfredo started to translate what I said.

"Just a second, Wilfredo," I interrupted. "I took three years of Spanish in high school, and you know sometimes I try to speak a little in class. Let me try to tell him. If I'm going to help him, I'm going to have to communicate in Spanish also until he learns how to speak English.

I explained the problem to Nicolás in Spanish, with occasional assistance from Wilfredo when I was literally stuck for a word. He nodded his head and indicated that he understood, especially after Wilfredo repeated in Spanish everything I thought I had said.

Nicolás hadn't been very talkative throughout the entire discussion. I later found out that it was not only because he was embarrassed by having to ask for help, but also because he had developed a raging sore throat overnight and could hardly speak.

"I'll tell you what I can do, though," I continued, speaking directly to him, oblivious to both his psychological and physical discomfort. "I have at least an hour between the time I get back from lunch until my afternoon class arrives. Why don't you come every day right after you finish your lunch?"

"I can tutor you out here in the library or in my classroom. I've helped other guys like that...helped them look up stuff in the library...proofread their term papers...let's do that...Okay? Then, when there's room in my class, I'll ask them to put you in officially."

Nicolás returned that day after lunch and for the next two days and started his lessons.

That Saturday, I left for California for a vacation and to visit my three sons who lived in Santa Cruz. When I returned nearly two weeks later, I noticed that my new student was no longer coming for his lessons. After a few days I became curious and asked Wilfredo if Nicolás had changed his mind about getting extra help or if he was unaware that I had returned from my vacation.

He explained to me that Nicolás had been transferred to MCC because his trial was going to begin in two weeks and he had to meet with his lawyer to prepare for it.

I had never asked an inmate about his case or what he had done or what his sentence might be. I had even made a point to tell the inmates in my class, individually and as a group, that as far as I was concerned they were my students and I was their teacher, and the fact that they were in prison was immaterial to me. I didn't want them to tell me about their cases or even discuss their cases with each other when I was around. But now, don't ask me why, I asked Wilfredo what Nicolás had done to land himself in prison.

He told me about how Nicolás had stowed away on the Bright Eagle, and what it was like for a week in the rudder compartment.

Then, knowing that his trial was about to start in a couple of weeks, I asked him what Nicolás' sentence might be if he was convicted.

"Probably life imprisonment," he replied.

I felt like someone had just punched me in the stomach.

When I finally got into my car at 3:15 that afternoon, I was the first one to pull out of the parking lot. My tires screeched as I took the downhill turns on Two Mile Drive at fifty miles an hour. I wanted to put as much distance as possible between me and the other teachers, who all took the same route home.

I didn't want anyone to ask me why I had burst into tears as soon as I had opened the door to my car. Hopefully no one had noticed. I couldn't stop crying...out of frustration...out of impotence...out of a profound sadness...I don't know. All I felt was a premonition that a terrible injustice was about to be inflicted upon someone that I believed, and still believe, was an innocent man.

Did I love him? No. How could I? I hardly even knew him.

At 9:30 in the morning on March 9, 1992, the 377th day of Nicolás' incarceration, his trial began. The legal process that he had wanted to get over with was underway...and over with astonishing rapidity.

Jonathan S. Sack, the Prosecuting Attorney for the United States, and Lawrence M. Stern, Nicolás' attorney, entered the courtroom, nodded to each other and took their seats to the right and to the left at their respective tables. Nicolás, dressed in the light-blue suit and a matching tie, white shirt and black shoes provided by his lawyer, walked in escorted by an armed uniformed officer and sat down to the left of his lawyer with the interpreter in between them. Although the members of the jury were not selected yet and in fact weren't even present in the courtroom, Nicolás was wearing neither handcuffs nor chains nor leg irons, because if they saw that he was already in custody, there was a very strong chance that they would automatically assume that he was guilty.

Everybody rose to their feet as the Honorable Judge Robert R. Merhige Jr. entered the room and sat down. He had just been assigned to the case three days earlier over the defense's objection that it would prejudice his client's right to a fair trial since Judge Johnson, who had presided over most of the preliminary hearings, was more familiar with it. Judge Merhige heard the objection and overruled it, and then ruled against the defense's motion to exclude charts and a scale model of the Bright Eagle, exhibits that Mr. Sack made available on Friday, three days before the trial.

Mr. Stern argued, "Judge, it is not just the model and the chart. Months ago we asked the government in front of the judge, 'please tell us who your experts are going to be and what they are going to be testifying so that we can prepare, so we can know in advance what kind of expert and help we have to get to analyze your expert evidence.' We asked for that. The government refused, and the court denied our request that they be ordered to do that. Now on the eve of the trial, they present us with these complex materials. We know they were going to call two kinds of nautical experts, they have given us all kinds of air temperature charts and routing charts, and I have no idea what these experts are going to say. They are going to get on the stand, and I am going to be completely unprepared to cross them, not because I didn't try."

The judge was sympathetic, but ruled in the government's favor, saying, "That is regrettable. I am going to permit them to use it. But I want you to know something: I am shocked at the attitude of this U.S. attorney's office. This is not a game. I have been here long enough to see that you all treat it as a real contest. I get to wondering whether prosecutors are being paid on a contingent basis. It is ridiculous. It is disgraceful. And it is unprofessional, from what I have seen so far. Now, I am going to let you use it, but if I feel that it is an unfair advantage, I am going to set any verdict aside. I can tell you that right now."

Shrugging his shoulders and displaying his empty palms to Nicolás, his attorney wordlessly indicated to Nicolás that he had tried but failed to get his motion approved.

"Is the jury here?" the judge asked the clerk, who replied affirmatively and then signaled the officer at the door to permit the prospective jurors to enter the courtroom.

A group of men and women shuffled into the room and silently took their seats in the jury box. Nicolás stared straight ahead, glancing at them every once in a while from the corner of his eye. His hands, clammy and visibly shaking, were clasped under the table on his lap.

"Jury is all present and accounted for, Your Honor," announced the clerk after he had taken role call.

"Swear in the jury," instructed the judge.

After the jurors were sworn in, Judge Merhige read the charges against Nicolás and then proceeded to ask them if they had heard or read anything about the case, if they were related by blood or marriage to the defendant or to the lawyers, or if they were acquainted with the lawyers. Everybody responded negatively. However, when he asked them if they themselves were or had ever been engaged in, or were related to anyone engaged in, the field of law enforcement, the responses were overwhelmingly positive with twenty friends and relatives of the jurors working in some type of law enforcement.

Continuing with this line of questioning he said, "...do any of you feel that anything you may have seen or heard in reference to law enforcement, or experiences that people close to you may have had, or you may have even had yourself, would in any way make it more difficult for you as a juror in a case like this...?"

Twelve people said yes, it would.

When he asked those who had not responded affirmatively if they would have difficulty rendering a true and impartial verdict because it was a drug case, thirteen people said yes.

Judge Merhige called a brief recess and went into his chambers with Mr. Sack, Mr. Stern and the clerk close on his heels. They each compared the responses of the jurors to the various questions and finally narrowed the list down to thirteen plus one alternate. The clerk informed them that the jury clerk had additional people available. They returned to the courtroom and after instructing the jurors that had not been eliminated to return the following morning at 9:15, Judge Merhige excused them and began questioning another set of people. After admonishing the second group that was selected not to discuss the case with anyone, he instructed them also to return the following day at the same hour.

A bewildered Nicolás stood up as the Marshal approached him in the nearly empty courtroom to take him back to MCC. He had sat in court all day, listening to the voice of the interpreter over his headphones, and it didn't seem like they had made any progress. He had looked into the eyes of each prospective juror for a sign of sympathy or compassion; he found nothing except a collection of mostly white faces looking at his own black one with cold contempt.

The dinner meal was over by the time he got back to MCC and, knowing it was useless to ask the officer on duty to get him something to eat, he took a shower and went to bed. He didn't expect to sleep, but the day in court had drained all of his energy. When he opened his eyes and stumbled to the toilet, he was surprised to see that it was already light outside.

By eleven o'clock the next morning, March 10, from the list of potential jurors not eliminated by the defense or the prosecution, the members of the jury were called by lot and seated in the jury box. Of these, sixteen were stricken by the defense or the prosecution and sent back to the central jury room. The remaining ten women and four men still seated stood up and were sworn in by the clerk. There was a Cavanaugh and a Kelly, a Cohen and a Katz, there was even a Grasso and a Cruz; they came from Islip and Valley Stream, Merrick and Huntington, from Brooklyn and Queens.

Judge Merhige studied each juror's face through his gold-rimmed glasses, making sure each man and each woman understood the awesome task that lay ahead as he admonished them as to their responsibilities. He instructed them that their function was to determine the facts, not to agree or disagree with the law, and reminded them that they were not to discuss the case with anyone outside the courtroom or even with each other, or read about it in the newspapers, or watch anything about it on television.

Smoothing the fringe of white hair on the back of his neck, he concluded, "Now you are going to find me, I can tell you in advance, you are going to find me moving these lawyers along. That is because I think justice is better served that way, if we move along. My experience is jurors don't mind serving, but they don't want to be sitting around...we are not going to waste any time."

At the judge's signal, the prosecutor rose to his feet. "Good morning, let me re-introduce myself. My name is Jonathan Sack. I am an Assistant U.S. Attorney here in the Eastern District of New York. I represent the United States. Assisting me during the trial is Special Agent Jack Conti with the U.S. Customs Service," he said gesturing to Conti.

Mr. Sack strutted towards the lectern in the front of the courtroom, his long legs covering the distance in a few strides. Ticking off on his fingers the points he was making, he briefly summed up for the jury the evidence the government was going to present in the course of the trial. He brushed away the strands of light-brown hair that had fallen over his forehead and concluded "...after all the evidence is presented, after you have heard all of the testimony, seen all the exhibits, I will have another opportunity to review that evidence with you and talk to you about what that evidence shows. And at that time I will ask you to return a verdict of guilty." He turned and returned to his seat.

"Mr. Stern, do you wish to address the jury, sir?" asked Judge Merhige, peering at him over the rims of his glasses.

"Thank you," he replied as he stood up and walked over to the lectern in front of the courtroom.

Nicolás held his breath as his attorney faced the jury box. After being incarcerated for three hundred and seventy-eight days, his fate was about to be determined by the words and skill of this stranger, this huge man in a rumpled dark suit, and the men and women who were finally going to hear his side of the story. His hands were clasped tightly in a silent prayer as his lawyer started to speak.

"Your Honor, ladies and gentlemen of the jury, my name is Lawrence Stern, and it is my privilege to be the court-appointed attorney for Nicolás Córdoba-Zapata, who is an innocent man. And Judge Merhige has already instructed you that the law presumes that. You, of course, don't know him. You will only know two things throughout the course of this trial: one, that he is presumed innocent; and two, whatever evidence the prosecution brings forth in the case.

"The case will be about the tension between those two things. And it is only going to be proof beyond a reasonable doubt that can satisfy that tension, can resolve it in favor of the prosecution. I haven't heard the prosecution's evidence yet, but if it is measured against that presumption, I am sure that you will vote not guilty.

"If you analyze the evidence, if you look carefully at the details, if you watch what you see and hear closely through the lens of that presumption, and you say to yourself, yes, but does that make him guilty, I think you will not be able to convict Mr. Córdoba-Zapata here of the crimes of which he is charged. Of course he is guilty of stowing away on that ship, of swimming into that rudder trunk. He was going to try to get into this country with 90 dollars to his name. And a craziness or courage, depending on how you look at it, born of desperation to get into the land of the free by hanging suspended over the sea for six days and six nights over a black hole. A place where, word had got around on the docks, you could get into undetected. The tragedy, of course, is that others knew that, too. And there was cocaine in that space. But that alone does not make Mr. Córdoba-Zapata guilty. Presence, proximity, nearness, closeness to that cocaine is not guilt beyond a reasonable doubt.

"You may see a lot of fancy charts and graphs and diagrams and documents, but none of that is going to go to the heart of the issue that you have got to decide. None of that is going to satisfy you, I hope, of the real doubt that you must have that my client is innocent."

Innocent...it's the same word in English and in Spanish, and Nicolás heard it both in his lawyer's voice and in his interpreter's almost simultaneously.

"Innocent," he thought to himself, "will they believe I'm innocent or have they already decided that I'm guilty? Have they already made up their minds that they don't like me because I'm black? Because I'm Colombian? Because I tried to sneak into the United States? Or will they believe me? Will they believe my story? Will they take pity on me...or feel sorry for me?"

In a way he was glad that he was here alone, thousands of miles away from his family and friends. He could just picture his mother sitting here in the courtroom while strangers determined his destiny. He was glad that she couldn't see him like this today.

Addressing the prosecutor, Judge Merhige directed him to begin to call his witnesses.

A stocky dark-haired man approached the witness stand and was sworn in by the clerk, who then requested, "Please be seated. Please state your full name and spell it for the record."

"Antonio González, A N T O N I O   G O N Z A L E Z."

Through direct questioning by Mr. Sack, Antonio González testified that he had been assigned to the harbor unit scuba team of the New York City Police Department based in Bay Ridge, Brooklyn, for the past four years. Confirming the fact that he was on duty on January 24, 1991, he related that his assignment that day was to "...go out and do a hull inspection" on the Bright Eagle that was located at the Stapleton Anchorage off Staten Island that morning.

Mr. Sack approached Officer González with an enlargement of a photograph which the officer acknowledged fairly and accurately showed the way the Bright Eagle looked that morning on January 24, 1991. Turning to the jurors, he displayed the photograph for their benefit also.

As Officer González explained how he and his partner, Tommy Burn, were setting up the lines to conduct the search of the back of the ship, he identified the area of the rudder and the rudder trunk in another photograph handed to him by Mr. Sack.

He then related how he and his partner had discovered Nicolás in the rudder trunk. "Myself and Tommy Burn, Officer Tommy Burn, went down the side of the ship, down to the hull. Worked our way down. You couldn't see anything, it was all by feel. So I swam to the rudder itself, went down the rudder. We got taken off by the current. We had to swim back, and we were just lucky that we found it again. So because it was so dark, even though we have a light, there is so much garbage in the water you can't really see. Got back on the rudder. Searched both sides of the rudder. Came back up to the rudder shaft to the water line, which is the rudder trunk there."

"What did you do when you got to the water line?" asked the prosecutor.

"Okay. I popped up. I popped up on one side, Tommy popped up on the other. I took my light and looked up and saw the duffel bags and..."

"What did you see specifically?" interjected Mr. Sack.

"I saw brown duffel bags. And then I saw...I just saw a face with two eyes just looking down. And as soon as I saw them, he kind of moved quickly. And I tried to just dump the air out of my suit so I could get down as quick as I could."

"What did you do then?" asked Mr. Sack.

"I told Tommy underwater, 'let's go. Let's finish this dive.' I signaled to him. We got out and went back to the inflatable, the small boat, and I told Mike Rivedinera, the safe tender, what we had saw. And he relayed the message back to launch 8."

Urging him to continue, the prosecutor asked, "What was the reason that you got out of the rudder trunk as soon as you saw what was there?"

"Well," explained Officer González, "I was surprised to see what I saw, and I was scared. I wasn't sure what was going to happen. So I just wanted to get out of there."

Lawrence Stern approached the witness stand. Now it was his turn to cross-examine Officer González in order to elicit information that would be favorable to Nicolás' defense.

"Good morning, Officer González," he began.

"Good morning."

"You were concerned, were you not, when you surfaced in the rudder trunk area that there might... when you saw somebody in there, that there might be weapons?"

"Yes."

"And that is because you were concerned that when a quantity of drugs is brought in places like that, there are usually weapons."

"Yes, I was worried about that."

Hoping that the jury would grasp his point, that Nicolás had no weapons and therefore was not connected with the drugs at all, Mr. Stern changed the direction of his interrogation.

After several overruled objections by the prosecution, he managed to elicit the information that the defendant was cold, tired, nervous and in bad physical shape. Trying to paint a picture for the jury of Nicolás as he appeared after a week in the rudder compartment, he continued to question González about the damp clothing found in his client's bag and the occasion when "an entire sandwich was left in the mouth of the defendant."

Jonathan Sack asked a few more questions on redirect examination and, after the judge excused Officer González, announced, "The government calls Sergeant John Cummings."

John Paul Cummings, sergeant and supervisor for the 24-man scuba team, responded to the prosecutor's questions, relating facts about his background and experience. He went on to tell of the telephone call that he received from Customs Agent Jack Conti requesting the search of the Bright Eagle.

Detailing the method of the investigation and the fruitless effort of the first team of divers, Sergeant Cummings' narrative finally arrived at the rudder trunk.

"Did there come a time when you received a message from the divers who were in the rudder area?" inquired the prosecutor.

"Yes."

"When was that, approximately?"

"Around noon. Little after noon."

"What was the message?" Mr. Sack prompted.

"Message was they saw packages and a person."

Sergeant Cummings stepped down and approached the large stand on which the prosecutor had just placed government exhibit 31, a diagram of the steering-gear room. Standing to one side so as not to obstruct any of the juror's views, he described it in detail, pointing to the stairwell, generator, steering-gear mechanism, stowage areas, manhole covers, planks on the floor, and the railing that went around the steering gear.

In response to the prosecutor's question about how the manhole cover was opened that morning, he reported, "A member of the crew was requested to get a wrench and have the nuts cracked and removed."

"How did that take place?" inquired Mr. Sack.

"Well," said Sergeant Cummings, "it took a while. It took I guess 20 to 30 minutes. Each nut had to be cracked with a hammer, and then moved all the way around because of the paint. And then after each nut was removed, the lid itself, the cover itself had to be hit with a sledgehammer to break the seal."

"Now, Sergeant Cummings," Mr. Sack continued, "what were you doing while this lid, this manhole cover, was being opened?"

"I was standing in this area and preparing for it to be lifted open."

"Did you have anything with you?"

"Yes, I had a shotgun that I got from Launch number 8."

"Were there any other guns drawn at the time?"

"The guns were drawn when the lid was being removed. Guys had their side arms out, designated guys. I had a shotgun, one other officer had a rifle."

"What was the reason you had a shotgun?"

"Well, we didn't know who was in there...for our protection."

The prosecutor continued to question Sergeant Cummings, asking him to identify the contents of the rudder trunk from photographs taken in the steering-gear room on the morning of January 24, 1991. When that was completed, he held up each item that had been removed from the rudder trunk, and one by one, asked the sergeant if he recognized the object and if the object was substantially in the same condition as when he had seen it on January 24. From the duffel bags that had contained the cocaine, to Nicolás' jacket and bags, to the inflatable raft with its collapsible oars, patch kit and hand pump, to Nicolás' flashlight, which had been floating in the water since he dropped it, and hearing protector, each item was confirmed and received in evidence.

When this lengthy process was completed, Sergeant Cummings described how he and the other officers had removed the items from the rudder trunk and then boarded Police Launch 1.

"Mr. Stern, do you have any cross?" asked Judge Merhige.

"Yes, Your Honor," he replied, stepping over to the lectern, where for the next ten minutes he attempted to have Sergeant Cummings describe the dangers that were present in the rudder trunk and the peril that Nicolás would have faced had he left the compartment as the ship lay at anchor in New York. He was trying to convince the jury that his client, unaware of the dangers of both the compartment and the ship's destination, was therefore innocent of any involvement with the drug shipment.

"Now, that day during the dive there was something called the reverse tide?" Mr. Stern asked the sergeant.

"Yes."

"Can you tell us what that is?"

"That is the Hudson River is constantly discharging into the ocean, and the tide changes sometimes and comes in from the ocean. So you have a surface tide, a surface current that may be going out, and when you get underneath a certain distance there may be a current coming in. So one current could be coming in and one going out."

"Is that a particularly dangerous current for you?"

"Somewhat."

"More dangerous than if the tides are going in one direction?"

"More dangerous than if it were slack."

"And one of the divers hurt himself?"

"Yes."

"What happened?"

"While he was under the ship, he was backing up. When he backed, he was going with the current, backing with the current, instead of fighting the current, and he hit his neck."

Turning to the inherent dangers of the rudder compartment, Mr. Stern asked Sergeant Cummings, "Now, when you were in there, isn't it a fact that the water was covering the rudder itself?"

"Yes."

"And although the rudder shaft would come up, all the way up to the top, the water was higher up in the rudder trunk than is illustrated on this diagram?"

"True."

"And, in fact, considerably higher; isn't that right?"

"Yes."

"And the sides of the rudder trunk were wet, weren't they?"

"Damp."

"Damp?"

"Moist."

"And was it sort of a rusty film on the side of the walls?"

"Yes. Somewhat."

"You were afraid of slipping, weren't you, when you were in there?"

"Well, there wasn't much room for me to move, and yes, it is...it wasn't much room. I was afraid I could possibly fall in."

"Okay. Thanks."

In his next line of questioning, Mr. Stern attempted to prove his client's innocence by bringing out the fact that Nicolás had no special equipment in the compartment that would be necessary to move the heavy duffel bags in the water. With the weight of the bags at close to one hundred pounds each, Nicolás' attorney tried to convince the jury that it would have been impossible for him to place them into the compartment in the first place, and, equally, if not more impossible, to get them out, considering the debilitated condition he was in and the perilous conditions of the water that January day.

"What equipment was available to you to carry out from the ship or from the hull anything you found there?" he asked Sergeant Cummings.

"Objection," interjected the prosecutor.

"Objection sustained," responded the judge.

Mr. Stern went on, "Did you have any equipment with you on the boat?"

"Yes."

"What did you have?"

"We had our dive gear, we have lines, cables, we have shackles, things of that nature."

"What is the purpose of the line and cable?"

"Well, we always, on a boat you use a line a lot of times. We use it...we use the line to connect the divers to keep in touch with the divers while they are under a ship. We use the line to tie things up."

Nicolás' lawyer tried again. "Did you have any equipment on the boat at all to aid you in removing things from the hull?"

"Objection," repeated Mr. Sack.

"Objection sustained," repeated Judge Merhige, adding, "It is completely irrelevant. He didn't find..."

"Your Honor..." started Mr. Stern.

"I said it was irrelevant," interrupted the judge. "Next question, if you have any."

Taking a different approach, Mr. Stern asked, "Have you ever carried large weights underwater as a diver?"

"Yes," Sergeant Cummings replied.

"And what...how do you do that?"

"Well, with the suits. We have a dry suit; it is possible to lift it sometimes just yourself. If not, you could put a lift bag on it and the bag fills with air and assists you in lifting it. Or, if it is that heavy, you can connect a line from our vessel to whatever you are lifting. And we have a winch on board that could lift it up."

Mr. Stern resumed his seat next to Nicolás, realizing that other than directly asking the sergeant how anyone expected his client to be able to lift and transport the duffel bags without any special equipment, there was nothing else he could do to strengthen his point.

On redirect examination, the prosecutor asked a question which was quickly answered.

"Let's move along, Mr. Sack," urged Judge Merhige. "Is that it?"

"That is it," answered the prosecutor.

"Well," exclaimed the judge. "There really is a God. All right. You may step down, sir. Call your next witness."

"The government calls Captain Jho Tae Ho," announced Mr. Sack, adding, "Your Honor, we will have a Korean interpreter, who is here."

"Try your own case, Mr. Sack," directed the judge, "but we want to get to the meat of whatever your case is. These folks are busy, they want to do their duty, but they don't want to be here for a week."

"I intend to, Your Honor."

Captain Ho of the Bright Eagle and the interpreter, Dolke Pak, were sworn in and took their places.

Under the prosecutor's direct examination, Captain Ho informed the Court that he had been a ship captain for ten years and had served in that capacity from July 1990 to June 1991 on the Bright Eagle. He identified the ship's log books and they were received as evidence.

"To your knowledge, Captain Ho, who boarded your ship while it was in Mamonal?" asked Mr. Sack, trying to ascertain who had access to the ship besides the captain and the crew.

"As soon as we arrived, the pilot was on board," related the captain through the interpreter. "And the pilot berthed our ship by the offshore terminal. Then immigration officer, customs agent, and the agent person from our company, and the cargo inspectors. They were on board. But also there were some shore workers along with loading masters."

"How long did any of the other people stay on the ship?"

"Those officers from Customs, Immigration and these people got off as soon as their process has been completed. But cargo-loading masters, loading masters and offshore workers and the agent person from the company, they were...they will remain until..."

"No, no," interjected Captain Ho in English, interrupting the Korean interpreter. "Loading master, cargo inspector, agent remained on board."

"Loading master, cargo inspector and agent, they remained until..." repeated the interpreter.

"Finish cargo," ended the captain.

"Finished cargo was loaded. And offshore workers remained until they connected the hose to the oil tank, and then they got off," concluded the interpreter.

For the next twenty minutes Captain Ho told of how the crew had been hired, explaining that he really had nothing to do with it and was unaware if any of them had a previous

criminal record. He related that he had informed the crew of
the ship's destination soon after he had received the orders by
telex, before they had left Mamonal, a port from which the
Bright Eagle had made several voyages to New York in 1990.
In addition, he admitted that none of the offshore workers
were searched when they came on board nor were there any
limitations to what they could bring on board.

"Are you aware of the provisions of the sea carrier initiative agreement that you made with Customs?" asked Mr.
Stern.

"When I was on the board, I used to know it very well,"
replied the captain.

"And you understood, did you not," Mr. Stern continued,
"that as part of that agreement Customs said that as long as
you comply with the measures that it recommended to protect
your ship, that Customs would regard that as favorable, favorable with respect to fines and criminal penalties, should drugs
be found on the boat later on?"

"Yes, I knew," Captain Ho said. He went on to tell of the
periodic inspections and searches he and the crew conducted
before the ship left port.

"When you searched the ship in Mamonal, you didn't
search the rudder trunk."

"No."

"You had been warned, though, about the rudder trunk,
weren't you?" pressed Mr. Stern.

"Although we didn't check the rudder trunk, we confirmed
that there is no, there is no opening from manhole to steering-
gear room, manhole to the rudder trunk."

"You mean you decided not to go look into the rudder
trunk?"

"Well, I am in charge of the ship as captain. I just looked
from outside that it was confirmed that nothing could be in
rudder trunk."

"Meaning the manhole cover was screwed on securely to
the manhole."

"Yes," agreed the captain without the assistance of the
interpreter.

"And that satisfied you there was no need to look."

"Yes," he answered, again directly.

"You didn't use a checklist during your search at Mamonal, did you?"

"Objection," interrupted the prosecutor.

"No," said the judge, "but I am going to limit your examination, Mr. Stern. You are just wasting time now. You have ten minutes to finish your examination."

"We used a checklist," admitted the captain.

"You used a checklist, did you not, it is in your log?"

"We don't make entries about using checklists. We only use...just make entries that we made inspections."

"Would you turn to the log book, sir, for January 18. Does it say there that your search of the vessel employed a checklist?"

"It is not written in the log book."

"Do you know how often after January 24 that you searched the vessel for drugs and contraband?"

"Objection."

"Objection sustained."

"Do you know that every time in the log book after January 24 when you conducted such a search you put down 'used checklist?'"

"I believe we didn't make any entries that we used a checklist," replied Captain Ho. "We only make entries that we made inspections."

"Mr. Stern," Judge Merhige admonished, "we can't wait for you to go through the log book now, unless the government had not given you access."

"It is in evidence," protested Nicolás' lawyer. "We will show that he..."

"You find it and you can read it," interrupted the judge. "You bet."

"Did you tell Customs that you searched the entire vessel?" continued Mr. Stern.

"I show to the Customs officer about our checklist of inspection."

"Did you tell them that you searched the entire vessel?"

"Yes."

"But that wasn't true, was it, Captain?"

"That is true."

"But you didn't search the rudder trunk."

"Rudder trunk is customarily not included in the area of a search."

Nicolás could see the point that his lawyer was trying to make and wondered how many ways the question was going to be rephrased until the members of the jury reached the defense's desired conclusion. He knew that he wasn't going to take the stand. Although it was his own decision, his lawyer had repeatedly advised him to remain silent, reminding him that he was presumed innocent and the burden of proof was on the prosecution. After the last two days in court, Nicolás wasn't too sure if his attorney hadn't been misinformed.

The next witness called was Senior Customs Inspector Lawrence Raffaele, who was in charge of the vessel-search team on January 24, 1991. He related how he had searched the Bright Eagle and even carried one of the duffel bags off the ship himself. Step by step Mr. Stern went over the chain of custody of the bags of cocaine; who handed them over to whom, who received them, and who signed for them in order to establish beyond a doubt that the duffel bags removed from the ship had not been exchanged for others or tampered with in any way.

Mr. Stern continued his cross-examination. "Now, those four bags you say came out of the rudder trunk at 12:30."

"Right," Inspector Raffaele confirmed.

"And at 1:30, about 1:30 or 1:40, you told the captain of the boat, didn't you, that he wasn't going to be in any trouble?"

"Objection," interjected the prosecutor.

"Objection sustained," agreed the judge. "That is immaterial."

"May I state my reasons at the sidebar, Judge?"

"Sure."

Mr. Stern and Mr. Sack approached the bench, out of earshot of the jury, and Nicolás' lawyer tried to explain. "At 1:30, ten minutes after that on the video tape that you are going to see, this Inspector Raffaele is seen and heard telling the captain, 'you are not in any trouble.'"

"What is relevant?" the judge inquired.

"That they assumed from the start that...the crew and captain had nothing to do with it. It is very important to establish for the jury that no investigation was done," answered Mr. Stern.

"I don't think it is any big deal. Why are we discussing it?" the judge asked rhetorically. "I will ask him myself."

"Were you in charge of any investigation?" the judge asked Raffaele.

"No."

"And did you tell the captain that, 'You are not in trouble,' as far as you were concerned?"

"No."

Mr. Stern continued, "Now, Inspector, if you are seen on the video tape, and heard on the tape telling the captain at 1:39 'you are not going to be in any trouble,' would that change your mind?"

"Objection."

"Well, no," said the judge. "Would it refresh your recollection?"

"It might have," agreed Inspector Raffaele, "because the captain was scared and I..."

"Do you think you might have told him that?" interrupted the judge.

"I could have. But I don't recall."

"And according to your records," Mr. Stern asked, trying to drive his point home, "that would have been about one hour, little over an hour after everything was taken from the rudder trunk."

"Yes."

For the next hour, Special Customs Agent Sean J. Mulkearns, the evidence custodian assigned to the Advance Target Unit in the SAC Newark Office, described how he had weighed, photographed, and secured the drugs removed from the Bright Eagle on January 24, 1991. In response to the prosecutor's question, he testified that the "148 kilo-size bricks weighed a little over 166 kilograms, or just a little over 366½ pounds." He then spelled out in great detail how he had transferred thirteen of the kilo-size bricks to the DEA for testing.

U.S. Customs Special Agent Jack Conti was called briefly to the stand to verify the chain of custody in the transfer of the thirteen bricks.

It was getting late and the judge was anxious to send everybody home. "We have got to quit soon because my court reporter got up before breakfast, and he is exhausted," he explained to Mr. Sack as the prosecutor began his direct examination.

When both the prosecution and the defense had completed their questioning after five minutes, Judge Merhige dismissed the jury, telling them, "Please be careful going home. Would you report in the morning at 9:15 to the central jury room? We can finish tomorrow," and reminding them, "Remember, now, no discussion with anyone. Don't read anything about it. Don't listen to anything about it."

After a brief discussion with both counsels, court was adjourned and the marshal escorted Nicolás back to MCC for the night.

Wednesday, March 11, 1992, dawned gray and grim.

When the officer came to tell him that the marshal was waiting downstairs, Nicolás got up from his cot and checked himself in the mirror. Although he couldn't do anything about the clothes his attorney had selected for him, at least he could be well-groomed. He had noticed some of the jurors staring at him during the trial, and he wanted to look his best. Patting his hair in place with his trembling hands, he resolutely squared his shoulders and followed the officer down the hall.

It was almost 9:30, and all the jurors had not yet arrived.

While waiting for them, Judge Merhige addressed the prosecutor and Nicolás' lawyer, expressing his dissatisfaction at how long everything was taking. "Gentlemen, we are going to get in the evidence and the arguments today, hopefully the charge, but that may be expecting too much."

Mr. Stern rubbed his beard and tried to explain, "We have been working pretty much around the clock. The lawyers, that is."

"I know, but I have got to consider a docket and consider how justice is best served. That is my responsibility. I have given you all the leeway I am going to give you. I am not going to give you any more. An hour and 16 minutes to cross-examine that captain. Could have been done in 15 minutes...I don't know. I am not going to put up with any more of it."

"I disagree with Your Honor," protested Mr. Stern.

"Of course you do. You have a right to," replied the judge. "I am sorry. I have another jury coming in the morning. I can't keep people waiting. We are going to run it the way I think it ought to be run to get the case over with."

"Okay."

"The jury is all present," announced the clerk.

"Good morning, ladies and gentlemen of the jury," began Judge Merhige. "We will be a little more strict than I was yesterday, because we have got to move the case along. I may have to limit counsel. We have a right to do it; that is all there is to it. That is the way justice is served. Call your next witness."

Special Agent Jack Conti resumed the stand and described his twenty-three years with the Customs Service and how the search of the Bright Eagle had been conducted. The prosecutor then asked about the papers that had been seized from Nicolás' wallet.

Nicolás' lawyer immediately rose to his feet and requested if he could approach the bench. "There are a few things in here which have no relevance at all to the case," he began.

"I don't know," replied the judge.

"Well, I think that if the government is intending to prejudice the defendant, because, for example, a football card that is found in his wallet has a different name on it..."

"Does it? Does it have Redskins? No, no. That might be...a different name?"

"Yes, Your Honor," interjected Mr. Sack, "several papers."

"Purely prejudicial, no relevance whatsoever," insisted Mr. Stern.

"It may be," conceded the judge.

"It has the same last name. Just the fact that he has a card, they are trying to prejudice him," Nicolás' lawyer continued.

"What else?" asked the judge.

"The same thing with a prescription, copy of a prescription blank."

"Indicative of using an alias?" inquired the judge.

"That is a different name," answered the prosecutor.

"That is very prejudicial. No relevance to this case," said Mr. Stern.

"No. Innocent people don't do that," retorted the judge.

"That is not true. Innocent people have things in their wallets from their friends and relatives," Mr. Stern insisted, and then objected to another card issued by the government of Panama. "I would object to this because the card was never opened. We were presented this card like this. We were never told that it opened. It looked like a closed card. This is a trick. We were given copies of this evidence without that, without that card opened. I can show you. I can show you the documents given to us by the government, Xerox copies... We were never given it physically. The agents always held it."

"That is incorrect," disagreed Mr. Sack. "The defendants were provided at least two opportunities in my office to review all the physical evidence."

"What else? What else?" asked the judge impatiently. "Come on, now. Let's go..."

The prosecutor resumed questioning Jack Conti, who held and identified Nicolás' *cédula*, his Colombian citizen's photo ID card, a football identification card in the name of Javier Rivas Zapata, and the rest of the papers that were seized from Nicolás' wallet.

Agent Conti then testified that the members of the crew were not interviewed after the cocaine was discovered and that no search was made specifically for cash or personal papers of the crew members either. In his cross-examination, Mr. Stern pressed this point. "Isn't it true," he asked, "that the *Sea Carriers Security Manual* states that the organized conspiracy generally moves large quantities, that is, ten to several hundred kilograms of marijuana, cocaine or heroin? These conspiracies involve several, if not all, crew members. Doesn't it say that, sir?"

"Yes," replied Agent Conti, "if that is what it says in the book, yes."

"We have got to move along, folks," prodded the judge. "We are going to get all the evidence in today if we have to send out for dinner for you, and probably the arguments as well."

"Isn't it also true that the *Sea Carriers Security Manual* advises carriers never to overlook the crew, never overlook crew involvement?" demanded Mr. Stern.

"Yes."

"Now...you took no latent fingerprints from the items you took from the...Bright Eagle?"

"No prints were taken. None."

"Made no attempt to lift prints off any items?"

"That is correct."

"And did you take the fingerprints of the crew members before you left the Bright Eagle?"

"No, I did not."

"And the *Sea Carrier Security Manual* tells you, does it not, Agent Conti, that if fingerprints are required as part of a carriers pre-employment application procedure, latent prints taken from the packages containing the illegal drugs may be compared and might lead to the arrest of the responsible crew member and his removal from the vessel. It says that in the *Sea Carriers Security Manual*, doesn't it?'

"If it is written there, yes."

"I will represent that it is written there."

"Okay."

"But you didn't do that?"

"No, I did not."

After a few more questions, Judge Merhige requested a bench conference. "I want the record to show," he began, addressing Mr. Stern, "I find most of the examination to be, although dealing with some relevancy, not all, its probative value in light of the method of examination is substantially outweighed by consideration of undue delay and waste of time, and that is what is going on. I don't want to tell people how to try their case, but you have now ten minutes to finish your examination. You can tell the Second Circuit that I cut you off. I have to cut you off in ten minutes. That is it. Let's go."

Nicolás' lawyer glanced at his watch and continued, "These rudder-trunk seizures, they usually involve divers, don't they?"

"Yes."

"These smuggling operations involves divers?"

"Yes."

"The danger...one of the greatest dangers of being in that rudder trunk was falling into the turning propeller, isn't that right?"

"I would say that was probably the greatest danger."

"Similar to the dangers that stowaways who jump onto the landing gear of airplanes from Cuba would suffer if they fell?" continued Mr. Stern.

"Objection," interrupted Mr. Sack.

"Objection sustained."

"Or the Haitians on the rickety boats."

"You have two minutes," advised the judge.

"Objection," repeated the prosecutor.

"Precisely two minutes," the judge warned again.

"You found no diving gear in the rudder trunk, did you?"

"Just the items that were found."

"Coming to the end, Judge," Mr. Stern told the judge.

"I know that. You have got one minute."

After three brief questions were answered, the judge interrupted, "All right, you have one more question, and that is it."

Immediately after that question was asked and answered, the judge declared, "That is it, Mr. Stern. You are through."

Nicolás' lawyer sat down.

The next person to take the witness stand was Adrian Krawczeniuk, a forensic chemist working at the Drug Enforcement Administration Northeast Lab in New York City, who described the sampling and testing methods he had employed and the results of the tests that he had performed on the drugs seized from the rudder trunk.

Following him was the next government witness, Philip Kimball, a naval architect and marine transportation consultant with C.R. Cushing & Company in New York City. Using diagrams, charts and a scale model of the rear part of the Bright Eagle that his firm had constructed, he described and explained the functions of the rudder trunk and the different water levels on the ship as the ship loaded with oil.

The defense objected to Mr. Kimball's testimony and requested it stuck from the record because it had not received notice of this expert testimony until the Friday evening before the trial and had therefore not had time to secure, let alone consult with, their own expert to be able to adequately cross-examine the witness.

The objection was overruled and the request was denied.

Special Customs Agent Manuel Marín was then called by the prosecution, and he translated some of the information on the papers removed from Nicolás' wallet.

James Glauner, Special Agent with the Drug Enforcement Administration, was called next as an expert on drug prices and purity, and he testified that the cocaine had a wholesale price of around two million dollars and a purity of eighty-five percent.

When he was finished, Judge Merhige turned to Nicolás' lawyer and said, "Now, Mr. Stern, you offer a tape."

Mr. Stern faced the jury and announced, "I am offering the video tape made by the government agents on the Bright Eagle on January 24, and I will now play the tape."

"Hot dogs, Cokes?" asked Judge Merhige.

"Two hot dogs and a Coke, please," a juror called out.

"Sometimes I wish that is what I was doing," replied the judge.

The courtroom was silent as everyone watched the television monitor.

When the video tape had finished running, Judge Merhige instructed Nicolás' attorney to call his next witness.

"Your Honor, defense calls Captain Pasquale Naczaro," announced Lawrence Stern in a loud voice.

Nicolás knew how important the testimony of Captain Naczaro was. He hoped that he would be able to convince the jury that the four bags of drugs were indeed inserted into the rudder compartment through the manhole cover on the deck above. Because nobody had seen him swim into the ship with his few possessions, he couldn't prove that he hadn't placed the drugs in the compartment.

Because the access plate had been so difficult to remove, the prosecution was using that fact to imply that it hadn't been opened for quite a while, and therefore Nicolás must have brought the drugs with him when he swam to the ship and he must have placed them into the compartment from below.

In an effort to refute this claim of the prosecution, Mr. Stern had secured Captain Naczaro, a former captain of a merchant ship and a full professor at the U.S. Merchant Marine Academy. In addition, the captain was a member of the American Master Mariners and the Society of Naval Architects and Marine Engineers.

After describing how the access plates were secured to the deck, the captain went on to say that when the plates are opened, "generally you will find that it is quite tight, and it takes a considerable effort."

"Now, if a plate like that had been opened recently..."
Nicolás' lawyer asked, "would it be difficult to re-open in a few
days?"

"Yes," the captain replied. "What happens, in particular
on ships more so than shoreside, if one is familiar with rust,
what happens is the condition is even more severe out at sea,
the oxygen in the air...moisture, particularly sea air, salt, it
causes it, steel to oxidize to some extent, and in doing so this
oxidizing, and it is a self-continuing thing, and, of course, it
makes it a little more difficult to undo. Also, it has a lot to do
with how tightly one secures it. Maybe a hundred-pound person would put limited pressure on it. Someone much stronger
can put an excessive stress on in tightening and makes it very
difficult to undo."

After several more questions, Nicolás' lawyer sat down
and the prosecutor stood up to cross-examine the captain, who
continued to insist that there was no way to tell if the manhole cover had been opened two days or two months ago.

"I have a question," declared the judge, interrupting Mr.
Stern's redirect examination. "Could you say whether it was
two days or two months?"

"No, I couldn't say," replied Captain Naczaro. "You couldn't
tell."

"But it could have been within days?" asked Mr. Stern.

"Yes," answered the captain.

Nicolás breathed a sigh of relief as the captain stepped
down. Hopefully, the jury now realized that the drugs could
have been placed from above the compartment by somebody
else.

The next witness for the Defense was U.S. Customs Special Agent Michael Bennett, who had boarded the Bright
Eagle on January 25, the day after Nicolás' arrest. He testified that in his report of the investigation, Captain Ho had
told him that "the stowaway must have entered the rudder-
gear area from under the water after removing a metal grid
that was over the entrance." This testimony was exactly opposite to the previous response to Mr. Stern's earlier cross-examination, when Captain Ho had stated, "There was no metal
grid."

Nicolás' lawyer hoped that the jury realized the captain's
conflicting statements.

Cydnee Blattner, the next witness for the defense, who
had been working as a legal assistant for the Legal Aid Society at the time in question, related what she had seen and
heard on April 30, 1991, when she accompanied Mr. Stern to
Wilmington, Delaware, to interview Captain Ho on board the
Bright Eagle. She testified that the captain had told them
that the offshore workers who had boarded the ship while it
was in Manomal "were not searched and that they were free
to go anywhere on the ship that they wanted to without supervision."

Mr. Stern recalled Agent Conti to the stand to identify the
rest of the items that were in Nicolás' wallet, hoping that the
religious nature of most of the cards would help offset the
prejudicial attributes of the other papers found there.

After the next witness, María McMahon, a staff interpreter in the Eastern District Courthouse, translated what
was printed on the cards, the jury was dismissed.

"Are there any motions?" inquired the judge.

"Yes," said Mr. Stern. "On behalf of Mr. Zapata I would
move for a judgment of acquittal. The evidence is insufficient
to prove guilt beyond a reasonable doubt based on the arguments that I have made at the Rule 29 juncture, and now with
the additional evidence of the defense...the case should be
dismissed."

"I will take it under advisement," replied the judge.

Following ten more minutes of discussion, Judge Merhige
ordered Nicolás removed from the courtroom and instructed
the attorneys to return the following morning at 8:30, reminding them, "We have got a tough day tomorrow, too."

"Good morning, ladies and gentlemen of the jury," began
Judge Merhige.

It was 9:45 in the morning of March 12, 1992. Nicolás had
been in custody for three hundred and eighty days.

"We will now hear counsel's closing statements," he continued. "We will take a break in between some of them,
depending on how long they take, although they have agreed
on a limited time. And when they finish all their statements,

then I will charge you as to the law and the matter will be given to you for your consideration."

"This is it," Nicolás thought to himself. His lawyer had told him that the jury would probably reach its decision today; the longer they took, the better chance he probably had of being acquitted. He had been awake all night, and although he had showered and freshly shaved and appeared calm on the surface, the dark smudges under his bloodshot eyes reflected his inner turmoil.

Praying fervently last night as he stared at the ceiling in his cell, he hoped that God would direct the minds and hearts of the jury so that he would be found innocent. Although his mother had no idea that he had been on trial all week, he knew that she prayed for him every day and he hoped that at least her entreaties would be heard if his weren't.

"May it please the court, ladies and gentlemen of the jury," the prosecutor began. Reiterating the government's case, he stressed the fact that it was not an accident that Nicolás was in the rudder compartment with the drugs; he was not there simply because of his "tough luck in picking the wrong port, the wrong night, the wrong tanker, the wrong rudder trunk to sneak into." He argued instead that Nicolás had been hired to safeguard the cocaine. "Think about it from the drug dealer's point of view... Drug dealers wouldn't leave their drugs in the control of strangers. They would leave drugs with members of their organization, people who work for them, people who have a job to do. People who for one reason or another can be trusted, especially when it comes to millions of dollars worth of drugs."

Displaying the photographs taken of the inside of the rudder trunk before anything had been removed, he pointed out that Nicolás' "things were all mixed up with the drugs, intertwined with the same pink and yellow line holding up the drugs." He told the jury that if the defendant had nothing to do with the drugs, he wouldn't have wanted his belongings together with the drugs. "But they were all mixed up. Why? Because it made no difference."

Arguing that common sense alone would tell the jury that if Nicolás had not placed the drugs in the compartment, then surely he would have encountered the drug dealers who did put it there. "After all, there wasn't that much time to do everything in Colombia. The ship arrived at about 11:00 in the

morning on January 17. As Mr. Kimball explained to you with
the diagram of the different water levels, the water level had
risen and covered most of the outside opening to the rudder
trunk by midnight, and the drug dealers had a lot to do, loading those three bags weighing over three hundred sixty
pounds altogether on the ledge.

"But let's say...the cocaine was already there... Why go
there? Why go on that ship? Why not go on the next ship or
the one after that?" he asked.

"As you can tell, the defense has suggested every which
way someone on board the Bright Eagle must have deposited
the drugs there: crewmen, even the captain, one of the Colombian people who boarded the ship to do work on the boat. That
is what they suggest. But does it make any sense?"

"Plain common sense, ladies and gentlemen...that is all
it takes to realize that the possibilities, the speculations, the
fantasies suggested...are ridiculous. Just a lot of smoke to
confuse you and obscure the facts of the case."

Referring to the papers seized from Nicolás' wallet, Mr.
Sack reminded the jury that they "should also consider some
small pieces of evidence that tell you a lot. Look at the papers
that the defendant Zapata had with him when he was arrested. He had a Colombian I.D. card in the name of Nicolás Córdoba-Zapata. He had a card indicating membership on a
soccer team. It was in another name, Javier Rivas Zapata. He
had a card from the Panamanian Ministry of Health, it was in
the name of Narciso Gómez, age 23, residence, Turbo. According to his Colombian ID, he was 24 in January of 1991, and
from Turbo, and he had a prescription from a doctor in Colombia. It was in another name: Guzmán. Why have so many
names? Well, it would certainly come in handy if you were
dealing in drugs, if you wanted to make it harder for somebody in law enforcement to know who you were."

As he concluded his summation to the jury, the prosecutor
repeated his argument that the defendant was "in the rudder
trunk to smuggle cocaine. It is that simple. It is the only thing
that makes sense."

Facing the jury box and looking at each man and woman
straight in the eyes, he asked them to return a verdict of
guilty.

Now it was up to Nicolás' lawyer to convince the jury of
his client's innocence.

He began by telling them that the government asserted that the crime was committed by his client.

"Why?" he asked them.

"Because in his wallet he had a lot of scraps of paper, a bunch of cards, including a football card from a relative named Zapata. He had a Xerox copy of a dermatological prescription, a Xerox that somebody gave him, something that could help him when he got here...a 20 peso Colombian peso bill...all his religious cards, other scraps of paper in his wallet. But most importantly, he had two identification cards with his name on them and his photograph. His seaman's license from Panama. And by the way, he knows about rudder trunks. He is a licensed seaman, ships out of Panama. His license has his picture, his name and picture on a Colombian identification card. What was he going, how was he going to...how was he trying to fool anybody if he carries this kind of identification? They are relying on scraps of paper in his wallet.

"You see," said Mr. Stern, "they are reaching. They are reaching because they know that the evidence in this case...points to someone else. We can't prove who, and it is not our function. All that a defendant can do is to plead not guilty, deny his responsibility, and hope, and leave it to you to ensure that in no courtroom in this country can there be a verdict of guilty when the evidence leaves open a reasonable doubt that another person or persons may have been responsible for this crime. And particularly so where the prosecution conducts virtually no investigation, and what they do give to you is unreliable."

How could Nicolás possibly have gotten the drugs into the rudder trunk, he asked the members of the jury. He couldn't have floated out there during daylight with a convoy of rafts and he couldn't have done it at night either due to the illumination around the ship. "If that stuff was brought into the rudder trunk by raft, it could only have been done with clearance by somebody on that boat that let it go through...clearance, high sign, look the other way..."

Arguing that Nicolás could not have swum out to the ship with the drugs, not only because the bags were too heavy but also because cocaine is water soluble, he asked, "And who is going to, what self-respecting drug smuggler is going to take the risk that cocaine, which dissolves like a sugar cube, is going to be dragged in the water for all that way to get it into the rudder trunk? Impossible. Impossible. Makes no sense at all."

He offered his own explanation. "The way the cocaine got in there, and the only reasonable way that it got in there, is through the inspection plate, the manhole cover. Very simple. There is no fear of the cocaine going through water. No fear of it dissolving. And look at this. One of the bags, one of the bags of cocaine is this one. Not even surrounded by vinyl. A porous nylon bag with lots of holes in it.

"The captain gets his orders for where he is going to go while the boat is at sea," Mr. Stern pointed out. Therefore, he reasoned to the jury, how could Nicolás have known where the boat was going to end up, how could he communicate this information to any confederates, "about whom there is no evidence, anyway?"

How could the defendant be guarding the cocaine, he wanted to know. "With what? A hunting knife?"

And why didn't he get out of the rudder trunk when he saw the drugs were there? Mr. Stern threw up his hands in amazement at the question. Nicolás didn't leave, he explained, because he thought he was lucky enough to make it to the ship undetected in the first place and he was not about to leave.

"Why not take advantage of the ledge, cut those bags, throw them into the sea and stay on that ledge in safety?"

Nicolás' lawyer paused and adjusted his glasses. He wanted the question to sink in before he told the jury that this was one of the crucial factors that showed that his client was innocent.

"Diver Cummings told you that the bags that you see here today, the duffel bags containing the cocaine, are in substantially the same shape as they were when they were taken out of the rudder trunk. Notice the bottom of this duffel bag. There is a slit at the bottom, and a nice even slit made by a hunting knife to find out what was in it. How did that slit get there?"

It got there because Nicolás wanted to find out what was in the bag without untying all the ropes. "Now, that slit can also be partially seen on defendant's exhibit Z5, a photograph of the bags as they are laying on the deck. And it can be seen, part of it can be seen on the video tape. I want to play that for

you now so you can see that the slit was already there in the
rudder trunk before the bag was removed."

Mr. Stern then answered the question that he was sure
was now in the jurors' minds: Why didn't Nicolás cut the bags
loose and throw them into the water as soon as he realized
what they contained? Whether he "knew it was two million
dollars worth or not, the agent testified, Agent Kimball testified, it is no secret that cocaine is a lot of money," and had
Nicolás thrown the bags into the water, his greatest fear
would no longer be the propeller but "death by drug smugglers."

"Now, what has the government shown you to refute, to
negate the reasonable doubt in this case? And, of course, that
is their job, to investigate. It is their job to look for the evidence. We don't do that. What techniques they use may not be
of your concern, but what they fail to bring in here that they
could use to establish proof beyond a reasonable doubt is certainly your concern.

"What were they doing on that ship? They were supposed
to be investigating this huge seizure of cocaine. But what do
you see them doing on this video tape after they take the
cocaine out of the rudder trunk? Here I am with a brick of
cocaine. Here is González with a brick of cocaine. Here is González and Cummings with a brick of cocaine. Here is González,
Cummings, and Raffaele with the duffel bags. You get a lot of
shots from 1:40 on the video tape to 2:30, almost an hour's
worth, and it skips. Skips. You know you don't have to watch
it for an hour, but you can tell by the time on the screen that
for an hour's worth of time these guys are using their time to
pose with the cocaine, not to go talk with the crew, not to
make an inventory list of what is in the bag...wasn't that
more important for a jury trial, proof beyond a reasonable
doubt, than pictures of officer González congratulating himself
and having others congratulate him?

"And do you remember Inspector Raffaele? I asked him,
Inspector Raffaele, 'At about 1:40 on that tape did you turn to
the captain and tell the captain, nothing is going to happen to
you?' Or, 'You are not going to get into any trouble?' Something like that. He said, 'Oh no. No, no. I wouldn't say that.'
Well, when I played you the video tape before, what I was trying to get to was to show you Raffaele actually saying that to
the captain only ten minutes after everything is removed from

the rudder trunk. They are sure that is it. 'Nothing is going to happen to you, captain.'

"You have heard already that they didn't bother to take any fingerprints of the crew...and they made no attempt to get any prints off of the items taken from the rudder trunk, which could prove positively one way or the other. And you heard the *Sea Carrier Initiative* and how important prints were. Don't overlook the crew, take prints.

"The captain leads them astray to the steering-gear room," Nicolás' lawyer reminded the jury, pointing to the diagram of the Bright Eagle. "Remember this? The captain is up in the office and...they get the call. Something is in the rudder trunk... The captain is with them, but they somehow make wrong turns. The captain doesn't know the way to the steering-gear room? Then when they get to the steering-gear room, the captain directs them to the wrong manhole cover...The testimony is that they went to this manhole cover first, and that led to a tank where people don't go, a completely void space. Why, if the captain is with them and there is somebody, and the divers are telling them something is in the rudder trunk, why do they go over here? This is the rudder-trunk manhole. Why is there this diversion? Because something is up.

"Ladies and gentlemen, I am going to close now. Your function is to act as a check. Please don't rubber-stamp this fiasco. You are the kings and queens of the facts, not me, not the judge, not the president, not Agent Conti. You. Nobody is above you. Nobody can question your verdict. Nobody knows about your deliberations. You can't say that the prosecution has given you evidence beyond a reasonable doubt...and that is your only concern... None of us was there."

The prosecutor stood up to deliver his closing statements, labeling the arguments of the defense as "a blizzard of irrelevant information... The defense is trying to get you to look at, to get hung up on anything at all but the facts of this case. I guess if you can't get rid of the facts, you try to hide them. Blow smoke. Cloud the evidence with all kinds of distractions."

He argued that the fundamental problem was that there was no evidence about how the defendant got to the Bright Eagle. There was no evidence that the drugs were put into the rudder trunk before, no evidence the drugs came in from on

board the Bright Eagle, there was no evidence that the defendant wanted to stow away for freedom, no evidence that he
came here to live out a dream.

"What testimony or physical exhibits did you see that
show any of that?" he asked the members of the jury. "When
you took your oath as jurors, you swore to base your decision
fairly on the evidence and on the judge's instructions as to the
law, and nothing else. Not sympathy, not prejudice, not fantasy, not the lawyers' questions, not on their arguments, but on
the evidence. You should ignore arguments that aren't based
on the evidence, that have no evidence behind them."

He reminded the jury that the defendant did not have
enough money to live on or "any names or numbers or
addresses of people to see in the United States. Nothing.
Nothing to start a new life. Zapata had plenty of names,
though. Different names." There is no evidence of how the
drugs got inside the ship. He asserted that the only evidence
is that the defendant stayed with the drugs all the way, put
himself at risk and kept the drugs safe, and the only explanation that makes sense is that it was his "job to stay with the
drugs until they, the drugs, got to New York safely.

"And I ask you," the prosecutor concluded, "to return a
verdict of guilty...on all the charges."

"Court will take a brief recess," announced Judge Merhige.

Nicolás rubbed his eyes with his fingertips and took a sip
of water. He glanced at the clock and saw that it was eleven
fifteen.

"Lies...lies...lies..." was all he could repeat silently during the prosecutor's closing remarks. There was no evidence
that proved how he had gotten into the rudder trunk, there
was no evidence that he was just a stowaway; there was just
the cocaine. "Yeah," he said to himself, "there's just the
cocaine and Javier's soccer card that the prosecutor keeps
waving in front of the jury's face, telling them that it "would
certainly come in handy if you were dealing in drugs." When
he had asked his lawyer why he hadn't used his brother's
death certificate and his own baptismal certificate to prove
that the card belonged to his brother, the lawyer answered
that he was sorry but he had forgotten.

Nicolás anxiously waited for the recess to end.

"Bring in the jury," directed the judge.

"It's almost over," Nicolás said to himself.

"All right," the judge continued. "You may be seated."

"Ladies and gentlemen of the jury," he began, "it now becomes my responsibility to charge you as to the law of the case, after which the matter will be given to you for your consideration. You have heard the evidence and the arguments. And it is your duty as jurors to follow the law as I am stating it to you, and to apply the rules of law, so given, to the facts as you find them from the evidence in the case. Regardless of any opinion you may have as to what the law ought to be, it would be a violation of your sworn duty to base a verdict upon any other view of the law than that given in the charge of the court. Just as it would be a violation of your sworn duty as judges of the facts to base a verdict upon anything but the evidence in the case.

"Now, if during the course of this charge I should make reference to my recollection of any of the evidence and it differs from yours, the oath you took requires that you take your recollection, and not mine...not mine, not counsels'.

"You know," the judge cautioned, "that you have got to perform your duty without bias or prejudice as to any party, and the law does not permit jurors to be governed by sympathy, prejudice or public opinion. Hopefully, not only in this court, but in every court in the country, all people who come before the court come as equals. And they are to be treated as equals. And that includes individual defendants, regardless of where they are from, or what their race is or religion.

"Now, what you are here for is not to determine the guilt or innocence of some third party, although that might...if it occurs to you that indicates a lack of evidence, you may consider that...but you are here to tell us whether the government has proven its case beyond a reasonable doubt. And if they have, then you must say so. If they have not, then you must say that as well and you must acquit.

"In your consideration of the evidence, the court charges you that you are not limited to the bald statements of the witnesses. In other words, you are not limited solely to what you see and hear as the witnesses testify. You are permitted to draw from the facts which you find have been proved such reasonable inferences as you feel are justified in the light of experience. In short, we didn't ask you to leave your good sense, your common sense, at the courthouse steps.

"A defendant is never required to prove that he is innocent. You, of course, may not speculate as to why a defendant did not testify. You may not attach any stipulation or any significance, rather, to the fact that a defendant did not testify. And you may not draw any inference, adverse or otherwise, against the defendant because he chose not to take the witness stand. It would be a violation of the oath you have taken."

Judge Merhige then commented in detail on each of the charges, explaining to the jurors that the defendant had to be a knowing and willing participant in an unlawful agreement and "must have intentionally engaged in, advised, or assisted in it for the purpose of furthering the alleged illegal undertaking." In addition, the defendant had to have "knowingly and willfully" imported the cocaine into the United States and he had to possess the cocaine "with intent to distribute, and that he did not possess it accidentally, carelessly, negligently, through inadvertent error or mistake, or for some innocent reasons, because, as I...as I have told you, mere presence, proximity to cocaine, is not in and of itself sufficient reason to convict.

"Now I have used the word 'negligently' and 'wilfully' from time to time, and the court charges you that the word 'knowingly' means that the act was done voluntarily and intentionally and not because of mistake or accident. The word 'wilfully' means that the act was committed voluntarily and purposefully, with the specific intent to do something the law forbids, that is with bad purpose either to disobey or disregard the law."

Finally the judge instructed the jury how to fill out the verdict forms and told the members that they were to select a foreperson. He reminded them, "The verdict must be unanimous. You are not to give any thought to what happens after your verdict, such as punishment and so forth. That is not your responsibility."

In conclusion, he said, "Now, please, I told you what seems like weeks ago that the moment of deliberation was a very precise one. Take as much time or as little time as you want. We will quit any time you want if you haven't reached a verdict in what you consider a reasonable time. We will just quit and come back tonight or tomorrow. Do justice. I have great confidence that you will.

"If you give... if you think the government has proven its case, don't you hesitate to say so. If you are not satisfied to each one, to each count, count you are considering, that they have proven it, and I mean beyond a reasonable doubt, say so. You can do no more, and the system is entitled to no less."

The jury withdrew. All the exhibits were brought into the jury room. The judge called a recess. Lunch was brought to the jury room, the lawyers left the building to get something to eat, and Nicolás was escorted to a small room off to the side of the courtroom and given a sandwich.

The jury returned a verdict at 3:14.

The jury took its place in the jury box.

"Mr. Clerk, you may make inquiry," said the judge.

"Yes, Your Honor. Mr. Foreperson, ladies and gentlemen of the jury, have you reached a verdict?"

"Yes, we did."

Judge Merhige told the foreperson to give the verdict forms to the Marshal and told the clerk to have the defendant rise. Nicolás rose to his feet and faced the front of the room. The clerk asked the jury how they found the defendant as to count one.

"We found guilty."

"How do you find the defendant Nicolás Córdoba-Zapata as to count two?"

"Guilty."

"As to count three?"

"Guilty."

Nicolás slowly let out the breath he had unconsciously been holding. His arms hung limply at his sides and he stared at the flag of the United States. His dream had become a nightmare.

The judge thanked and dismissed the jury and requested Nicolás to remain standing. Judge Merhige turned in his seat and looked directly into the defendant's eyes.

"Nicolás Córdoba-Zapata, on the verdict of the jury, the court adjudges you guilty as charged in counts one, two and three of the indictment. You may be seated."

The judge explained to Mr. Stern that he would set the date for sentencing after the pre-sentencing report was completed; it usually took about two and a half months, but might take more because his client was from Colombia. Then he thanked the attorneys and told the marshal to remove the defendant.

Nicolás entered the small room and took off the suit, shirt, tie and shoes that his lawyer had brought for him to wear at the trial and put on the orange jumpsuit that he had worn that morning on his way to court. Without being asked, he stretched both arms in front of him and the marshal snapped the handcuffs on his wrists and then attached the leg irons and chains to his ankles. Then he followed the marshal to the waiting van and went back to MCC.

As he walked towards his cell, several of the inmates that he had spoken to during previous stays at MCC intercepted him and asked him how the trial had gone. Unseeingly, he walked past them. He just wanted to be alone; he didn't want to talk about it...he didn't even want to think about it. He didn't want to hear their questions and he didn't want their sympathy.

Grown men cried like babies when they came back from their trials. He had seen men of all ages, races and nationalities sitting alone in their cells or surrounded by their buddies in the multi-purpose room, with tears streaming down their cheeks when they returned from being sentenced. He had vowed to himself on the first day of the trial that he would not be like one of them. Never in his life had he cried...not when his grandmother died, not even when his brother Javier, whom he loved so much, had died in his arms. He was not about to cry now.

Five days later, at one o'clock in the morning, the officer on duty woke him up and told him to pack up his things. He hoped that he was being transferred back to FCI Otisville.

The slanting rays of the sun peeking over the mountain awakened Nicolás as the bus pulled into the parking lot at FCI Otisville. Sighing with relief, he felt almost glad to be there. At least the surroundings were familiar to him. He was used to the routines and he knew a lot of the men there. The food was certainly better than at MCC, and he could spend time outdoors and play soccer again.

Despite having been found guilty, at least the trial was over and he didn't have to worry about its outcome. Taking a deep breath of the chilly early morning air, he entered R&D, where he impatiently waited for the processing to be completed so that he could return to his housing unit.

"Turbo, how ya doin'?"

"How's it goin', bro'?"

A gauntlet of handshakes, high-fives and hearty slaps on his back greeted Nicolás as he entered the dining hall for lunch. The warm feeling that he had felt when he got off the bus grew inside him, and he realized that he actually felt better than he had in months. He piled his plate high with food and looked around for an empty chair.

"Turbo!"

He heard a familiar voice calling his name and walked over to a table where Wilfredo and some other guys that he had met the last time he was at Otisville had saved him a place.

"Well, what happened...tell us," they demanded.

Nicolás, who hadn't eaten a decent meal in over a month, didn't stop chewing to answer, but just pointed his left thumb down in response.

"Oh, no!" they all groaned in unison.

When he finished eating, he told them everything that had transpired during the trial. They commiserated with him and expressed surprise that he had been convicted.

"My lawyer's going to ask for a new trial," he told them confidently. "He told me I shouldn't have any problem getting acquitted. I just have to be patient and wait a few months. Meanwhile they'll probably let me stay here."

After one of the men noticed an officer walking over to them as they lingered over the remnants of their meal, they stood up and started to leave the dining hall. Nicolás and the others picked up their trays and walked towards the exit. "Did you guys start playing soccer yet?" he asked one of the men.

"No, it's still too cold, but we're trying to get the team organized...maybe all-Colombian if we can get enough good players. You're going to play again, aren't you?"

"Sure," he replied.

The men separated outside in front of dining hall, most like Nicolás going down the hill towards the housing units, and a few going up the hill toward the Education building for their afternoon classes.

"Hey, Turbo, are you coming back to school?" Wilfredo turned around and called after him as they walked in opposite directions.

"Not if I can help it," Nicolás shouted back. "Right now all I want to do is sleep for two weeks."

Two days later it snowed all day and all night, and Nicolás, with his hands deep in his pockets and his green knit cap pulled down over his ears, was escorted with the other inmates to and from his unit and the dining hall.

Exactly fourteen days later it was April Fool's Day...four hundred days since he had been arrested. Nicolás returned to his unit, plopped down on his cot and started unsnapping his white jumpsuit. He had been up since five o'clock in the morning, the hour when all the A.M. food service inmates were awakened every day. It had been dark, and he could still see his breath in the chilly air as he stumbled behind the other unfortunate inmates who had been pressed into service.

"Working in the kitchen and dining hall is bad enough," he muttered, "but being on the early shift makes it even worse. Maybe I'll try to get a job in Recreation...or maybe as an orderly in the Education Department," he thought, stretching his arms above his head and yawning. "Those guys only sweep and wash windows all day...and they don't have to wake up at the crack of dawn to do it, either. That's what I'll do. He slid between the sheets and drew his blanket up to his neck. "I'll go over to Education after lunch and see if I can find a job there."

"Sit right over there in the library. I'm busy right now," the education specialist told Nicolás when he knocked on the Plexiglas door to her office and told her that he wanted to work as an orderly.

Figuring he was going to be waiting for a while, he walked over to the librarian and requested one of the magazines on the shelf.

"Hey, man, what are you doin' here?" Wilfredo asked upon spotting his friend sitting at a table absent-mindedly turning the pages of the magazine.

Nicolás explained that he wanted to get a job as an orderly so he could get out of Food Service; he didn't mind having a job, but just didn't want that one.

"Oh," his friend said, surprised, "I thought you were here so Miss Carol could start helping you again with your English."

"Oh, yeah," Nicolás said distractedly, not wanting to admit that he had forgotten all about it. "Yeah, maybe I will."

"There she is now," said Wilfredo, pointing to her as she came through the double doors with the rest of the teachers.

"Miss Carol," Wilfredo beckoned.

"Hello, Mr. Córdoba," I said, greeting Nicolás as I approached the table. "Welcome back. Are you ready to start your lessons?"

Seeing his blank expression in response to my question, I repeated it in Spanish.

"Sí...sí...uh, yes," Nicolás lied.

He really wasn't ready...he'd never be ready for school. He had hated it when he was younger and he still hated it now, maybe even more. But this wouldn't be exactly like school, he reminded himself. It would just be him and Miss Carol with nobody there to laugh at him or make fun of him if he made a mistake. Somehow he was sure she'd never laugh at him.

Nicolás followed me down the hall to my classroom and waited outside the teachers' lounge next door to my room while I hung up my ski jacket. Inmates weren't allowed in the teachers' lounge except to mop the floor.

He peered in curiously. He watched me pull various books off the shelves in my classroom as I tried to decide which ones I wanted to start him on.

Some of the guys in his unit were in my morning class, and he had overheard them saying that I was really nice... and different. They said that I treated inmates like people instead of criminals, not like some of the other teachers, and especially not like the officers. There were only a few of them that he thought acted decently to him.

"Here, Mr. Córdoba," I said in Spanish, placing a workbook in front of him as we sat down at my desk. "We're going to start with this book. We're going to work on your handwriting and we're going to talk a lot, in English and in Spanish.

Remember, if you don't understand something, or if I'm going too fast, or speaking too quickly, tell me. I'm willing to help you, but you have to do the work. It's up to you...if you don't come, I can just sit here and relax or mark some papers. If you come, I'll help you. And when there's an opening for another student, they'll put you in my class. Do you understand?"

Nicolás nodded his head.

"No, tell me you understand. Say it, don't just nod your head, tell me in English."

"Yes," he said softly, nodding his head again.

Nicolás came every day after lunch and stayed until most of the students in the afternoon class had trickled in and it was time for me to start teaching. He greeted the incoming men as they entered, and then with his manila folder containing his workbook, some lined paper and two pencils tucked under his arm, he left the Education Department and headed back to his unit to change from his institutional clothes, which were required for daytime students, to a more comfortable sweat suit.

He sat at the edge of his bed and took the workbook out of his folder. Each page had a different letter of the alphabet and photographs of objects that started with that letter. The book had no words, but I had labeled each picture in English and in Spanish and he struggled to pronounce the unfamiliar vocabulary. I had told him that it was very difficult to learn English...but he was determined to try.

Putting the workbook aside in frustration, he took out the paper on which she had written the letters of the alphabet that he was supposed to trace and then try to write. Writing had always given him trouble, and his hand trembled as he grasped the pencil tightly and tried to copy the letters.

"Come on, Turbo, let's go. We've got an hour before the count."

He looked up in surprise as one of the guys on his soccer team rapped on his door; he couldn't believe it was three o'clock already. Quickly he took off the jumpsuit he was still wearing and threw on his red sweat suit and rushed out the door.

Nicolás came for his lessons every day after he ate lunch. He even found himself skipping lunch, on the days when his unit had to eat last, in order that he would have time to meet with his teacher. The only days he didn't go was when it was foggy. During "adverse weather," as it was called, the inmates were only permitted to leave their housing units when they were escorted to the dining hall for their meals.

Then one day he didn't show up. He had been placed in Segregation for refusing to re-mop the dining room floor that he had just finished washing and which he thought was perfectly clean.

Two weeks later, on June 10, he was officially placed into my class and started the next morning when he got out of Segregation.

Nicolás sat his desk in the front corner of the room near my desk. Now, for the first time, he had to share his Miss Carol with fifteen other inmates who also needed my individual assistance and guidance. He watched them out of the corner of his eye as they sat next to me and I went over their lessons. He wasn't happy about it...not happy at all.

He continued to come after lunch for additional help. That was the only time he had my undivided attention, and we both knew that he learned more in those forty-five minutes than he did during the three hours he sat in class every morning.

"It's nice having someone to talk to," he told me, "someone that not only listens to me, but someone who makes me feel like I'm a person, not just another inmate in a green jumpsuit, even if it's only for a few hours every day."

The only other person that had ever taken this much time with him or had been so kind and patient with him had been his grandmother, and he found himself eagerly looking forward to the time that we spent together.

Nicolás and I sat at my desk and went over the lessons in the workbook; he was on his second one now. After we checked it, I dictated a dozen or more words in English, which he would write in his notebook. Then we practiced his new vocabulary words. I had tried to lend him one of the picture dictionaries from the classroom to take back to his cell so that he could study it in his free time, but it had been confiscated during one of the shakedowns of his unit, even though I had written a note giving him permission to borrow it.

We talked and talked and talked, sometimes in English, mostly in Spanish, about anything and everything. Nicolás told me about his daughters and some of the things that he had done in Colombia. I told him about my divorce in 1982 and showed him photographs of Eric, Michael and Richard, my three sons.

"How old are they?" he inquired, after closely studying their pictures.

I replied that Eric was twenty-seven and that Michael would be twenty-five in November and Richard twenty-two in December.

"And how old are *you*?" he asked curiously. He sounded surprised that my children were almost the same age as he was...one was even older.

"Fifty-one," I answered. "I just turned fifty-one a few weeks ago."

Nicolás peered intently at my face. "You sure don't look fifty-one...maybe forty-one, forty-two at the most."

We didn't mention my age...or my children...again, but we continued to sit in my classroom every day after lunch and go over Nicolás' lessons and talk and talk...and talk.

On Friday, July 17, there was adverse weather and all classes were cancelled. On Saturday morning, I left for a week's vacation with my brother's family and two of my sons at St. George Island in Florida. When Nicolás returned eagerly to school that Monday, he found an inmate, my assistant, teaching the class.

"Where's Miss Carol?" he asked, hoping that he sounded nonchalant.

"Oh, she went on vacation...she'll be back next Tuesday," the aide replied.

Nicolás swallowed hard and sat down.

During the break he walked down the hall and asked the typing teacher, Mrs. Demeter, if she had any room for him in her afternoon class.

"You're lucky," she informed him, "three of my afternoon students just went to MCC. Give me your name and number and I'll tell them to register you. You'll start tomorrow...your name should be on the computer by then.

"I can't believe it!" exclaimed Wilfredo when Nicolás excitedly told him the news. "You? You, who can't stand to go to school, are now going to GED class in the morning and Typing class in the afternoon? You?"

Nicolás didn't have the heart to remind his friend that he was still going for private lessons after lunch also. He didn't want to disillusion him completely.

I returned from vacation the following Tuesday, rested and with a great suntan. "Did you miss me?" I asked the class, laughing, as I stuck the roses I had brought from home into a large plastic mug I kept on my desk. I knew they had probably enjoyed my vacation as much as I had because my assistant was less demanding and they could sit around and spend time discussing their cases, their favorite topic.

"Nicolás, do me a favor," I requested, handing him the container of flowers, "please put some water in this for me."

Walking to the water fountain at the end of the hall with his nose buried in the flowers, Nicolás inhaled deeply. "This is what makes her different," he thought to himself. "She doesn't have to bring these flowers in here...but she knows that this is something that we miss...something that is beautiful."

Somehow he had never noticed that a few of the other teachers also brought in flowers from time to time.

"Hurry up, Nicolás," I urged him, looking at my watch at the end of the morning session. The late bell, that signaled the end of the ten-minute activity move was about to ring. That was the only time that the inmates were allowed to walk freely from one building to another, to return to their units, go to their classes or go to the gym before the compound was cleared.

Nicolás smiled at me. He had been waiting to tell me his surprise...hoping I'd be proud of him. "I'm in Typing class in the afternoon," he told me proudly in Spanish.

"That's great!" I said, grabbing his hand and shaking it. "That's terrific!"

I was really pleased...and he could tell. He walked down the hall with a grin on his face and stared at his hand.

The next morning when I checked my class roster to take attendance, I noticed that Nicolás' name was no longer on it.

"That's strange," I thought. Even when a student was transferred to MCC his name still appeared on the roster, which was run daily.

When Nicolás showed up after lunch for his customary tutoring session, I was even more confused than ever.

"What's going on?" I asked him.

Sheepishly he told me that he had a problem in Typing class the previous afternoon and that he had not only been taken out of Typing class but out of my class as well.

"What on earth did you do?" I asked him. "It couldn't have been all that bad if they didn't put you in Segregation.

I knew that he was no angel, but I had never had any problem with him in my class.

"I was just sitting there," he explained, "minding my own business, typing my lesson, when I decided that I wanted to get a drink of water...the water fountain is right outside the classroom, you know."

I nodded and said, "So?"

"Well, the Typing teacher, she called out my name as I was walking out the door, but I just kept on walking...the water fountain is right there...I wasn't going anywhere, I just wanted a drink."

"Oh, Nicolás," I sighed in exasperation. "We're finally making great progress in your lessons and I was so glad that you're taking Typing."

I knew that although his handwriting had improved over the last six weeks, it would never be great, and knowing how to type would really help him...even before he got out of prison and certainly after.

"Oh, Nicolás," I repeated, my disappointment plainly visible in my face and audible in the tone of my voice.

In a way, I blamed myself. I had allowed him to get up and get a drink or walk back and forth to the library every half-hour or so. I knew that he couldn't sit still any longer than that, let alone pay attention to the lesson for more than a half-hour at a time without taking a break. He had told me about his previous experiences in school and I tried to make his lessons as stress-free as possible by breaking them up into small doses.

"Can I still come after lunch...and can you still help me?" Nicolás asked hopefully.

"Sure," I replied, smiling at him. "I don't see why not... you never gave me any trouble. I'll try to talk to someone... maybe they'll change their minds and at least put you back in my class. I don't want to lose my star pupil."

Throughout the summer, Nicolás continued to come every day after lunch and our lessons continued. In between the workbook drills and during the penmanship exercises and after we had gone over his new vocabulary words, we talked. And talked. And talked. Sometimes in English but mostly in Spanish, we talked. He told me about his voyage on the Bright Eagle. I told him about the movie I had seen that weekend. He told me about his grandmother and the way she had dragged him to church with her twice a day. I told him about growing up in Brooklyn and going to the Catskill Mountains every summer and about my brother's bar mitzvah. He told me about some of the women he had known in Colombia. I told him about my ex-husband and what it had been like, living in the suburbs with him and my three sons.

He noticed that I had lost a lot of weight since February when he had first met me. I noticed that he had the whitest teeth and the most beautiful smile I had ever seen.

I started wearing dresses to work every day. After losing forty-five pounds in the previous six months, I had purchased a whole new wardrobe to show off my new figure; my old clothes literally fell off me when I tried to wear them.

On Tuesday, September 15, after several requests on both of our parts, Nicolás was again officially placed in my class. He sat in the same seat near my desk that he had occupied previously; it seemed as if he had never left.

"Te quiero."

"No, you don't," I told him...in Spanish, to make sure that he understood me.

"Te quiero," he repeated.

"No, Nicolás," I protested. "You don't love me. Maybe you like me because I'm helping you. Maybe you're grateful to me because no one has ever helped you before. But you don't love me."

"But I dream about you every night and I think about you all the time," he persisted.

"Well, stop dreaming and stop thinking...please," I added in a gentler voice, seeing the pain in his eyes.

"But I love you...I'll love you forever," he insisted, oblivious to my protestations.

It was a few minutes after noon and we were sitting at my desk in the classroom. Through the open doorway I could see some of the afternoon students who had just finished their lunch; they were entering the Education Department and taking seats in the library down the hall.

"It's impossible, Nicolás," I said, placing my hand on top of his as he opened his mouth again to speak.

"It's not just because it's against all the regulations here...and I would be fired and you would be put into Segregation for God only knows how long. It's not because you're an inmate, it's not because you're black...you know that doesn't matter to me," I explained firmly, trying to make him understand my reasoning. "It's just...it's just that I'm too old for you. You know how old I am. I'm fifty-one...and a half. And what are you...maybe twenty-five...twenty-six?"

"I'll be twenty-six in a few weeks," he acknowledged. "Pero no me importa...but I don't care."

"Nicolás, I like you...very much," I admitted.

"But a relationship between the two of us is impossible. I'm old enough to be your mother. In fact, I'm even older than your mother...maybe six or seven years older than her. I have children your age...one's even older than you. You know that—you've seen their pictures. No, Nicolás, it's impossible," I concluded, trying to close the subject by opening his book to the next page so that we could continue our lesson where we had left off.

"No, nothing is impossible," he insisted, shutting the book again. Then, taking a deep breath, as if he were about to dive from a high cliff into the ocean, and speaking too rapidly for me to interrupt but slowly enough so that I could understand, he continued, "I only know that I love you and I've waited my whole life for someone like you. Ever since I saw you for the first time, in February, I've been praying to God to bring us together. I know that you can have me put in the Segregation for even saying these words to you, but I have to say them, I have to tell you how much I love you, if it's the last thing on earth I do."

I was dumbstruck, thinking that he had harbored these feelings towards me for the past seven months.

"Just think about it," he pleaded.

I let out a long drawn-out sigh of resignation. "Okay," I finally agreed just as two inmates entered the classroom and took their seats, waiting for the class to begin.

"I"ll see you tomorrow, Mr. Córdoba," I said as Nicolás reluctantly stood up to leave.

He exchanged greetings with the incoming students and left the room.

Hoping that my face was not revealing the emotional state I was in, I somehow managed to to get through the afternoon. The fourteen students took turns sitting beside me at my desk while I corrected their work from the previous day, chatted with them for a while so they could practice their English, and assigned them new pages in their workbooks.

I had practically calmed down as I walked across the parking lot with the rest of the teachers at 3:15. That was, at least, until I happened to glance over towards the rec yard as I was inserting the key into my car door. There was Nicolás, sitting on top of one of the tables at the edge of the rec yard, watching me through the fence, thirty yards away.

Turning around to face him, I matched his stare. He nodded his head imperceptibly in a silent farewell and I got into my car and drove away.

I couldn't go home. That was the last place in the world I wanted to be. I needed time to think and a place to think where no one would bother me. As I had done so many times in college when I had worked on my Latin homework in the noisy school cafeteria where I could concentrate better, I headed for the most crowded place I could think of: the Food Court at the recently opened Middletown Mall. There, surrounded by a few hundred shoppers, I knew I would be able to sort out my feelings and decide what to tell Nicolás.

As soon as I got there, I called my boyfriend and told him that I had stopped at the mall, which was the truth, and that I was going to do some shopping, which was a lie...the first of many.

"Okay, Shorty," he said amiably, only too happy to make himself a cheeseburger and continue watching "Ophrah" undisturbed.

Armed with a large Diet Coke, I marched resolutely over to one of the tables at the far end of the Food Court and sat under a pair of royal palm trees that had just been planted

there. It was my favorite spot in the mall because of its tropical setting.

"This is crazy," I thought to myself. "I must be crazy for
even thinking there could be a possibility of a relationship
between me and Nicolás. Sure, it's great for your ego to have a
man tell you that he loves you. Mackie's only said it two or
three times in the last nine and a half years, and even then I
had to practically drag the words out of him. But Nicolás is an
inmate and hasn't had a relationship with a woman since he
was locked up almost two years ago—any woman would look
good to him.

"Maybe he's just using me. He's all alone. His whole family is in Colombia. He doesn't even know anyone in the United
States. He probably just wants some link, some connection to
the outside world. He's handsome...very handsome. I've
heard half the inmates and even some of the officers call him
Eddie Murphy...right to his face, although I can tell that it
annoys him. He's tall and he looks like he's in great shape
too...even though it's practically impossible to tell what's
under his green jumpsuit.

"Sure, any middle-aged woman would be flattered to have
a great looking guy half her age attracted to her. But I don't
feel middle-aged and I know I sure don't look middle-aged.

"How could we have any kind of a relationship...other
than a friendship? And even that isn't allowed. No, this is
crazy. Maybe I could write to him once in a while, cheer him
up a little. But he can't write back to me...he can hardly write
more than his own name, and here am I with two college
degrees. This is ridiculous.

"He's from a different country where they speak a different language and, even though my Spanish is okay because I
studied it for three years in high school thirty-five years
ago...before Nicolás was even born...his whole way of life, his
way of thinking is different from mine. His country has different customs, different foods, different values and practices
than the those in the United States.

"This is insane," I laughed to myself. "This afternoon
Nicolás tells me that he loves me and here I am, a few hours
later, thinking that I'll be living with him in Colombia when
he's released. Why, he himself told me that he could receive a
life sentence. How I could I let myself fall in love with someone that I can never live with...maybe never even see until he

gets out of prison... if he gets out of prison?"

After arguing with myself for three and a half hours, I finally decided what to do.

Maybe the sane thing to do would have been to tell Nicolás that I was very flattered, but that I could never be more than his teacher and that we should forget that our conversation had ever taken place. Instead, I listened to my heart, which felt like an unfurled flower about to burst open with the first rays of the morning sun.

I finished the rest of my now warm and diluted Diet Coke and got up from the table. Then I rode the escalator down to the mall's lower level, marched into the B. Dalton bookstore and bought a paperback Spanish-English dictionary. I had a feeling that I was going to need one.

My morning students were all assembled and Nicolás was already sitting at my desk when I entered the classroom the next morning. His jacket was draped over the back of the chair next to mine like he owned the place.

We went over his previous lesson and neither of us mentioned yesterday's conversation. I was beginning to think that I had imagined the whole thing, when in the middle of plural nouns he asked me if I would go away with him for a weekend when he got out of prison.

"Sure," I replied, thinking that we both must be crazy.

"Could he have read my mind?" I wondered. I hadn't even told him what I had so soul-searchingly decided the day before.

He smiled at me and my stomach did a flip-flop.

One by one, each of my students took their turn at my desk, while Nicolás glowered at them from behind the pages of his notebook and pretended to work on his lesson. At eight-fifty, when the loudspeaker announced the ten-minute activity move, most of the students left the room to stretch their legs, use the bathroom or smoke. Nicolás slid back into the seat next to me.

"Take a break... take a break," Olympia called to me as she passed by my open doorway on her way to the teachers' lounge next door. We, like the inmates, also had a ten-minute break every hour.

Although there were other students in the room, this was the only time that Nicolás and I could just talk to each other instead of working on his lessons. When the rest of the class

returned ten minutes later, Nicolás reluctantly returned to his
seat, the closest he could sit to me without actually sitting at
my desk. There were no assigned seats, but the men automatically sat in the same chair every day and this was the one he
had assumed for himself.

We sat together and talked an hour later at the next
break, again not even mentioning our conversation of the previous day, but both of us realizing that a decision had been
reached and that our relationship had irrevocably changed.

A week later as Nicolás walked past me on his way out of
the classroom at the end of the day's session, he pressed a
piece of paper into my hand. Flustered and scared to death
that someone had noticed, I nervously shoved it deep into my
purse as I headed to the teachers' lounge to get my jacket and
go to lunch. I didn't even look at the paper until four hours
later when I was finally sitting in my car in the parking lot at
the Middletown Mall. It was becoming my home away from
home.

I had been afraid to take the piece of paper out of my
purse while I was still at work. Not only were there large convex mirrors and cameras all over the place, but the contents of
your pockets, your purse and your briefcase were subject to
inspection at any time.

A tiny plastic card fell out of the compactly folded sheet of
loose-leaf paper as I opened it. It measured an inch by an inch
and a half and it was printed in Spanish. Superimposed over a
photograph of a man and a woman walking hand in hand was
the following poem:

> Cuando te conoci
> Tuve temor de hablarte
> Cuando te hablé
> Tuve temor de mirarte
> Cuando te miré
> Tuve temor de abrazarte
> Cuando te abracé
> Tuve temor de besarte
> Cuando te besé
> Tuve temor de quererte
> Y ahora te quiero
> Sólo quiero no perderte.

Fifteen minutes later, after consulting the Spanish-English dictionary purchased only a few days before, I finally

translated the poem which said:

> When I met you
> I was afraid to speak to you
> When I spoke to you
> I was afraid to look at you
> When I looked at you
> I was afraid to embrace you
> When I embraced you
> I was afraid to kiss you
> When I kissed you
> I was afraid to love you
> And now I love you
> I only don't want to lose you.

I still have that tiny plastic card—it's on the table right next to my bed.

Taking the dictionary out of the glove compartment again, I translated the letter that had been wrapped around the card. I realized immediately that it wasn't in Nicolás' handwriting.

"He must have dictated it to another inmate who wrote it for him," I thought to myself. "But it's the words and the feelings that are important, not in whose handwriting it is."

And what words! Telling me again how much he loved me and how much he thought about me and how much he was suffering because he loved me so much!

"Oh, Nicolás," I sighed aloud, "I am falling in love with you, too."

That was it. I was hooked.

"Will you go on vacation with me when I get out of prison?" he asked a few days later as we sat at my desk after his lesson.

"Sure," I answered matter-of-factly, as if we were going to make hotel and airplane reservations for the following week. "Where shall we go?"

"I was thinking we can go to Florida...or maybe Mexico, someplace on the ocean where we can swim and walk along the beach. Would you like that?"

"Ummmmmm," I replied, thinking that if he had suggested the moon or Timbuktu, my response would have been equally agreeable.

The following week, Nicolás and I were sitting side by side at my desk and were in the middle of a vocabulary lesson. Using a Spanish-English picture dictionary, I was trying to teach him the English words for various kinds of foods by showing him the pictures and then by saying the words several times in English. He was then supposed to repeat them after me in English, but instead, he said something in Spanish.

"¿Qué?" I asked him, also in Spanish. "What did you say?" He repeated his question.

"What?" I asked again.

"This is definitely a case of the blind leading the blind," I thought to myself as he took the book out of my hands trying not to show his exasperation with my lack of comprehension.

He flipped backwards through the pages of the dictionary until he finally found the one he had been searching for. Holding the book in his hand, he pointed to the picture of a bride and groom, then pointed to me and then to himself, and then back at the picture to make sure I understood what he meant as he repeated his question.

"Yes," I replied, nodding my head at the same time to make sure that he understood.

Under the desk, his hand found mine and our fingers intertwined. We could not embrace each other or kiss. We could not even let our eyes reveal what we were feeling. We didn't have to.

A few days later, I told Mackie that I was moving out.

He couldn't believe it.

Maybe it was because he didn't realize that this time I really meant it. For the last nine and a half years, every time I had expressed my dissatisfaction with his lack of a job or his refusal to go on a vacation or his resistance to try anything slightly creative in the bedroom he would tell me, "If you don't like it, you can leave." He knew full well that I had never lived by myself and was afraid to live alone. In fact, whenever I visited my sons in California and had to stay alone in a motel room, I couldn't fall asleep until I had piled all the chairs and tables against the door and turned on both the television and the bathroom lights.

But being afraid to live alone didn't prevent me from thinking about moving out. Four years earlier, I had even got-

ten as far as hiring a moving company and was ready to relo-
cate to Georgia to live with my brother and his family. Two
weeks before the big day, I told Mackie of my imminent plans.

He swore up and down that he loved me and promised me
that he would change.

Hah! Not enough.

Four years later he still hadn't gotten a job, and when we
finally went on vacation together, we drove to the New Jersey
shore, only four hours away, where he spent nearly every
waking hour of the three days we were there looking for bar-
gains in all the t-shirt shops on the boardwalk. There were fifteen of them.

You would have thought that the fact that ever since the
day Nicolás had told me he loved me I had been getting
dressed and undressed in the bathroom and had refused to
have any sexual relations would have given Mackie a hint
that something was amiss, but I guess it didn't.

Either he was relieved that I was disinterested or he was
afraid to broach the subject and learn the truth.

Although we were still inhabiting the same house, in my
mind and my heart I had already left. It was six o'clock on a
Friday evening. I had been out in the garden pulling weeds for
two hours when Mackie walked over to ask me what I was
planning for dinner.

"I don't know," I replied. "I haven't even thought about it."

Sensing some not-so-latent hostility in the tone of my
voice, he asked me what was wrong.

I told him that I was leaving him and that I would move
out as soon as I found someplace else to live.

"Why, Shorty, why?"

"I've had it," I answered. "I'm going to look in the paper
for an apartment... even a room for rent. I've got to get out of
here."

"But, Shorty..."

"And don't call me Shorty anymore either," I interrupted.
"My name is Carol, it's not Shorty. I'm not your Shorty, I'm
not anybody's Shorty. Just leave me alone."

"But why? What's wrong? What did I do? What happened?"

"Nothing... nothing. I just want to get out of here."

"But why?" he pressed on relentlessly. "Do you have another boyfriend? Did you meet someone else? Is it someone at work?"

"No!" I replied instantly.

Although I'm sure he was thinking that I had gotten involved with one of the corrections officers or somebody else that worked at FCI Otisville, he was getting too close to the truth.

"No, there's nobody else," I lied. "I'm just very unhappy and I want to get out of here. I want my own place and I don't want to live with you; I don't want to be with you anymore."

I bent down and started yanking out more weeds. I certainly couldn't tell him the truth. I couldn't tell anybody... anything.

Not only was it not permitted to act in a less than professional manner towards an inmate, if anyone were to find out that Nicolás and I were planning to get married when he was released from prison, I would get fired immediately. Worse than that, I wouldn't be able to find out where he was incarcerated and we would lose contact with each other for ten, fifteen, twenty years or, God forbid, forever.

Not only could I not tell anybody, I could not allow any of my emotions to surface, lest anyone even guess our feelings for each other.

Every morning, the very first thing I did when I came into the Education Department was to check my class roster to make sure that Nicolás hadn't been transferred to MCC or a different institution during the night. On the rare occasions when I arrived after the students, as soon as I spotted his brown jacket draped over the chair next to mine as I walked down the hall, I breathed a sigh of relief knowing that he was still in my class.

"Good morning, Mr. Córdoba," I said as Nicolás, giving me a nearly imperceptible smile, entered the already filled classroom.

"Good morning, Miss Carol," he replied casually.

I always greeted all the students in a similar fashion and it would have been more noticeable not to exchange pleasantries. Nobody heard the unspoken words of love in our voices nor saw our hearts about to explode out of our chests.

Nicolás sat down next to me and we squeezed each others' hands under the desk in our private "good morning." We reviewed his lessons for twenty minutes or so with our fingers intertwined under the desk, and then he reluctantly gave up his seat so that I could work with another student.

As soon as the bell rang for the ten-minute activity move, he immediately sat down next to me again so that we could talk about what really mattered...us...and the wonderful future we would have together when he got out of prison. If we were lucky, and all the other students had left the room to smoke or to stretch their legs, we would desperately steal a soundless kiss or two, apprehensively listening for the sounds of their returning footsteps or voices approaching from the teachers' lounge next door.

Nicolás continued to come to class every morning and after lunch for his individual lessons. The only days that we didn't see each other was when there was "adverse weather" or weekends. I sat in my classroom on those days, preparing lessons or doing paperwork, quietly going crazy knowing that Nicolás was only a few hundred feet away.

Three weeks later, on October 7, I left for California to attend my cousin's wedding in San Francisco and visit my sons in Santa Cruz. I had made the reservations and paid for my plane tickets months before and couldn't change my plans. I didn't know how I was going to survive nine days without seeing Nicolás. I could hardly make it through a weekend.

I cried all the way to California...and back.

Fifteen minutes after the airplane landed in Chicago, where I was to change planes on my return trip to New York, all flights were canceled, ground crews were not allowed on the tarmac, and the entire airport was closed down because of a thunderstorm so severe that the walls of the terminal shook.

I should have realized that it was a portent of things to come.

Not even bothering to go home, I went straight to FCI Otisville directly from the airport, only to find it completely shrouded in a fog so dense that the floodlights above the parking lot resembled hovering flying saucers. Needless to say, the inmates were not permitted to attend classes.

After an interminable staff meeting, the teachers were permitted to return to their rooms to catch up on their paperwork. I practically flew down the hall to my classroom to check my class roster. I discovered that Nicolás was in Segregation. Again.

After asking one of the teachers who knew him, I found out that Nicolás had been taken out in handcuffs from the Education Department the day after I had left for California. Instead of standing up and returning to the classroom when the ten-minute break was over, as Ms. Suzanne Brown, the Education Specialist, had told him to do, he had remained seated in his chair in the library, speaking to another inmate. It was bad enough to refuse to obey a direct order of a staff member, but to make matters even worse, as she approached him for the second time to tell him to get back to class, he had scooted down the hall still sitting in the chair, which was on wheels, while uttering uncomplimentary comments in Spanish under his breath.

The Education Specialist was not fluent in Spanish, but she had understood enough to know that he wasn't telling her how nice she looked that day.

Pressing the button on her two-way radio, she called for assistance. Two officers entered the library less than a minute after her call and led Nicolás away. Although she would have been more than happy to personally escort Nicolás to Segregation, she was not allowed to leave the department.

"Suzie, you know I'm the only one that can teach him," I reasoned. "Let him stay in my class."

I tried my best not to sound too anxious. I was in Ms. Brown's office trying to persuade her to put Nicolás back on my roster. Since she was the person who had taken Nicolás out of school, she was the only one who could put him back in.

"No...I've had it with that guy," she replied. "No...I've had it," she repeated angrily. "That Córdoba's nothing but trouble. Doesn't he give you problems in class?"

"No," I insisted. "The only problem he gives me is that he can't sit still for more than twenty minutes or so, and I've got to let him walk around a little so he can come back and concentrate...that's all. Come on...give him another chance. He's already been kicked out of all the other classes he's eligible for...if I don't teach him, no one will."

"Oh...all right," she reluctantly agreed, obviously against her better judgment. She knew that I had worked miracles with other students that nobody had wanted, teaching men who had never gone to school and who couldn't even write their own names.

"Okay...I'll give him one more chance...but if he messes up just once, he's out for good. Do you understand?"

"Thanks," I replied, silently breathing a sigh of relief.

I had gone to bat for inmates before...switching them from my morning class to my afternoon class after they had told me they couldn't wake up early enough and were afraid that they were going to be sent to Segregation for coming late to school, writing notes to the doctors in the Health Services Department requesting eyeglasses for inmates who needed them, proofreading the letters they wrote to judges and helping them get appointments with the prison psychologist or chaplain when I saw that they were severely depressed or had received bad news from home.

This wasn't the first time I had tried to help an inmate and I was sure it wasn't going to be the last. But this was the first and only time I had a personal reason to help one of them.

The next day, it was still foggy and classes were again canceled. We attended another lengthy staff meeting, read newspapers, completed crossword puzzles, and more than caught up on our paperwork. If we, the teachers, were going slightly stir-crazy, the inmates must have been climbing the walls.

I had not seen Nicolás since the day before I left for California...eleven long days earlier.

The fog finally lifted at 2:30, a half an hour before the teachers were supposed to go home. It didn't pay to open the Education Department for just thirty minutes, so it stayed closed while the rest of the activities resumed on the compound.

As I walked towards the exit with the other teachers, I wondered when Nicolás would get out of Segregation. Subconsciously sensing something, I turned my head back towards where I had just come from and saw Nicolás out of the corner of my eye. With a rag in one hand and a plastic spray bottle in the other, he was washing the windows on the doorway leading to the chapel, which was next door to the Education

Department. He was staring at me, almost as if he were mentally compelling me to turn around to see him.

The next day he was back in class. There was no need for words...except to repeat Ms. Brown's warning.

The only thing that mattered was the two of us and the love that was growing stronger and stronger every day. We tried not to think that we might never see each other again..it was too painful to even contemplate.

I still was searching for someplace to live. It was easier said than done. After checking the "Apartments for Rent" in the Sunday papers for the last few weeks, I realized that while there was no scarcity of places to live, the rents were equal to or more than what I was paying for the three-bedroom house I was currently living in. Although I had been paying all the bills for the last few years, I realized that I now had to save as much money as possible for the future. Nicolás was not only penniless but had no training to secure any kind of a decent job upon his release.

I didn't know what to do. I felt like I was adrift upon a vast ocean with no set course, no navigational charts and no idea of where I was headed or how long it would be until I would see land again.

Nicolás was due to go to court again in a few weeks, at which time he would receive a sentence of between ten years, the mandatory minimum, and life in prison.

"Don't worry...I'll be out in a year...maybe a year and a half," he said again and again, trying to reassure me that even if he received a long sentence, he would definitely win his appeal and would be out of prison in a year.

I believed him. "I could stand it for a year," I told myself bravely.

With that time frame in mind, I searched for a temporary, inexpensive apartment. By the end of October, when I still hadn't found one, I realized that I would be better off if I sold or got rid of everything I owned in order to live in a furnished room. I figured that all I really needed were my personal items and some clothes.

"I don't even need all my clothes...just the summer ones," I reminded myself. "Wasn't I going to be moving to Colombia, South America, to be with Nicolás when he got out of prison in a few months?"

I didn't care if Mackie stayed in the house we had been renting for the last seven years. I just wanted to get as far away from him and everything associated with him as quickly as possible. Now he would have to be responsible for paying the rent and all the other bills, instead of me.

Living in the same house with Mackie had turned into a nightmare. Even though I insisted that he sleep in a different room, he sat at the foot of my bed, night after night, red-eyed and crying, begging me to reconsider my decision, preventing me from even closing my eyes. I would take refuge in the bathroom, the only room with a lock on the door, where I would sit on the floor in my bathrobe and write letters and poems in Spanish which I hoped to give to Nicolás one day.

Between not sleeping enough at night and not eating enough during the day, I was falling apart. The few hours I that I managed to sleep were filled with bizarre dreams and nightmares that awakened me with my heart pounding in my chest.

For the first and only time in my life, I lost weight without trying. I didn't even have to diet. I could hardly eat anything and was existing on grapefruit juice, Diet Coke and coffee. I almost passed out twice at work, once right in front of Nicolás just as I rose from my chair to go to the bathroom. I don't know if he was more concerned about my health or more angry with me for not eating, but whatever the reason, he insisted that I have a snack, either a piece of fruit or a bagel, every morning at the ten-o'clock break.

As if I didn't have enough to do during the day and to think about all night, I returned to the bookstore and purchased a Spanish grammar book in order to reteach myself what I had studied in high school thirty-six years earlier. Luckily, my three years of Spanish classes had given me an excellent grasp of the language, and I had not only assisted my teacher in grading all her classes' exams, but I had also tutored fellow students who were having difficulties in learning the language.

The lessons in the book I bought were self-explanatory, and I found that I had remembered more than I had forgotten. Nicolás and I spoke only in Spanish, and I wanted to understand what he was saying as much as I wanted to communicate my thoughts to him. He tried hard to be patient with me...speaking very, very slowly and drawing pictures or rephrasing his sentences in simple words that he thought I would understand whenever I stared at him with a blank expression on my face.

I hadn't given up trying to teach him English. We still went through pages and pages in his workbook every day, and he still practiced his handwriting and English vocabulary. But it was just easier and faster for me to speak Spanish than for him to learn to speak English. Besides, I had a feeling that after he served his sentence, he would be deported and not be permitted to live in the United States again, in which case I would have to be fluent in Spanish.

The grammar book helped, but what I really needed was someone to tutor me in conversational Spanish. I could read and write Spanish very well and understand it fairly well, but I sounded like the world's worst gringo whenever I opened my mouth and tried to speak it.

I was trying to figure out how I could get some help without enrolling in college again when I literally bumped into Rina in a supermarket in Middletown. She was from Honduras, and as a volunteer for LVA, Literacy Volunteers of America, I had tutored both her and her sister. Although we had lost touch with each other a year after our tutoring sessions ended, we greeted each other affectionately.

We brought each other up to date on what we had been doing for the past year, then we parted with the promise that we'd stay in touch and get together for lunch on my next day off. I didn't tell her about Nicolás...that was still my deep dark secret that I couldn't tell anyone.

As soon as I got home, I had a brainstorm! If I had been a cartoon character, a light bulb would have lit up above my head. I picked up the telephone.

"Rina," I began. "Do you remember how I used to help you with your English...how we used to go over what to say to the waitress in a restaurant and how to ask for different cold cuts and salads in the supermarket?"

"Sure," she recalled, laughing...reminding me that she used to ask for crab salad because she couldn't say shrimp salad. "I remember...why?"

"Well," I explained, "I need someone who can tutor me in Spanish."

"But you already know Spanish," she interrupted.

"I know, Rina," I agreed, "but I only know book Spanish...I want to know real Spanish, the language and the expressions and the way people really speak. I need someone to teach me these things and to correct me when I say something wrong...someone to help me with my pronunciation. Can you do it?"

I held my breath, hoping that she'd say yes.

"Sure," she agreed, immediately. "But I just have one request. Can you come to my house for the lessons?"

"Of course," I replied. "That's no problem at all."

As an LVA tutor, we were not supposed to meet with our students at their homes. Not only were there apt to be too many interruptions and distractions, but we were told that it was for our own safety to meet in a library or college facility.

The next day after work, instead of going home I drove to Rina's house for my first lesson. She greeted me with a cup of hot coffee and a warm hug. I asked her if we could speak only in Spanish while I was there, so that I could practice and so she could correct my pronunciation.

We sat down at the dining room table while we talked about our jobs and our families. She introduced me to her children as they each came home from school. I also spoke to them in Spanish. I think they thought I was a little strange, speaking to them in a language which was difficult for me while knowing that they spoke English as well as I did.

A month later, as I was standing at the front door about to leave, I asked her almost as an afterthought if she knew anyone with a spare room to rent. Grabbing me by the arm, she led me back into the living room while at the same time telling me that she herself owned a second house in which she rented rooms.

"That's great!" I exclaimed. Although I still hadn't found an inexpensive apartment, I had started to sort and pack the things I wanted to save. "Is there a room available? How much is the rent? Where is it? How soon can I move in? Do you want a deposit right now?"

I couldn't believe it. Here I was trying for months to find a cheap, temporary place to live, and Rina had exactly what I was looking for. Well...not exactly.

"Don't get too excited," she warned me. "The house is small, old, not at all like the one I live in, and it's in a very bad neighborhood."

That was an understatement. "Crack Alley," as the local newspapers had dubbed the street, was a block away from the house.

When I met Rina at the house the next day in order to see the room that was available, she apologized not only for its appearance, but also for its location. I didn't care, I just needed to get out of where I was living.

I was relieved when she told me that she would move all her stuff to one side of the garage in order that I could lock my car inside. My biggest fear was that someone would slash the roof of the Mustang convertible that I had just purchased that April and steal it.

She told me that the other tenants, a married couple and the husband's brother, were from Guatemala, and another man, a countryman of hers, was from Honduras. She assured me that they were all good, decent people and that I had nothing to worry about. Only Laz, the fellow from Honduras, spoke a little English, which was a distinct advantage for me because I would be forced to speak Spanish all the time.

As she led me through the house, I noticed the unmade bed and the solitary sofa and Formica table in the living room. Cockroaches of various sizes and colors scurried out of sight as we entered the kitchen. There were even more of them upstairs in the unheated bathroom and tiny bedroom which was to be mine if I wanted to rent it for $150 a month.

I gave her a check for the first month's rent and asked her when I could start bringing my things over. It felt like a weight had finally been lifted off my shoulders.

The next morning, when I told Nicolás about the place I had found, he was both relieved that I was moving out of the house that I had been sharing with Mackie and worried because I would be sharing living arrangements with complete strangers. I didn't dare tell him about the condition of the house or about the cockroaches or the neighborhood. He couldn't do anything to help me, and he had more than enough on his mind already.

When we said goodbye each afternoon, we never knew if we would see each other the next day or ever again. The date of his sentencing, which had originally been set for the middle of August, was rapidly approaching, and he told me that he was going to be sent to MCC in a few days. On Monday night, November 16, he was transferred to MCC.

I didn't see his jacket on the back of his chair as I walked into my classroom the next morning. As soon as I spotted "9N" as his housing unit on my class roster, I knew that the day that we had dreaded with such fearful anticipation had arrived.

If I hadn't promised Nicolás that I wouldn't cry, I would have fled from my classroom in tears. If it had not been necessary to assume a cheerful facade, so that no one could even guess that we loved each other, I never could have made it through the next few hours, let alone the days.

At 9:30, Tuesday morning, November 17, Nicolás was standing in front of Judge Merhige. At the same time, I was on my knees in the ladies' room in the Education Department at FCI Otisville, praying that my husband-to-be would receive the mandatory minimum sentence... or even less if that were possible.

"Is there any statement you would like to make to the court? Do you know of any reason why the court should not now pronounce sentence?"

"No," Nicolás replied.

"Let me just say that, one, the motion for a new trial is denied. I can't find any valid reason where I could legitimately, as a judge, deviate from the guidelines. Whether I approve of the guidelines or not is of no consequence. They are there; they are the law, and I am sworn to uphold the law."

Judge Merhige then ordered Nicolás "delivered to the custody of the Director of the Bureau of Prisons for confinement for a period of 121 months on each of the counts, to be run concurrently. He informed Nicolás about his right to appeal and recommended, upon Nicolás' request, that he be confined to an institution in Florida.

The judge looked at Nicolás' attorney. "Anything else?" he asked.

Mr. Stern shook his head.

"Thank you very much," said the judge, and, striking the gavel once, called the court adjourned.

A marshal escorted Nicolás back to MCC. It was only a matter of time until he would be sent to his permanent facility. It could be in a few days, a few weeks or even a few months. He could be shipped out from MCC or sent anywhere in the country while he was waiting.

Nicolás didn't think he'd ever be sent back to FCI Otisville. He dreamed about his Miss Carol every night. One week passed. Another week passed. He remained in MCC.

On December 1, I picked up the roster expecting to read "9N" next to Nicolás' name as I had for the past two weeks and gasped when I saw that he was no longer in MCC. He was in R&D... at FCI Otisville.

"He's back... Oh, my God... he's back... he's back," I kept repeating over and over to myself.

I called the roll and checked off my students' names with a trembling hand. I tried not to become overly optimistic because very often after the inmates were sentenced, they were kept locked up in Segregation until they were shipped out. If that happened to Nicolás, we would never be able to see each other again.

"Carol, are you ready?" Olympia called to me on her way into the teachers' lounge.

"I'm coming... I'm coming," I said distractedly. All I could think about was how I could get to see Nicolás.

We started walking down to the Officer's Mess, a dining room off to the left of the inmates' dining hall, to eat lunch. I buttoned up my navy wool coat and wrapped my striped scarf around my neck as I walked past the floor-to-ceiling windows of the inmates' dining hall. Turning my head to the right as I hurried to catch up to the other teachers, I spotted Nicolás facing the window just about to put a forkful of food into his mouth. Our eyes locked.

I forced myself to keep on walking.

At lunch, somehow I managed to swallow some soup and a slice of bread. With Nicolás in MCC and no one to remind me to eat, I had been living on nervous energy and little else, and I wanted to be able to tell Nicolás that I had eaten something... just in case he asked me... just in case he could actually come to see me.

After twenty minutes, one of the Education Department officers got up from the table and asked if any of the teachers wanted to go back with him. They were only allowed a half-hour for lunch, while we had a full hour and then some.

"Sure," I replied, hoping that he or anyone else wouldn't notice how jubilant I had become in the last half-hour.

"I've got papers to go over also," announced one of the other teachers, also getting up from the table. I breathed a silent sigh of relief, thankful that I wasn't the only teacher going back early to the department.

After removing some student folders from the filing cabinet, I sat at my desk and tried to concentrate on them or on anything that would take my mind off my fear that I wouldn't be able to see or speak to Nicolás again. Although I kept on telling myself that I was lucky that he had come back from MCC and I that I should be satisfied that I had seen him, I kept listening for the Education Department's doors to open and kept looking down the hallway to see if he was coming. Twenty minutes later, when I had finally resigned myself to the fact that he probably couldn't come, and I was correcting some papers, I suddenly looked up and saw Nicolás standing right in front of my desk.

"Oh, my God...oh, Papi," I exclaimed breathlessly.

I nearly leaped out of my chair as he grabbed my hand and led me to the middle of the room, away from the open doorway. We clung to each other and kissed, and for five minutes the only sound in the room was the beating of our hearts. We reluctantly tore ourselves away from each other, afraid that the afternoon students would be arriving any minute. We sat down at my desk.

"Oh, Papi, you lost so much weight," I exclaimed, stroking his cheek. We were no longer "Mr. Córdoba" and "Miss Carol," but "Papi" and "Mami" in the familiar Colombian custom of a husband and wife.

"I'm okay, Mami, don't worry," he assured me.

Abruptly, he stood up to leave, telling me that he was not permitted to attend classes until he was assigned to a regular housing unit, which would probably be in a few days.

"¿Cuánto?" I asked him, grabbing his hand so he had to answer me. "How much time did you get?"

"Ten years," he replied hurriedly, and rushed towards the door before I could say anything else. "I've got to go now...I'll try to come after lunch tomorrow."

"Ten years...oh, my God...ten years," I repeated desolately.

I couldn't believe it.

After convincing myself that I could stand a separation of a year...now I would have to wait almost ten years. With earned good time, he would probably only have to serve 85% of the ten years. And the months he had already been incarcerated would be included in the ten years. It still seemed like an eternity until we would be able to live together.

I didn't know how I was going to face all those years alone, so I did the only thing possible: I didn't think about it.

Could I have changed my mind and returned to my former existence? Could I have gone back to Mackie, who still persisted in calling me at work several times a week, begging me to come back and even sending flowers, which I immediately dumped into the garbage. Could I have told Nicolás that it was just too much to ask me to wait for him...to put my life on hold for the next ten years? Could I have told him, "Sorry, I just can't do it," and then walk away from him as if nothing had ever happened between us?

Sure, I could have done it...if I could have stopped breathing and if I could have stopped my heart from beating.

Nicolás had not just become a part of my life, he was life itself. For the first time in I didn't remember how long, I had a purpose to my life, a meaning to my existence. For the first time in my life I had somebody who loved me completely and unconditionally with all his heart and soul, somebody who told me constantly how much he loved me, somebody who swore that he would give up his life for me, somebody who promised to love me forever and to make me happy for the rest of my life.

In spite of all the present frustration and future separation, I couldn't turn away from Nicolás and go back to where I was and what I was before we met. In spite of everything, no one had ever made me happier.

Nicolás came to see me the next day. It was after lunch and we had only a few minutes for a fleeting kiss and a brief conversation before he had to return to his unit.

"Will you wait for me?" he asked a few days later, after he had been assigned back to my class.

"Of course," I said. "As soon as you know where you'll be designated, I'll hand in my notice of resignation and then after the thirty days that I have to wait, I'll move to whatever city they send you. I'll write to you every day and I'll get another job and visit you every weekend."

"Then we can get married," he reminded me. "You don't work for the Bureau of Prisons...you never did. And when you're no longer teaching at the prison, you'll just be like anyone else, and we'll be able to get married.

"Don't worry, Mami," he said, "everything will turn out okay. I'll win my appeal and get out in a year or so."

I nodded, afraid to voice my lack of confidence in the ability of Nicolás' court-appointed attorney to win an appeal if he hadn't even been able to have Nicolás acquitted in the original trial.

I tried to remain enthusiastic and optimistic not only to bolster my own courage, but also to raise Nicolás' spirits. He was very superstitious and truly believed that negative thoughts led to negative consequences.

Nicolás came to class every morning and every day after lunch, and we talked and talked.

We had no idea if he would be shipped out in a day or a week or a month, and we tried to squeeze a lifetime into every minute that we spent together.

Christmas was rapidly approaching. I purchased a live Christmas tree and brought it home to share with my new housemates. We got along well from the first day, and they were very patient and amused by my halting Spanish, helping me with my pronunciation and telling me the Spanish words for everything around the house. Instead of putting my large color TV in my bedroom upstairs, I had placed it in the living room where they could also watch it, and on Saturday nights I sat with them watching "Sábado Gigante," a Spanish language program emanating from Miami.

They appreciated the Christmas tree, and I was more than glad to buy it because they were poorer than poor, living on the barest minimum wages and sending nearly every cent that they earned home to their even poorer relatives in Guatemala and Honduras. Knowing that they couldn't afford to buy anything, I brought over extra sets of lights and decorations, which they gladly hung on the tree and around the living room.

I brought six other sets of multicolored miniature lights to the prison. Nicolás and the other students strung them up all over the walls and ceiling of my tiny classroom. Not only were we permitted to decorate our rooms for Christmas, but the prison officials looked the other way if the candy canes that were hanging up around the room "disappeared" and had to be replaced every day.

Every hour when we had a ten-minute break, I shut off the overhead fluorescent lights in the classroom and the class and I sat listening to the cassette tape of Christmas carols that I had brought from home, while the lights flashed all around us. Students from other classes poked their heads in the doorway and sometimes sat down for a few minutes, enjoying the peace and tranquility of the moment.

Nicolás and I sat at my desk, holding hands in the darkness. Although we knew we wouldn't be able to be together on Christmas Eve or Christmas Day, we were happy that he hadn't been sent to another prison yet and that we could celebrate the holiday together.

"Happy New Year, Mami," Nicolás greeted me in English as I returned to class on January 4. It was like a miracle...not that he said something in English, but that he was still at FCI Otisville.

I tried not to think about him leaving. I didn't think I could face the class, not seeing his face in front of me.

On Friday, January 15, he came to class wearing blue canvas slippers instead of the black oxfords that the inmates were issued.

"I'm leaving any day now," he told me. "My name is on the 'Call-out' sheet and they told me to pack up my things."

I held on to the edge of my desk, unable to say anything because I was afraid that the only sound that I would be able to utter would come out as a sob.

"Don't worry, Mami, I'll find a way to get in touch with you. I'll tell you where I am...and...and you'll quit your job and be able to visit me...don't worry."

Just because I wanted the morning to last forever, it flew by. When the loudspeaker directed the inmates to return to their housing units to get ready for the noon meal, I said goodbye to my students and stood up from my desk.

Nicolás was standing in the center of the room waiting to kiss me goodbye.

"Don't cry, Mami...don't cry, please," he begged, kissing me again and again. "Everything will turn out fine...don't worry."

Then, after kissing me one last time, he took a deep breath to steel himself and walked out of the room.

Numb and almost in a daze, I managed to get through the next few hours.

I cried all weekend.

Classes were canceled on Monday, January 18, in honor of Martin Luther King, Jr.'s birthday.

"I don't know why I even want to go to work, anyway," I told myself, peering through the windshield at the fog enveloping the entire mountain as I pulled into the parking lot at 7:30 the next morning. "Nicolás isn't here—God only knows where he is. And even if he is still here, he won't be able to come to class because of this fog."

I sat at my desk in my empty classroom and tried to concentrate on the papers I was grading.

"Ten-minute activity move...ten-minute activity move... all AM students report to Education at this time...ten-minute activity move."

I couldn't believe the announcement. The fog had lifted and the inmates were let out of their cells to resume normal activities. Holding the class roster in my trembling hands, I looked up as Nicolás walked into the room.

"Good morning, Mr. Córdoba," I said, still unable to believe that Nicolás was actually in front of me.

"Good morning, Miss Carol," he replied softly as he took off his green knit cap. I noticed that he had on a brand-new dark brown winter jacket.

"Why did they give you a new jacket?" I asked him. "Does that mean that you're going to stay?"

I knew that although the judge had agreed to recommend that he be designated to a prison in Florida, the Bureau of Prisons could send Nicolás anywhere in the country.

"I don't know," he sighed dejectedly. "They just gave it to me and I took it...I didn't ask why."

While the class watched a video about the life of Martin Luther King Jr., Nicolás sat next to me at my desk. I had brought an illustrated book about the famous civil rights leader to read to the class after they watched the video, with the hope that they would attempt to read it by themselves from time to time, once they were familiar with it. Translating the words on each page into Spanish, I read the book to Nicolás. I had no sooner reached the last page when I heard the announcement that all inmates were to return to their units. The movie wasn't over yet, and all the men groaned as they reluctantly got up and started putting on their jackets. It was only 10:30, twenty minutes before the class was supposed to be officially over. The fog had rolled back in...and looked like it was going to last for at least a week.

We hurriedly kissed goodbye after the other students had left, and started walking towards the door.

"Are you leaving today?" I asked him.

He shrugged his shoulders and sighed, "I don't know." Then, squeezing my hand once, he turned and left.

It was still too early to go to lunch, so I gathered up the papers on my desk, put the students' chairs back in place, and went into the teachers' lounge next door to get my coat. As I came back into my room a few seconds later, I saw Nicolás standing there, waiting for me.

"This is it," he said softly. "The officer at the door told me not to go back to my unit."

"Oh no...oh no...oh no..." I stammered as I burst into tears.

He took both of my hands in his and held them tightly. "No...no...don't...don't cry...don't worry, we'll be okay... everything will turn out fine."

Then we wrapped our arms around each other and kissed. Both of us realized that it might be our last kiss for a long time...or forever. Then he let go of me, and without another word walked out of the room.

PART THREE

"Come on, Carol," Olympia called out from the hallway. "Let's go...we'll be late for lunch."

Quickly, I wiped the tears off my cheeks and rushed from my room and out of the Education Department. I didn't even turn around to see if Nicolás was waiting at the entrance to the Administration Building with the other inmates who were going to leave that day—I knew I couldn't bear to see him standing there.

With shaking hands, I fumbled in my purse until I found the small bottle of pills I kept there. It contained mostly aspirin and some antihistamines, but I had also thrown in a few Valium tablets that I had not taken on my last airplane flight when I had decided to be brave and not take them. I was definitely not feeling very brave now. In fact, I felt that I was going to pass out on the sidewalk, right then and there. Opening the bottle as I walked to the Officers' Mess, I shook the contents into my hand, found one of the tranquilizers and popped it into my mouth. I chewed it dry; it was bitter. I knew it would make me numb. That's exactly what I wanted to be...numb...so I wouldn't be able to feel anything...anymore.

Once in the dining room, I washed down the remains of the pill with a cup of coffee and pushed the food around on my plate so it would appear that I was eating.

After what seemed like hours, I returned to the Education Department and went through the motions of teaching my afternoon students. Luckily, I rarely taught group lessons, and it was an easy matter of helping the few students who asked me to go over their lessons. What was not easy was trying to keep my eyes open with ten milligrams of Valium taking effect...but at least I wasn't crying...yet.

Nicolás huddled together with the other inmates who were also about to be shipped out. The chill that went through him had nothing to do with the seventeen-degree temperature outside the "sally-port," the glass enclosure at the entrance of the administration building. He turned around and faced the Education Department a hundred yards away, hoping that he could see me as I left the building on my way to lunch.

He had almost given up after waiting over ten minutes, when suddenly the doors opened and the teachers filed out in a small group, walking behind the officer who was escorting them to the Officers' Mess.

"There she is," he exclaimed to himself as he watched me walking inexorably further and further away. "Turn around, turn around...please," he begged silently. "Let me see your face one last time."

But I didn't turn, and finally the only thing he could see was a tiny figure in a long, navy coat with a brightly-colored scarf trailing behind in the wind as I turned the corner and entered the dining room.

"Oh, God," Nicolás shuddered to himself, "please...please let us be together soon."

It was three o'clock and all I wanted to do was go home, but I still couldn't leave because, in addition to the classes I taught in the morning and afternoon, I also taught an ESL, English as a Second Language, class from five to eight in the evening.

When I got home to my tiny roach-infested room I looked at the photographs of Nicolás that were on my dresser, on the table near my bed and on the wall.

He had given me a few Polaroid photographs of himself, taken at the prison, just for me. I had gotten them enlarged into eight-by-tens. The only place that I could look at them was in the privacy of my room, where nobody knew about Nicolás or even knew where I worked. I was almost paranoid about anybody finding out about us and still lived in fear that Nicolás would be sent to a prison at the other side of the country and wouldn't be able to contact me and we'd never be able to find each other again.

After taking a shower, I got into bed, leaving on the overhead light so that I could look at Nicolás' pictures next to me.

I cried and cried and didn't think I'd be able to sleep at all, but my physical and mental exhaustion combined with the residual effects of the tranquilizer I had taken earlier and I finally fell asleep.

By three o'clock in the morning, I was wide awake again. I opened my eyes and, like a weight crushing me, I remembered that Nicolás was no longer at FCI Otisville.

"God only knows where you are, Papi," I sobbed to myself, holding Nicolás' picture close to my chest.

At the same time as I lay there crying in my bed in New York, Nicolás was wide awake and staring at the ceiling from his bunk at USP Atlanta.

Right after I had disappeared from view, Nicolás and the other departing inmates had been escorted into the Administration Building and downstairs into R & D. Once there, he stripped off his clothes and stood stoically with his arms and legs apart while he was searched. Then, instead of the green clothes he was used to, he donned the tan shirt and slacks that designated inmates wore and slipped his feet back into his blue canvas slippers.

A few minutes later, two corrections officers entered the room to assist in processing the inmates for departure.

"Córdoba!" a voice called out.

Nicolás walked over with his hands already outstretched in front of him. One of the officers secured handcuffs to his wrists and attached them to the chain that he had just wrapped around Nicolás' waist while another officer clamped the leg irons around his ankles.

When the rest of the inmates were similarly restrained, the officers who would accompany the group picked up the stacks of completed paperwork from the desk and ordered the inmates out of R & D and onto the waiting bus.

Nicolás tucked his head down into the collar of his jacket as a blast of cold air whipped around him. He would have liked to dash into the bus to escape the biting wind, but the man in front of him, to whom he was chained, was taking his time in getting on the bus.

Within an hour, the bus arrived at the airport and Nicolás and the other inmates boarded the awaiting plane. Not being a commercial airline, there were none of the usual amenities associated with the flight. There were no pretty flight attendants or in-flight movies, the inmates weren't allowed the use of the bathroom, and the only meal served was a sandwich, which they had to eat hunched over at the waist in order to reach it in their fettered hands.

Nicolás had no idea where he was heading or even if he was being sent to his final destination, where the Bureau of Prisons had designated him to serve the rest of his sentence.

The sky was already a deep indigo when he deplaned and got onto the bus waiting on the tarmac at the airport in Atlanta. He took a deep breath and tried to stretch his arms and legs as far as his restraints would permit. The air, while not balmy, was decidedly warmer than it had been in New York, and Nicolás hoped that he was in Florida, as he had requested.

The bus pulled up in front of an old, multi-storied building in the middle of the city and dropped off its passengers. Nicolás looked up at the barred windows and hoped that he wouldn't be staying too long. He had heard many inmates' stories about this place...none of them good.

After being processed, he was handed a sandwich and a small container of juice. Although it was only a few minutes after six o'clock in the evening, he had arrived too late for the dinner meal, which was served at three in the afternoon. All the meals were served early in Atlanta...breakfast was at five and lunch was at ten o'clock in the morning.

It didn't matter to Nicolás; he couldn't eat anyway.

Sighing to himself, he opened the container of juice and drank it in one gulp. He wished he had a picture of me that he could look at right then. It seemed like it was weeks, not just that morning since he had last seen my face. He passed his fingers over his lips, remembering our last kiss, and wondered when or if he would ever kiss me again.

In his bunk at last, he lay on his back, folded his arms under his head and stared at the ceiling. He couldn't sleep.

Every hour he got up from his bunk, walked over to the bathroom, took a sip of water from the water fountain and returned to his bed, where he lay awake, staring into space. One of the officers, noticing Nicolás' hourly treks across the dormitory, asked Nicolás if he'd like to work as an orderly, as long as he wasn't sleeping anyway.

Nicolás agreed immediately, not especially because he wanted to work, but because he figured that the endless night would pass more quickly if he were busy doing something instead of just lying on his bed thinking too much of things that he couldn't do anything about. So while the rest of the inmates in the huge dormitory slept, Nicolás washed the floors and scrubbed the bathrooms and tried not to think.

Like an automaton, I went to work each day, teaching my GED classes in the mornings and afternoons, and my ESL classes in the evenings, but it wasn't the same. Something was missing and that something was Nicolás. Even though I had been teaching at the prison for two years before I had ever met him, now that he was gone, my job there was just a job, nothing special...nothing that would change the world or the lives of the inmates I was teaching.

"Maybe that's how I should have thought of this job," I berated myself. "Maybe I should have been like the other teachers...just open the books, teach the lessons and not talk to the inmates as if they were just like people on the outside... not listen to them when they wanted to tell me about their wives and children...not help them with their letters and their problems. Maybe that's how I should have been."

But it was too late for that now.

A week and a half after he left FCI Otisville, Nicolás got word to me that he was all right and that he had been assigned to FCI Tallahassee.

"Thank God," I cried. Our prayers had been answered: he was in Florida.

I typed up a short letter of resignation and delivered it to Randy Brown at BOCES and to Diane Loeven, the Supervisor of Education at FCI Otisville. Both Suzanne Brown, the Education Specialist, and Oliver Brown, the new Assistant Super-

visor of Education, agreed to write letters of recommendation
for me, to help me search for a new teaching position.

My resignation didn't come as a surprise to anyone there,
especially after they had heard me arguing with Mackie on
the telephone and had seen me dump into the garbage the
flowers he continued to send to me at work. They knew that
with my three sons living in California and my brother living
in Georgia, Mackie had been the only reason I had remained
in New York. With him out of the picture, there was no reason
at all to stay.

I telephoned my brother David and asked him if his offer
was still good. For at least the last nine years he had been trying to convince me to pack up everything and come down to
Georgia. He had a huge house on five acres, and he and
Stephanie, my sister-in-law, were more than willing for me to
live with them.

He assured me that I would be welcomed. He was both
relieved and happy that I had finally ended my relationship
with Mackie. He didn't know anything about Nicolás. I was
saving that bit of news to tell him in person.

According to the contract I had signed with BOCES, I had
to give one month's notice of my resignation. During my last
month at FCI Otisville, I plunged into my work with more
enthusiasm than ever, perhaps because I knew that the end
was in sight and there was finally some direction in my life.

Rina was sad when I told her I would be moving out in a
month, especially when I told her that I'd be moving to Georgia. We promised to keep in touch by telephone and through
the mail, but we knew it wouldn't be the same and realized
that we'd probably never see each other again.

Two weeks before I was to leave New York, I received the
application to be on Nicolás' approved visiting list. I answered
all the questions, signed it and mailed it back the next day,
hoping that I would be approved. There was nothing I could
do but wait.

Two days before I left, the teachers and staff had a
farewell party for me, held during lunchtime in the Education
Department instead of at the Chinese restaurant where we
usually celebrated, because I had to teach in the evening. It
was a bittersweet farewell because I had become friends with
many of the people over the past three years that I had

worked there, and we had visited each others' homes and shared many good times together.

Friday, February 26, was my last day at work. After work, I got into my car at three o'clock and slowly drove around the parking lot to take one last look at FCI Otisville. I thought about Nicolás and all the other inmates I had taught over the past three years, and hoped that I had helped them. Then I drove straight to Headlines, the beauty parlor that I had gone to for the past eight years, where Vicky refused to take any money for my haircut and frosting.

"It's a going-away present," she said, hugging me good-bye.

From there, I crossed the street to the Chinese restaurant for my last meal there. I smiled to myself when I opened my fortune cookie and the message read, "You will be traveling and coming into a fortune."

It felt like all the pieces of my life were finally coming together, almost as if it was preordained, and when I filled the gas tank of my car and the total came to $12.05, a chill went through me...for I had lived at 1205 Avenue R in Brooklyn for twenty-one years.

As soon as I returned to my room in Middletown, I put two photographs of Nicolás in my wallet. For the first time I was free to acknowledge our relationship.

It was seven degrees above zero when I awoke at six o'clock the next morning. There was snow piled on the side-walks, but the roads were clear. I had been anxiously watching the Weather Channel for the last few days, hoping that there wouldn't be a snowstorm to delay my departure. Now that the day was finally here at last, I wanted to be on my way.

I had figured that if I left Saturday morning and stopped driving each day before it got dark, I'd be able to reach my brother's house in southern Georgia by Monday. He lived in Bainbridge, one hour's drive north of Tallahassee.

All I had to do was put a few days' worth of clothes, some toiletries, and my CD player and television into the car and I'd be ready to leave. Moving companies had quoted ridiculous prices to transport my things to Georgia, and rental companies told me that I couldn't attach a trailer to the back of my car because it was a convertible. Because of this, for the past several weeks, I had been making daily trips to the post office to mail my books, dishes, household items and clothes that I was going to keep. I had given away to the Salvation Army ten huge plastic bags filled with all the rest of my clothes. I had sold or given away all my furniture and other household items.

Nicolás was going to win his appeal and we would be leaving for South America by the end of the summer. I didn't want to be encumbered by any furniture or excess clothing.

The only things I couldn't ship or take with me in my car were the Baldwin baby grand piano which my parents had purchased when I was twelve and a three-story electrified wooden dollhouse that I had constructed fifteen years earlier. Although he was still upset that I was leaving, Mackie had assured me that he would take care of them and hold them for me until I had a place of my own. Maybe he thought that if I had some link with him, there was still a chance for a reconciliation.

Luckily, Lazarus, one of the men who shared the house in Middletown, was able to carry my television set downstairs. In order to get it into the car, where it took up the entire back seat, I had to let down the top of the convertible while he placed it in from above. I covered the television with large towels and a quilt, hoping that no one would realize what was underneath them and slash the top of my car to take it out while I was eating or sleeping.

I said goodbye to Laz and shook his hand. He had helped me a lot, not only with moving all the heavy things in and out of my room but also with my Spanish.

The post office was still closed when I got there to retrieve my mail for the last time. Although I was eager to get on the road while the weather was still good, I decided to wait the half-hour until it opened, so I went around the corner to Dunkin' Donuts for a cup of coffee and a bagel.

"I just can't get away from the BOP," I told myself, laughing silently as I spotted Oliver Brown, the Assistant Supervisor of Education, sitting at one of the tables. I joined him there and we chatted for a while, mostly about Friday's bombing of the World Trade Center. He wished me good luck and I left, remembering his admonition the day before "not to get so emotionally involved" with inmates if I worked in a prison again; his declaration was that the inmates "are criminals first and people second." I wondered to myself what he would have said if he had seen Nicolás' pictures in my wallet.

There was no mail waiting for me at the post office and nothing to keep me in New York.

Taking a deep breath, I popped Meatloaf's "Bat out of Hell" into the cassette player, cranked up the volume, and put my Mustang into drive. I was on my way. At last.

With each mile that passed, I could feel all the tension and worries of the past few months slipping away. For the first time in six months, I was relaxed and carefree. I wasn't concerned about not having a job or where I would live, and I no longer had to worry that somebody would find out about Nicolás and me. Although I felt sometimes that I was poised at the edge of a diving board about to plunge into a swimming pool of unknown depth, I was more than willing to leap into it, even though the pool might turn out to be empty.

"A new month and a new life," I told myself as I reached the city limits of Bainbridge, Georgia, just as the sun was going down on March 1.

I honked the horn all the way up the long driveway, and David, his wife Stephanie and my niece Jessica all rushed out to greet me. I made it!

Twenty minutes later the phone rang. It was Nicolás.

After much crying and laughing and assuring him that I was okay, he told me that I had been placed on his list of approved visitors and that I could come to see him on Thursday.

"Thursday? Why Thursday...why can't I see you tomorrow or Wednesday?" I hadn't seen him since January 19 and wasn't sure that I could stand another two days...especially now that he was only an hour away.

He reminded me that FCI Tallahassee, like the other correctional facilities, did not have regular visiting days on Tuesdays or Wednesdays.

"Oh," I said, remembering the regulations at FCI Otisville, which now seemed a million miles away.

"Just rest, Mami...sleep and take it easy for the next two days. We'll see each other Thursday. I love you, Mami...just rest, okay?"

I hung up the phone and, with an idiotic grin plastered on my face, turned and faced my family which was still in the kitchen trying hard not to eavesdrop. It was easy enough for Stephanie and Jessica—they didn't know any Spanish—but my brother, who had done his doctoral research in South America and was fluent in Spanish, had understood the entire conversation.

"Okay, so tell me, who's this Nicolás?" he began, folding his arms across his chest.

So I told him. Everything.

He didn't approve of the relationship, not only because Nicolás was black and a convicted felon, but also because he was also half my age.

"Like, tell me something I don't know," I said to myself.

He wasn't exactly thrilled either when I told him that, hopefully, Nicolás would be his brother-in-law in the very near future. To no avail I tried to tell him how much Nicolás and I loved each other and how alike we were in so many ways, in spite of all our differences.

I realized that my brother's, and indeed my entire family's, concern and disapproval stemmed from their love for me and from their desire not to see me hurt. But I knew that the only thing that would hurt me was to not see Nicolás and to not marry him and not to be with him for the rest of my life.

There were already some people in line on the steps leading up to the entrance of FCI Tallahassee when I arrived there at 8:15 Thursday morning. I had always marched right past the waiting lines of visitors on my way in to work at FCI Otisville, never realizing that one day I would be one of them. Now that I was, I only prayed that I would be processed without any difficulties and be allowed into the visiting room.

"Is it your first time here?" the woman in front of me asked.

"Yes," I replied. "Is it that obvious?"

I guess it was, because while most of the women were wearing simple skirts and blouses, and even blue jeans and sweat shirts, I was decked out in high heels and a black and white silk dress that I had bought on sale for $165. The "Visiting Regulations" pamphlet that Nicolás had mailed to me stated what kinds of clothing were and weren't permitted and even stipulated that dresses and skirts "will not exceed three inches above the knee in length." My dress reached five inches above my ankles—I wasn't going to take any chances.

"Don't worry...it's nothing," she assured me. "The first time is always the hardest. You'll get used to it."

One by one, the visitors were summoned by an officer into the lobby. It was almost like waiting to be seated at an expensive restaurant.

By the time it was finally my turn, my heart was pounding almost audibly in my chest. With a clammy hand that I hoped wasn't visibly shaking, I filled out and signed the obligatory "Notification to Visitor" form, in which I not only had to list my name, address, phone number and car license number, but also had to declare if I had in my possession, among other things, such items as firearms, explosives, weapons, ammunition, metal-cutting tools, narcotics or alcoholic beverages.

I wondered if anyone ever checked "yes."

"You need to bring a clear purse next time, Ma'am," instructed the officer, as I handed him the small floral makeup case that I had just purchased the day before. It contained my car keys, my driver's license, and about twelve dollars worth of loose change.

"Yes, sir," I replied immediately, "I'm sorry...I didn't know."

"It's okay, Ma'am...just bring it in next time."

"Next time," I repeated to myself. "I haven't even had this time yet."

I took off my watch and set it on the counter and slipped off my shoes. Then I walked back and forth, as directed, under the arch of the metal detector. I didn't expect it to ring, but I knew that some of them were so sensitive that even the under wires of my bra could set it off.

It didn't beep.

"Give me your right hand, please."

I stretched out my arm and the officer turned the palm side down and stamped the top of it with an almost invisible liquid.

"Okay, let's go," beckoned the officer to me and to three other women who had just been processed.

A heavy door was buzzed open and our small group was ushered inside a short narrow passageway. The door noisily clanged shut behind us.

The ink on my hand glowed under the blacklight lamp mounted on the outside of the glass enclosure, where several corrections officers sat, completely surrounded by television screens. After each of the women in my group had passed her hand under the light, the door to the visiting room slowly opened and I walked inside.

Inside the larger of the two rooms, there were about thirty square tables with seats attached, like the tables at McDonald's. A color television mounted on the far wall was above a small carpeted enclosure for children that was surrounded by a short wrought-iron railing. At the opposite side of the room, close to the entrance, was the officers' station, which was set up higher on a platform. The adjoining room contained an assortment of vending machines that dispensed soda, coffee, cigarettes and food, which could be heated in two microwave ovens in the large room. There were two bathrooms, one for men and one for women, each with a sign reading, "VISITORS ONLY."

I sat at one of the tables and tried to stop shaking, at least on the outside. I looked around the room at the other visitors waiting for their husbands or sons or fathers to arrive and peered through the windows at the side of the room to see if I could spot Nicolás. In addition to the one that I had entered from, there were two other doors that led to the prison compound, and I didn't know which one Nicolás would be using.

After five minutes the inmates started arriving at the visiting room. They stopped at the desk to hand over their ID cards to the officer while their wives and children waited patiently and sometimes not so patiently to greet them.

Ten minutes later, when Nicolás still hadn't arrived and practically all the other tables were filled with inmates and their families, a wave of panic washed over me as I told myself that all my worst fears were going to come true.

Then suddenly there he was, opening the door and walking over to the officer's desk. I couldn't speak. I couldn't even move. I felt as though my heart were going to explode inside my chest. We wrapped our arms around each other and kissed and kissed. Again. And again.

We couldn't speak, but we didn't have to because we could feel our bodies trembling with a mixture of love and relief. For the first time since we had met over a year ago, we didn't have to hide our feelings for each other.

Still holding hands, we sat down at one of the tables and talked and talked and laughed and cried and talked some more. We were oblivious to everyone and everything around us. The fact that there were over a hundred people in the same room that could be watching us and listening to what we were saying was completely inconsequential as we gazed into each other's eyes and told each other how much we missed each other and how much we loved each other.

"Visiting hours are over. Visiting hours are over!" announced an officer banging on the desk.

I could hardly believe it. It was 3:15 and I had to leave.

Nicolás stood up and pulled me to my feet. "I'll see you tomorrow, Mami," he said, crushing me to his chest. We hungrily kissed each other goodbye, knowing that these last few minutes of the visit were the only time that we could show the slightest passion. The "Visiting Regulations" expressly stated that, "Embracing and kissing by members of the immediate family is permitted only upon arrival and departure within the limits of acceptable conduct. Any excessive display of affection between visitors and inmates which may tend to embarrass others will not be permitted and may be cause for termination of the visit." In other words, Nicolás could be put into Segregation and I could be prohibited from seeing him. That was the last thing in the world we needed.

Finally he held me at arm's length and took both of my hands in his own.

"I love you, Papi," I said as I kissed him one last time before I tore myself away. "I'll see you tomorrow."

Blinking back my tears, I placed my stamped hand under the blacklight once again and followed the rest of the visitors through the double set of locked doors and back into the lobby.

"You have to sign out, Ma'am," instructed the officer at the desk, pointing to the large green ledger book that I had signed in the morning.

I found the line with my name and signed it.

"Bye... see you tomorrow," I said, turning to leave, as if I had done this every day for the last ten years.

I returned the next day, but I couldn't visit him on Saturday or Sunday. If it had been allowed, I would have visited Nicolás every day, but inmates were only allowed eight visits a month. According to the "Visiting Regulations" pamphlet issued by FCI Tallahassee, I could only visit Nicolás every other weekend, when visits were on an "odd/even basis... determined by the last digit of the inmate's five-digit register number."

I didn't mind. At least we could be together once or twice a week.

At each visit we sat and talked. Sometimes we played cards or dominoes or watched the music videos on MTV. We were just happy being together.

Most of the time we made plans for our future. Nicolás had filled out all the official documents requesting permission from the Bureau of Prisons, the Immigration and Naturalization Service and the warden of FCI Tallahassee for us to get married as soon as possible. As directed by his case manager, I had even mailed a letter to his unit manager stating that I loved and wished to marry Nicolás.

After several weeks, Nicolás still hadn't received a response to his application. Finally, he was told that the INS had given its assent to our marriage and that he just had to wait for the warden's approval.

We waited. And waited. Then one morning in the visiting room, the warden unexpectedly appeared.

"Speak to him... speak to him now before he leaves," Nicolás urged, almost propelling me out of my chair.

As soon as the warden had finished talking to the officer at the desk, I approached and asked him if I could have a few minutes of his time. I explained that Nicolás had filed all the necessary paperwork for us to get married and, although he had gotten approval from Immigration, he still hadn't heard anything from him or the Bureau of Prisons.

The warden replied that he hadn't received the paperwork yet and that he would look into it.

I thanked him and returned to the table, where I translated the warden's response to Nicolás.

"Don't worry, Mami," he said. "We'll find out soon."

"Remember, Papi...don't call me," I said as we kissed goodbye that afternoon. "I'm going down with my brother and his family to visit my cousin Andrea and her husband Howie in Cape Coral for a few days. We'll probably be back April sixth...that's Tuesday night."

I was reluctant to go anywhere at all, knowing that I wouldn't be able to speak to Nicolás. Nobody had informed me about "call-forwarding" or "call-waiting" or about any of the other wonderful services of the telephone company, and I didn't think I could survive almost four whole days without speaking to Nicolás. But Andrea and I had become very close over the past few months. She had been the first one in my family that I had told about Nicolás, and I hadn't seen her since December.

"That's good, Mami. Have a good time and enjoy yourself," Nicolás said as he kissed me goodbye. "I'll call you when you get back."

Four days later, I was not in the house more than five minutes when the telephone rang.

It was Nicolás. He started speaking to me very rapidly in Spanish, instead of in his normally calm voice.

"Wait, Papi...wait," I interrupted. "Habla despacio... speak slowly...please."

He started again...slowly this time.

"Mami, the warden just gave us permission. We can get married next week."

"Next...next week?" I managed to sputter.

The last time I had gotten married, it had taken ten months to prepare for it. Just the consultations with the caterer alone had taken over three months.

"That's wonderful, Papi," I exclaimed, laughing and crying simultaneously.

Without pausing to take a breath, I started rattling off the questions as fast as they popped into my head.

"What do I have to do?"

"Where can I get the license?"

"Can the prison chaplain perform the ceremony?"

"I don't know, Mami," Nicolás replied in a somewhat bewildered voice. He had never been married before and didn't realize that these things were so complicated. "I'll speak to Mr. Gavin, my case manager, in the morning. Then I'll call you and let you know."

When the telephone rang at 10:30 the next morning, I picked it up by the second ring.

"Carol, do you have a pencil and paper?" Nicolás asked.

I knew this was serious because he only called me "Carol" when he wanted me to pay close attention. Although my Spanish was much better than it was a few months ago, I still had trouble understanding all the words... especially over the telephone where I couldn't see his lips making the sounds.

"Okay, Mami, write this down."

By the time he had finished telling me everything that I had to do, I had filled up two sheets of paper. Our wedding was scheduled for the following Tuesday, April 13, and I had six days to do everything.

First I had to find a minister that would be willing to come to the prison to perform the ceremony, then I had to find out where the city of Tallahassee issued the marriage licenses, pay for and get the license, have my signature on it notarized, bring the license to the prison for Nicolás to sign, get his signature notarized, figure out what size ring Nicolás wore, buy two wedding bands, have them engraved and buy a dress.

In six days.

"Okay, honey," I assured him. "I'll try to do as much as I can today... don't worry."

It was Wednesday and I wouldn't be able to see Nicolás until Thursday. I figured that I had about eight hours to get everything done... or at least started.

The first thing that I did was look in the yellow pages of the Tallahassee telephone directory, under "Churches," to find a minister. There were five and a half pages of churches listed in the phone book, encompassing sixty-three different religious affiliations. Should I call them alphabetically or just go "eeny meeny miney mo?" It seemed like an insurmountable task.

After receiving three negative responses from the first churches listed under "A," I turned to the last page, hoping I'd have better luck starting with "Z." The words "Universal Unitarian Church" nearly leapt off the page. I remembered that my Uncle Arthur had been a Unitarian and that its followers had seemed humanitarian and liberal. I called and the minister, Reverend Dr. Jayson Hays, immediately agreed to come to the prison and perform the ceremony.

Securing the license was as complicated as I had anticipated. The only positive aspect was that there was no mandatory blood test, as there had been in New York when I had gotten married the first time thirty years previously. I only had to pay the fee and have my signature notarized. The only problem was that Nicolás also had to have his signature notarized the very same day as I got the license, and he couldn't exactly go down to the Leon County Courthouse.

I didn't know how I could do it, but there had to be a way. Nicolás and I weren't the first couple to ever get married in a prison, and somebody had to know how to get all the documents signed. Suddenly I had a brainstorm. I called FCI Tallahassee and spoke to Nicolás' case manager. Between the two of us, we finally figured out a solution.

Thursday, the next morning, instead of going directly to the prison to visit Nicolás, I first went to get the marriage license and had my signature on it notarized. As I left, the clerk reminded me that I had to have the license with Nicolás' notarized signature on it back in her office by three o'clock that afternoon or the license would not be valid. I assured her that I'd return before three.

Then I went right to the prison, which was less than ten miles away, where Nicolás met me in the visiting room. With him was the secretary from his housing unit, who notarized his signature.

After his signing, Nicolás and I sat and talked about everything else that had to be done before the big day. We had both agreed that we wanted simple gold wedding bands, one-quarter of an inch wide. Nicolás insisted that they be in eighteen-carat gold instead of fourteen-carat, explaining to me that in Colombia all jewelry was made of at least 18K gold. I told him that it would be difficult, and more expensive, to find rings like that, but that I would try. I also explained that buying a ring for me would be an easy matter of trying them on to determine the right size, but getting the correct size for him would be much harder, if not impossible.

"Nothing is impossible, Mami," he told me.

Hearing his words, I had to smile to myself, because he had said the exact words to me almost a year ago when I had told him that we could never have any kind of a relationship because he was in prison...and now look where we were.

Taking the aluminum foil from the container that had covered the food I had just purchased from the vending machine, Nicolás twisted it and coiled it into a ring. After making several adjustments, he slipped it on and off the ring finger of his left hand.

"Here, Mami," he said, handing the piece of foil to me. "This is the size I need. Just take this to the jewelry store and you'll know what size to buy for me."

I looked down at my watch.

"You'd better go now," Nicolás said, seeing me glancing at the time.

"But, Papi, I have to bring the license back by three and it's only one o'clock, and, besides, the office is ten, fifteen minutes away from here at the very most," I protested.

"No, Mami," he insisted, standing up and pulling me to my feet at the same time. "Go now...you want to make sure you get there on time, and, besides, you have a lot of other things to do."

He was right...as usual. And although I would have loved to have stayed there all day, or at least until two-thirty, I reluctantly kissed him goodbye and left.

"You made it!" remarked the clerk, as I walked back into her office at one-thirty, waving the signed and notarized license high in the air like a victory banner.

"Sure," I answered. "No problem."

From there, I headed to the Tallahassee Mall, a mile away, to purchase our rings. I figured it would take about a half-hour, and then I could spend the rest of the afternoon looking for a new dress to wear for the wedding.

"I'm sorry, Ma'am, we don't carry 18K wedding bands. But we can order them from a catalog. You'll probably get them in two or three weeks."

I tried another and then a third jewelry store in the mall and received the same answer.

"Uh oh," I said to myself. "This is going to be harder than I thought."

I returned home and consulted the Yellow Pages again. All the jewelry stores in Tallahassee told me the same thing...no, they did not have 18K gold wedding bands in stock and, yes, they could order them and deliver them in two to three weeks.

I was starting to panic.

Then I remembered that my sister-in-law had recently purchased a pair of earrings from Kres Jewelers, a small, but expensive, shop right in Bainbridge. Thinking that I had nothing to lose, I called and asked if they had any wedding bands in eighteen-carat gold.

"Yes, we do," was their reply.

"In stock...in the store?" I asked incredulously.

"Yes, Ma'am," was the answer.

"I'll be right there."

In ten minutes I was at the jewelry store and ten minutes after that, I had selected and purchased the two rings. I tried mine on to make sure that it fit and used the strip of aluminum foil to get the correct size for Nicolás. Then I handed the clerk the paper on which I had written what we wanted engraved on the inside of the rings. Mine was to say "N.C.Z to C.A.R 4-13-93" and Nicolás' was to say the opposite, "C.A.R. to N.C.Z. 4-13-93." Ken, the owner of the store, assured me that I could pick the rings up on Monday afternoon, the day before the wedding.

Whew!

Although the next day was Saturday and it was our weekend for visitation, I didn't go to see Nicolás because we wanted to separate the eight visits so that there wouldn't be more than four or five days between them. Besides, I wanted to go to the store to look for a wedding dress.

The night before on the phone, after I had related the trials and tribulations of finally getting our rings, I had asked Nicolás what color dress he wanted me to buy for the wedding.

"Blanco," he said.

"White?" I asked, surprised.

"Sí...white," he repeated, half in English and half in Spanish so that I'd understand. "White."

So I bought a white dress...a long cotton dress with pearl buttons, puffed sleeves and an embroidered bodice. As soon as I tried it on, I felt like a bride.

Luckily, Stephanie had to do some shopping also that day, so we had trooped down to the store together with Jessica in tow to pick out the dress and petticoat and even pantihose, "just in case Nicolás and I can get married."

I hadn't told anyone in my family that in four days I was going to become Mrs. Nicolás Córdoba.

My three sons were worried about me because they thought that Nicolás was too young, and nearly everyone else in my family had already voiced their disapproval of both Nicolás and our entire relationship. My brother had even suggested that I see a psychiatrist, or at least a therapist, in order to find out "why I was entering into these self-destructive relationships with men who were dependent on me."

I admitted to him, and even to myself, that my relationship with Nicolás was certainly different and unusual, but no one could or would ever be able to convince me, or Nicolás for that matter, that our love for each other was not normal or that we were both crazy.

Well, maybe we were...but just crazy about each other.

It was Monday, the day before the wedding, and Nicolás and I sat at our usual table near the entrance of the visiting room, each wrapped up in our own thoughts.

"Papi, I have to tell you something today...before we get married...a secret about me...something I've never told you before," I said.

"Oh, my God, what is it?" he whispered, afraid to ask me out loud.

"I can't iron very well...in fact I'm lousy at it," I replied, laughing at the expression of relief on his face.

I had just wanted to break the tension we both felt, not scare him, and I felt guilty seeing how serious he still was.

"Are you nervous?" I asked him.

"No," he lied.

"Me neither."

Hah!

He squeezed my hand and gave me a little smile. He knew exactly how I was feeling.

Half-heartedly, we tried to play cards, but couldn't concentrate. Both he and I knew that we were taking a big step—actually more like a giant leap—and that our lives would be changed as well as joined forever.

We had no doubts, no last-minute reservations about what we were about to do. We just had a lot of uncertainties about the future and about things that we couldn't control. Nicolás' lawyer had expressed confidence that he could win the appeal that was due to be answered in May. And if not, he could always appeal to the Supreme Court. Because of this, we didn't know how much more time Nicolás would have to spend in prison. It could be a few months or a year, or even six and a half more years—we had no idea. We didn't even know if he would be deported after he served his sentence or if he would be permitted to remain in the United States. All we knew was that we loved each other and that we wanted to be together—wherever—for the rest of our lives.

I smiled sleepily to myself as my alarm awakened me at six o'clock the next morning. This was the big day. Quietly, I tiptoed downstairs to get some grapefruit juice, trying not to wake up Ginger, my brother's overly friendly springer spaniel, who would then wake up the entire family. My brother had told me that he was going to go fishing with some of his buddies that morning; I was glad that he was going to be out of the house when I left. I wasn't in the mood to have any confrontations.

After taking a shower, curling my hair and putting on my makeup, I put on my new dress. Then for the tenth time that morning, I made sure that I had tucked safely in my purse both the marriage license and the text of the ceremony, which I had compiled from two different books and written myself in English and in Spanish. I wanted to make sure that we both understood what we were getting into.

Finally, I slipped both wedding bands on: one on the ring finger of my left hand and one on the right. Inmates were permitted to wear a wedding band, but were not allowed to receive presents. I didn't consider Nicolás' ring a present, but I wasn't going to take any chances and have one of the officers tell me that I couldn't bring it into the prison.

On my way out of the house, I walked into the kitchen to put my glass into the dishwasher and spotted my brother standing at the sink.

"Where are you going all dressed up like that?" he asked.

He knew there were no visitations on Tuesdays and Wednesdays.

"You don't want to know," I replied, hurriedly dashing out the door.

Just as I started the car and was about to turn into the driveway, David came running out of the garage, yelling to me that I had a phone call.

"Oh, God, no," I said to myself. "Something's gone wrong...it was too good to be true...something's gone wrong and we can't get married today."

I picked up the phone with a trembling hand. It was Reverend Hays.

"What's the matter? Is something wrong?" I asked nervously.

"No, no," he assured me. He told me that he had just wanted to confirm the time of the wedding and find out, again, exactly how to get to the prison.

I gave him the directions and reminded him that he had to bring his driver's license with him because he couldn't enter the prison without presenting a photo ID.

Breathing a sigh of relief, I slowly walked out of the house. My brother, sitting at the table as I passed through the kitchen, watched me in stony silence.

I arrived at the lobby of FCI Tallahassee at nine o'clock. Mr. Gavin, Nicolás' case manager, was already there, waiting to escort me and the minister inside. I had already mailed a letter to Mr. Gavin with Reverend Hays' name and address so that he could check out his credentials beforehand.

Twenty-five minutes later, a breathless Reverend Hays dashed up the entrance staircase and into the lobby.

"I've heard of the groom having cold feet, but never the minister," quipped Mr. Gavin as the officer at the front desk checked Reverend Hays' identification.

"Is Nicolás nervous?" I asked his case manager as the three of us walked through the double set of doors and into the visiting room.

"Oh, yeah," he answered, raising his eyebrows and grinning.

"Let's have the ceremony outside," he suggested as soon as we got inside.

Taking advantage of the fact that there was no visitation that day, a drug education class was being held in the visiting room and we couldn't use it. I felt the stares of all the inmates and the officers teaching the class as I walked past them in my now very obvious wedding dress.

Although the patio area at FCI Tallahassee is still part of the official visiting area, it's like a different world, with tables and benches both in the large open area and under a metal canopy, and with trees, grass and even a small playground with a sandbox for the children. It is very different from the "patio" areas of most of the other prisons, which usually consist of concrete floors, concrete tables and benches and twelve-foot-high cement block walls topped with hook-like bars, two-feet high.

Reverend Hays directed me to stand opposite him under the canopy, facing the trees, just as Nicolás, wearing sharply creased khaki pants and a white tee shirt, entered the far end of the patio escorted by another corrections officer, who, with Mr. Gavin, would serve as a witness to the ceremony.

Without a word, Nicolás walked over and stood at my right side. We both held copies of the ceremony so that he could follow along in Spanish what Reverend Hays said in English. After his opening remarks and our declaration that we came there to get married by our own free will, it was the moment to exchange vows. Nicolás' hands were damp and trembling as he took mine into his own and said in Spanish, "Yo, Nicolás, te acepto a ti, Carol, como mi esposa, y prometo serte fiel en lo próspero y en lo adverso, en la salud y en la enfermedad, y amarte y respetarte todos los días de mi vida."

Then, looking into his eyes, I took Nicolás' hands into mine and said, in English, "I, Carol, take you, Nicolás, to be my husband. I promise to be true to you in good times and in bad, in sickness and in health. I will love you and honor you all the days of my life."

We exchanged rings, intertwined our trembling hands together, and recited the Lord's Prayer in Spanish.

Then Reverend Hays continued, "Inasmuch as Nicolás and Carol have consented together in marriage, and joining hands and exchanging rings as symbols of that marriage, they are now husband and wife."

"Husband and wife"...next to "I love you," are the three most beautiful words in any language.

We turned and faced each other. Then Nicolás spread open his arms and wrapped me inside while we kissed and kissed and kissed.

We knew that "excessive display of affection" was not permitted, but this was our wedding day, and these few minutes were the only "honeymoon" that we were going to have until Nicolás was released from prison.

After a minute, I wiped the tears off my cheeks and Nicolás and I shook the hands of Reverend Hays and the two witnesses, who had just finished signing the marriage license and were now smiling and congratulating us.

We embraced one more time.

"I love you, Mami," Nicolás said to me, kissing me again.

Mr. Gavin looked at his watch and cleared his throat.

I blinked back my tears. It was time for me to go, and we wouldn't be able to see each other until Thursday.

"I'll call you tonight," he said over his shoulder as one of the officers led him out of the patio area and back to his unit, while the other escorted me back outside to the lobby.

I signed my name in the visitor's log and looked up at the clock so that I could enter the time of my departure. It was nine-fifty. The entire wedding had taken less than twenty minutes.

As soon as he left the visiting room, Nicolás walked over to the commissary. He had about fifty dollars left in his account and with it he bought four six-packs of soda and bags of potato chips and fritos. When he returned to D-South, the barracks-like housing unit that he shared with seventy-nine other inmates, his friends and countrymen, who had known that he was getting married that morning, immediately gathered around him.

They slapped him on the back and shook his hand and congratulated him. Nicolás beamed with happiness.

"What are you so cheerful about?" asked another inmate, who had just been told the news. "A marriage here is only a piece of paper. It isn't like a marriage on the outside...you can't go places together, you can't be together all the time...you even have to wait until you get out of prison to have a honeymoon."

"I don't care," he replied. "I love her and she loves me and even though I'm in prison and she's on the outside, in our minds and hearts we're together. That's where it counts."

One of the inmates started beating on a small drum, another produced a guitar and started playing and singing. They all danced around Nicolás, who in the center of their circle was dancing and clapping his hands to the rhythm of the drum.

"Jingle bells...jingle bells..." he sang, seemingly oblivious to the song they were singing.

"Why are you singing 'Jingle Bells?'" one of the men asked. "It's not Christmas."

Nicolás ignored the man's question and kept on singing. In Colombia, where the festivities lasted more than a month, Christmas had always been the happiest time for him...and he was even happier now.

An officer walked over and asked what all the commotion was about. The men told him. He looked at Nicolás and then at the floor, which was littered with some fritos and an empty potato chip bag.

"Córdoba!"

"Yes."

"You've got ten hours extra duty...clean this mess up!"

"Okay...okay."

"Here, let me do that for you," said one of the men, trying to take the broom out of Nicolás' hands. "It's your wedding day; you shouldn't be sweeping on your wedding day."

"No, it's okay, it doesn't matter," he replied.

Nicolás looked down at the floor and at the broom in his hands. Then he looked out the window. It was spring, and the sky was blue and the sun was shining and it was warm.

"Everything is going to turn out fine," he told himself. "For so many years I dreamed of coming to the United States and starting a new life...a life that I thought was over when I was arrested. Now I'm married to the woman of my dreams... a woman who loves me as much as I love her...a woman who will wait for me until I get out of prison. And that's all we have to do...wait."

He started sweeping. The sun's rays, filtered through the slats in the windows, splashed stripes through the dust and onto the walls and floor. He turned around and felt the warm sunshine on his face and smiled.

The bright sun glared off my car's windshield as I walked through the nearly empty parking lot. Here I was, on my wedding day, all dressed up and all alone. I looked back at the prison, hoping that I'd see a glimpse of Nicolás through the fence as I had after some of my visits. Seeing the deserted patio area, I forced myself not to cry. Then I got into my car and drove to the courthouse to file the license. The clerk had told me that either I or the minister could mail it in, but I was not about to take any chances, not with something this precious. I delivered it by hand and waited for it to be filed and stamped with the official gold seal of the State of Florida.

"Now we're officially married," I sighed to myself, relieved that everything had gone relatively smoothly. It had been an emotional and hectic week, and I felt physically as well as emotionally drained. Although I was bursting with happiness, there was no one that I could share it with, no one to tell my good news, no one that would congratulate me and tell me how happy they were for me.

This was the happiest day of my life and I was all alone. No one except Nicolás and Reverend Hays and the two witnesses, strangers to me less than a week ago, even knew that Nicolás and I had just gotten married.

There was nothing left for me to do but go home, but I didn't want to go back home. I wanted to stay in Tallahassee because my husband, my brand-new husband of one hour, was in Tallahassee, and even though I couldn't visit him or even see him, I couldn't bear to drive sixty miles away from him.

"We should be kissing and embracing and dancing and drinking champagne now," I told myself bitterly.

I knew that it was going to be different being married to a man who was in prison. I knew that it was going to be difficult, too. But I didn't realize how desolate I would feel. I was riding an emotional roller coaster. I was either at the height of happiness or in the depths of despair. There were no plateaus...no times in between to relax...no times to just live a life that I had once thought of as normal.

Nicolás says I'm a *bruja*. That's the Spanish word for witch. I know it sounds like an insult, but coming from him, as superstitious as he is, it's a compliment.

I think he's right. I told him that as soon as I'd find a job in Tallahassee, he'd be transferred from FCI Tallahassee to a different institution. And that's exactly what happened. I hadn't been employed since I left New York. Living off my savings and my brother's hospitality was keeping me fed, taking care of my bills and providing a roof over my head. Free from the worry and pressure of a job, I was able to write all day and visit Nicolás Mondays and Fridays and sometimes on the weekends, too. I thought this pleasant arrangement would last until Nicolás got out of prison, which would probably be in a few months...after he had won his appeal.

Then one day, my brother told me that it would be a good idea if I moved to Tallahassee, found a job and got my own apartment. I'm sure it seemed like a good idea to him, but it seemed like a lousy one to me. However, I had to admit even to myself that my savings were rapidly dwindling, mostly due to the car payments I was making on my Mustang convertible.

Although I still hadn't received the Georgia and Florida teaching certificates that I had applied for as soon as I left New York, I knew that they would come soon, so I looked for a teaching job, even though I knew that I'd never be able to match the $32,000 that I had been making.

Finally, I was hired as a teacher's aide at five dollars an hour at a summer program for the children of migrant workers. It was only for six weeks and I didn't get a chance to teach, but at least I was working in a school again.

Because I was working Monday through Friday, I could only visit Nicolás every other weekend, when it was our turn. I hadn't realized how fortunate I had been to see him during the week. On the weekends, because no visitors were allowed on the grounds of the prison before eight o'clock in the morning, I had to wait in line across the street. After the first day, when my car was the twelfth in line even though I had arrived at seven-thirty in the morning, I started getting there at six-thirty in order to be near the front of the line.

Sometimes even that didn't help, because visitors that came with families dropped someone off at the entrance to hold their place in line before they parked the car, while I, who was alone, had to first park and then get in line.

It was bad enough seeing children running to the entrance, but it was more pathetic to see wives, girlfriends and even elderly mothers and grandmothers running through the parking lot in order to get to the front of the line. Everybody knew that if they didn't get processed and into the visiting room by nine-thirty, they wouldn't be able to get in until eleven because of the ten-o'clock "count" when all activity in the prison came to a halt while the inmates were counted.

Being fourteenth or fifteenth in line could make a difference in seeing someone for six hours or four hours. And if those few hours were all that you saw each other all week—or in some cases all month—it made a big difference. Fortunately I lived only an hour from the prison. But some families lived ten or fifteen hours away and travelled all night and slept in their cars in the parking lot because they couldn't afford to stay in a motel.

I was lucky, and I didn't even realize how lucky I was until one day when I went to visit Nicolás...and he wasn't there.

I didn't panic. I didn't even cry.

It was 10:30 on July 16, a Friday morning, and I had just completed my third interview at Keiser College, in Tallahassee, for the position of Admissions Officer. Although they had told me that they'd reach a decision and call me that afternoon, I knew that I had gotten the job. The prison was only five minutes away, so instead of going home to wait for the phone call, I decided to surprise Nicolás and visit him.

Because it was mid-morning and a weekday, there was no line outside and I walked right into the lobby. Everything went smoothly until the officer at the entrance desk called Nicolás' housing unit in order to tell his unit manager to send Nicolás to the visiting room.

"Would you have a seat, please," the officer at the desk said to me, indicating the group of chairs in the lobby.

"Is anything wrong?" I asked anxiously. My heart started hammering in my chest as I repeated over and over again to myself, "Please let him be okay, please let him be okay."

"No, nothing's wrong, Ma'am, just take a seat," he assured me.

I strained to hear his end of the conversation as he made several phone calls. Finally he said, "Okay, you can go in now."

"Thank God," I said to myself, and looking calmer than I felt, I breathed a sigh of relief and walked into the visiting room. I bought a Diet Coke for myself and orange juice for Nicolás and sat down at "our" table to wait.

Five minutes, then ten minutes passed, still no sign of Nicolás. I reasoned to myself that he was taking longer than usual because he hadn't known I was going to visit him that morning. All the other times he had known in advance and had been showered, shaved and dressed an hour before visiting hours started.

When twenty minutes had elapsed and he still hadn't arrived, I asked one of the officers at the visiting-room desk if he could have Nicolás paged. Maybe he was outside in the rec yard. He told me he'd see what he could do.

I started to worry again. I just had a feeling that something was wrong. As soon as the officer walked over to the table where I was gripping my soda with both hands to keep them from shaking, I knew that my worst nightmare had come true.

"Mrs. Córdoba, you have to leave the visiting room," he said to me in a quiet voice.

"Why...why...what's wrong?" I managed to ask.

"The lieutenant will speak to you outside, Ma'am. Would you please leave now."

Oblivious to the curious stares of the other couples in the visiting room, I forced myself to remain calm and walked out of the room. Standing at the desk in the lobby was a very tall, thin officer who told me that Nicolás had been transferred to another institution. In fact, he had just been transferred that very morning, probably at the same time that I was walking into the visiting room.

"Where...where is he? Where is he being transferred to?" I asked. "Can you tell me where he's going so I can visit him?"

I knew, both from my experience of working at FCI Otisville and from the stories of other wives, that inmates and their families were never told the destination when an inmate was transferred.

"Can you just tell me what state he's being sent to so I can make arrangements to see him this weekend?" I pleaded.

"He's being transferred to Jesup," he said, relenting.

"Jesup?" I asked. "Where's Jesup?"

I wasn't going to stop until I found out exactly where they had sent my husband.

"That's in Georgia, Ma'am," he said.

"Georgia," I repeated aloud. "Thank God."

Nicolás could have been transferred anywhere in the country, but he was being sent to Georgia, and although it was a large state and I lived at the most southern part of it, at least I'd be able to drive there to visit him.

My brother's office was five minutes away from the prison. I rushed over to find out if he had a map. I had no idea where Jesup was, but tomorrow was Saturday and I was going to drive there, no matter how far it was, to see Nicolás. We looked at the map and I was thrilled to see that Jesup was only four and a half hours away, about two hours south of Savannah, Georgia.

"Take it easy," I told myself on the way home, as I made a mental list of everything that I had to do before I left the next morning.

The telephone was ringing as I opened the door. It was the Director of Keiser College, with whom I had had the interview that morning, telling me that I had just been hired and that they wanted me to start immediately.

Nicolás was right when he called me a witch.

As soon as I hung up, I called Information and got the telephone number of FCI Jesup, which I immediately called to find out if Nicolás was there. The officer who answered the phone checked and told me that Nicolás hadn't arrived yet. In spite of what he had just told me, I dashed upstairs to my room, pulled my suitcase out of the closet and started packing. In order to get to the prison by seven-thirty, I figured that I'd have to leave no later than two o'clock in the morning—especially since it was the first time and I wasn't sure exactly where it was.

I could hardly believe how calm I was. For the past ten months, my biggest fear was that Nicolás would be sent to another prison and I'd never be able to find him again. But now that he had actually been transferred, I was serenely packing a suitcase and calling motels in Jesup to find out if they had any vacancies for Saturday night.

Perhaps if the lieutenant hadn't informed me of Nicolás' destination, I would have been panic-stricken by now, but he had, and so I wasn't. Maybe I was so tranquil because we were married now, not that it was any guarantee that I'd be informed every time he was transferred. In fact, a wife couldn't call the Bureau of Prisons and demand to know where her husband had been sent. He, himself, had to call her to give her

that information...and some men chose not to...for various
reasons.

I had a feeling that Nicolás was more upset than I. He
knew that I was expecting to visit him the next day, and now
he had no way to tell me not to come. We had talked about the
possibility of this happening and he had always assured me
that he would try to call me as soon as possible from wherever
he was.

"Oh, Papi," I sighed to myself, "you must be going crazy
worrying about me."

It was getting dark outside as I put my suitcase into the
trunk of my car, then went upstairs and took a shower. My
alarm clock was set to wake me at one A.M. and I wanted to go
to sleep early. I picked up Nicolás' latest letter, one he had
written a few weeks ago, and started to reread it...for perhaps the twentieth time. Although I wrote to him at least one
letter every day, his letters were few and far between and all
the more precious because I knew how long and hard he
labored over them.

I still had a silly grin on my face when the phone rang
and startled me out of my reverie.

"You have a collect call from Nicolás Córdoba," the operator announced. "Will you accept the charges?"

"Yes!" I agreed before she had even finished the sentence.

"Hi, Mami, how are you?" Nicolás asked casually.

"Papi, where *are* you?" I replied, ignoring his question.

"In Tallahassee," he answered, starting to laugh.

"Oh no you're not," I told him. "I went there this morning
to surprise you and you surprised me instead. Where are you?
I want to visit you tomorrow."

"No, Mami, don't come. I'm in Atlanta. Don't come to see
me here."

"But, Papi, it's not that far. I can stay at a motel and see
you Saturday and Sunday," I argued.

"No, Mami, don't visit me until I get to Jesup. It's really
bad here, and I don't want you to come...just rest and relax
and wait until I get to Jesup to visit me. Okay? I'll be there in
about a week."

"Okay," I reluctantly agreed. I had heard stories from
wives of other inmates who had visited their husbands in
Atlanta, and I realized that Nicolás wanted to spare me the
aggravation that they had gone through.

"Okay, I guess I'll have to take my suitcase out of the car," I sighed.

"You're crazy, Mami," he said, laughing.

"Yeah," I answered, "crazy for you."

That's what we always told each other when one of us had gone overboard in demonstrating our feelings.

We said it a lot.

"Don't worry, Mami," he said just before he hung up, "I'm fine. Go to sleep. I'll call you tomorrow."

I hung up the phone, turned off the light and tried to go to sleep. Even though I was disappointed that I couldn't visit Nicolás the next day, I was thankful that he was all right and that I'd be able to see him soon.

The phone rang at ten o'clock. It was Nicolás. He called again at ten-thirty. "I love you, Mami," he told me. "Go to sleep, okay?"

"I've been trying to," I replied, laughing.

At six-thirty the next morning he woke me up, telling me how much he loved me. I asked him again if I could visit him, but he insisted that I wait.

So I waited.

I started working that Tuesday as an Admissions Officer at Keiser College, making half the salary I had made in New York and working twice the hours. But at least I was working. Not only did I need to save money and pay my bills, but now I would also need money for motels and meals when I visited Nicolás...whenever that would be.

Finally, right after work on August 6, I headed for Jesup. Nicolás had called me as soon as he had arrived, three days before, but because my job was new, I couldn't take any time off. Besides, they didn't "believe" in personal days, or in sick days either, for that matter.

My suitcase, containing among other things five outfits with their matching shoes, an iron and a can of spray starch, was already in the trunk of my car. I placed the map of Georgia, the route highlighted with a fluorescent pink marker, on the empty passenger seat beside me. I took a deep breath, turned up the volume on the radio and was on my way. After driving myself down from New York, a trip of merely one hundred and ninety miles seemed like a short excursion.

Five and a half hours later, after I had crisscrossed the same highway three times and was still unable to locate the motel that I had called the night before, I headed towards the main road that ran through Jesup in search of a place to sleep. Luckily I found a relatively inexpensive room that was vacant for the next two nights at the Pride Inn on Highway 301 South, four miles away from the prison.

There were at least fifteen cars, vans and pickup trucks lined up on the side of the highway when I arrived at the prison at seven o'clock in the morning. I sleepily got out of my car and asked the woman in the first car what time people usually arrived to get in line.

"Four-thirty or five o'clock in the morning," she replied.

"I guess I'm going to have to wake up earlier," I told myself. I used to pride myself for being the first visitor to arrive and the last one to leave when Nicolás was at FCI Tallahassee. Maybe I was trying to show him and the rest of the world how much I loved him. Even though Nicolás told me that it was crazy to be rushing to see him when he wasn't exactly about to be going anywhere, I had heard him bragging about it to other inmates and their families.

It was after nine by the time I got into the lobby. The processing of visitors was even more stringent than at FCI Tallahassee. Not only was my picture taken and laminated onto an ID card, but even the fingerprints of my right hand were recorded on the same card, which was used at every visit. I was thankful that I didn't have to race to be at the front of the line, because an officer, who stood at the entrance of the parking lot, had handed each visitor a consecutively numbered visitor's form and it was strictly first come, first serve.

Twenty minutes after my name was called I was finally escorted into the visiting room, where I sat down to wait. Nicolás and I hadn't seen each other since the Fourth of July weekend, and all I wanted to do was rush into his arms and kiss him for an hour. But all I was able to do was give him one brief kiss and say hello when he walked in.

FCI Jesup was a much newer facility than FCI Tallahassee, and the visiting room reflected this. Instead of chairs grouped around tables, there were rows of identical seats arranged against the walls and interior waist-high partitions.

Gone were the trees, flowers and playground of the outside patio area that were at the prison in Tallahassee. They were replaced by concrete walls, concrete tables and benches which glared brightly in the August sun.

In addition to the cameras hidden behind domes of smoked gray glass inside the visiting room and the large convex mirrors mounted at strategic locations both inside the room and outside in the patio area, there were cameras mounted high on posts outside in the patio area, which moved from side to side and up and down as they tracked the movements and actions of the inmates. It was almost like a scene from a science-fiction movie about a futuristic totalitarian society...but it was real.

Most of the inmates, including Nicolás, thought of the visits as psychological torture. For six hours the inmate and his visitor lived under the constant scrutiny and observation of not only the corrections officers in the room and those observing the TV monitors in the "Control" room, but also the other inmates and their families who surrounded them. With people sitting only a few feet away, there was no such thing as a private conversation. Because each inmate was strip-searched both before and after each visit, many inmates refused to let their families visit them rather than subject themselves to this humiliating procedure.

Despite the efforts of many organizations involved in prison reform, there were no conjugal visits. There was never even a minute of privacy for a husband and wife. These organizations had lobbied Congress and urged that inmates in federal prisons be able to earn the right to receive conjugal visits, just like the inmates in state prisons who had committed more violent crimes. The Bureau of Prisons, nevertheless, remained adamantly opposed.

Because of this, each visit was filled with physical as well as psychological anguish. Not only could an inmate and his wife or girlfriend not demonstrate the slightest amount of affection towards each other, every word, every action, every embrace, every kiss was observed and noted.

Once, in our newly-wed exuberance, we had exchanged the briefest of kisses, not at the arrival or departure times that were designated for kissing, and Nicolás received a "shot," a written memo that stated his infraction of the rules, warning him that we would lose our visitation privileges if we were to kiss again when it was not permitted.

I saw Nicolás Saturdays and Sundays for the next three months. I visited him every weekend, driving to Jesup on Friday afternoon right after work and returning home Sunday night. I told Nicolás that I understood how he felt about the visitations, but reminded him that seeing each other under these circumstances was better than not seeing each other at all. He reluctantly agreed.

I knew that he suffered as much as I did when I had to leave at the end of each visit. He usually had to forcibly stop kissing me as an officer stood right behind us, told us to "break it up" and ordered Nicolás to stand against the wall with the other inmates.

"I'll see you next week, Papi," I told him, as I tore myself away from his embrace. We held each other's gaze as long as possible as I and the other visitors were herded towards the exit at the opposite end of the room. I smiled at a little girl dressed up like a princess and her brother who was dressed as a tiger. It was October 31, Halloween, and they had worn their costumes to the prison to show them to their father. As I walked towards the exit door, I caught Nicolás' eye once more and we waved goodbye.

As an Admissions Officer at Keiser College, I had to work until eight o'clock on Thursday nights. I would spend nearly six hours of every day on the phone, trying to set up appointments for prospective students to see the college, but personal phone calls were frowned upon and were supposed to be only for emergencies.

As soon as I heard Nicolás' voice on the phone, I had the feeling that something was wrong. In a voice quavering with emotion, he told me that he had been taken in handcuffs from his housing unit that morning into Segregation, where he had been questioned for several hours by one of the lieutenants and an officer from the internal security division of the Bureau of Prisons. Through an interpreter, they had asked him about me, about where we had met and about our relationship both while he was incarcerated at FCI Otisville and at FCI Tallahassee.

"Mami, you might lose your visitation privileges," he said quietly.

"What? Why, Papi?" I demanded to know, starting to cry in spite of the fact that I was at work sitting in my office where everyone could see and hear me. "What happened? Why are they asking now? I've been visiting you for nine months. Why did they all of a sudden decide to investigate our relationship now? I answered every question truthfully on the Visitation Application form. The Bureau of Prisons and the INS and the warden at FCI Tallahassee even gave us permission to get married at the prison. What happened?"

"I think that your old boyfriend," Nicolás explained, "you know, Mackie...the one that you told me you trusted with your piano...the one who sold your piano and everything else you had and kept the money for himself... Well, I think he found out somehow that we were married and he called the prison at Otisville. I think that's what started this whole investigation."

"But, Papi, we did nothing wrong," I reminded him. "I don't work at the prison anymore...and even when I taught at FCI Otisville, I was working for the State of New York, not for the Bureau of Prisons."

"I know, Mami," he told me. "We'll have to see what happens. You're still coming to see me on Saturday, aren't you?"

"Of course," I assured him, wiping away my tears.

"I'll call you tonight after you get home, okay?"

"Okay," I agreed, taking a deep breath as I tried to pull myself together.

I just wanted it to be eight o'clock so that I could get out of there and go home. My apartment, which I had moved to a month ago, was less than a mile away and all I wanted to do was fling myself down on my bed and wait for Nicolás to call.

"Just prepare yourself, in case you can't visit me on Saturday," Nicolás advised me when he called an hour later. "Don't worry...we'll just have to see what happens."

"Didn't they tell you anything?" I asked him.

"No...nothing," he replied.

Two days later, at four-thirty in the morning, mine was the first car waiting in line outside FCI Jesup. I tilted the seat back and tried to take a nap, but in spite of the fact that I had slept less than an hour that night, I couldn't fall asleep.

At eight-fifteen I took my seat inside the lobby with the other visitors and waited for my name to be called so that I could be processed and escorted into the visiting room to see Nicolás. Then, and only then, would I know that everything was all right.

"Carol Córdoba," the officer at the entrance desk announced.

"Oh, thank God," I said to myself, almost crying with relief.

"May I speak to you for a minute...outside?" asked another officer, coming from around the desk and intercepting me before I reached it.

As soon as we passed through the outer doors, he took me to the side of the entrance and said quietly, "I'm sorry, your visiting privileges have been terminated."

"Terminated," I repeated, stunned.

I couldn't believe it. Even though Nicolás had told me to prepare myself for this possibility...even though I had been telling myself for the last three days that this might happen, I still couldn't believe it actually had come to pass.

"Can't I talk to someone? Can't I speak to the warden... or to the captain or a lieutenant?" I asked him. "I live five hours away and I'm here right now. Isn't there anybody I can speak to?"

I was trying to remain calm. I didn't cry.

"No one wants to speak to you now," he told me, then added in a kinder voice, "I hope everything works out. You're really nice...I wish everyone was like you."

After thanking him for the compliment and telling him that I wished all the officers were as nice as he was, I got into my car.

And cried all the way home.

Strength and courage. That's all you can pray for. All the way home, in between crying and picturing Nicolás waiting in vain for me to arrive, I prayed for strength to do everything in my power to see him again and for courage to face the future alone if I failed.

I didn't know how I was going to survive if I couldn't visit him. We knew that he wasn't going to be released from prison any time soon because he had lost his first appeal in May and the Supreme Court had refused to even hear his second appeal.

I could hardly breathe. It felt like my heart had been torn out of my chest. The possibility of not being able to see him was bad enough, but now that it was a reality, it was too painful to bear. If it wasn't for the fact that Nicolás would be utterly devastated by my death, I would have driven headlong into the nearest and biggest tree. I realized that he needed me just as much I needed him, and I couldn't do it.

As soon as I got back to my apartment, Nicolás called. Realizing the state I must have been in, he had been trying to reach me every few minutes for the past half-hour. When I picked up the phone, I was crying so hysterically I couldn't even speak.

"Mami, don't cry...please, Mami, don't cry," he kept repeating over and over again until I finally calmed down enough to listen to him.

"Ten paciencia, Mami...have patience," he continued. "We'll be okay. Go to church...read the Bible. I promise I'll write to you every day...and I'll send pictures every week. We'll be okay...I promise."

"But, Papi..." I said, starting to cry all over again, "I want to see you, I want to be with you...I want to feel your arms around me...I want to feel your lips on mine. I can't survive if I can't visit you."

"Don't think about the visits anymore...don't remember them and don't talk to me about them...ever," he answered, more sternly this time.

"There are women that have it much worse than you, Mami," he reminded me. "There are women that live in other countries, far away from the United States, women that are too poor to visit...women who haven't seen their husbands for five, ten, fifteen years or more. You'll be okay...we'll write to each other and speak to each other every day...don't worry."

"I know, Papi," I conceded, "but I'm not them...I'm me. I can't help how I feel."

"Just promise me you won't cry, okay?" he said.

"Okay," I agreed. Then I hung up the phone and burst into tears.

I realized that the only way that he could cope with not being able to see me was by not thinking about it. Indeed, this was the way he survived being in prison all these years: by not thinking about the past or dwelling on what might have been. But I wasn't like him. I couldn't just turn off my thoughts and let this happen to us. I couldn't and wouldn't rest until I had exhausted every possible means to get my visitation rights reinstated. The only problem was I had no idea where to start.

In between crying and speaking to Nicolás on the phone, I spent the entire weekend writing a three-page letter to the warden of FCI Jesup. In the letter, I explained how Nicolás and I had met and developed our relationship. I told him that I had truthfully answered all the questions in my application to visit Nicolás and that we had even received permission to get married at FCI Tallahassee. In closing, I asked him to allow me to speak to him in person as soon as possible or to at least call me to tell me why he had terminated my visitation privileges.

Before going to work that Monday morning, I made a copy of the letter at the post office and mailed the original to the warden. I didn't know what else I could do except to open the lines of communication with the Bureau of Prisons so that they would understand and see my point of view.

By the time I got to Keiser College at nine, I was a physical and mental wreck. If I had slept or eaten anything during the last forty-eight hours, I didn't remember doing so. Luckily, most of my work was conducted by telephone, so nobody saw what I looked like...except María, the Admissions Director, who told me I "looked like hell." I didn't go into details when she asked what was wrong. I just told her that I was having "some personal problems." Although I tried, I couldn't be the "bubbly, bouncy, cheerful" Admissions Officer over the telephone that she wanted me to be. I wasn't that good an actress.

I hadn't said anything to my family. They didn't approve of my relationship with Nicolás in the first place, and in the second place I didn't want their sympathy or to hear their I-told-you-sos. My brother, who slept at my apartment whenever he was "on call" and had to be near the hospital, came on Sunday night, took one look at me, and wrote a prescription for an antidepressant, a strong one. Numbly, I walked around like a zombie, went to work and even slept at night. I didn't even cry all the time.

By Tuesday, it was obvious even to me that I couldn't function as an Admissions Officer. I could hardly function at all. María told me that she was going to have to let me go if I didn't get my act together soon. She thought I was going through a nasty divorce; I didn't care to tell her what was actually happening. Then she told me that Mr. Keiser, *the* Mr. Keiser of Keiser College, was visiting the Tallahassee campus and that he wanted to talk to me.

I walked into the Executive Director's room, figuring that I was about to get the official ax, but instead I found myself blubbering and telling a very kind and sympathetic Mr. Keiser the entire story of me and Nicolás: how we had met and gotten married and about my recent loss of visitation privileges.

"Look, take a leave of absence," he suggested. "Two weeks without pay, and do everything you can to get this situation resolved. You said you sent a letter to the warden yesterday? Use our fax machine; make sure he gets it today. Use our copier if you want to, anything you need, just ask."

I thanked him profusely. I couldn't believe he was being so nice to me and so helpful.

Just as I was about to leave, he asked, "Have you spoken to Pete Peterson...the Congressman from our district?"

I had seen a photograph in the hallway of Pete Peterson and Mr. Keiser shaking hands in front of the college, so I knew who he was referring to.

"No, I haven't," I admitted.

"Well, he has an office right here in Tallahassee. Why don't you go down there, give them a copy of the letter you mailed to the warden and see if they can help you?"

At last, I had somebody that might be able to help...and if he couldn't help, maybe there were other Congressmen or Senators or Governors... My mind started to whirl. I finally had a plan of action.

"That's what I'll do," I told myself, shaking my head to clear it from its antidepressant-induced stupor. "I'll go to the library and look up all the names and addresses of Congressmen, Senators, Governors, members of Senate and Congressional judicial committees... I'll even write to Kathleen Hawk,

who is the new Director of the Bureau of Prisons...and I'll
write to Janet Reno, the Attorney General of the United
States. I'll write to President Clinton if I have to. Somewhere
there has to be somebody who will listen to me...somebody
who will realize how cruel it is to prevent me from seeing my
husband for the next six years. Somewhere there is someone
who will help me...someone who will reinstate my visitation
privileges."

And that's exactly what I did.

Keiser College fired me on December 17th. I didn't blame
them.

It was a week before Christmas and I was out of work. I
hadn't seen Nicolás for a month, but now I would have time to
write letters, time to make phone calls, time to plan what to
do next.

Nicolás called every day. We laughed and joked and told
each other about our dreams and endlessly declared how
much we loved each other.

Encouraged by my efforts to try to get my visitation privileges reinstated, he started filing formal complaints to the
prison officials. After weeks of telling me that there was nothing we could do and that I should stop trying to fight the currents, he finally agreed to try to fight the decision. Known
officially as an "Administrative Remedy Appeal," which was
the only way he or any inmate could have an issue brought
before the Bureau of Prisons, each form was typewritten in
English by fellow inmates who were trying to help him. After
thirty days, when he received an unfavorable reply, he filed
another complaint and then another, each one which was
heard by a higher and higher level of the Bureau of Prisons'
administration.

Spurred by Nicolás' efforts, I redoubled mine. I devoted
every day and every evening to writing letters and making
phone calls. Although the staff of Congressman Peterson had
contacted the Bureau of Prisons, instead of waiting until they
received a reply, I decided to write to the Bureau myself. I
wrote to the Southeast Regional Office in Atlanta and to
Kathleen Hawk, the Director of the Bureau of Prisons in

Washington, D.C. I even sent a letter to Janet Reno, the
Attorney General of the United States.

I wrote letters to all the members of the Senate and the
House Judiciary Committees and to some of the Congressmen
and all the Senators of New York, Georgia, and Florida, the
three states I had lived in. Every letter I sent included copies
of the letter that I had originally written to the warden and
copies of correspondence I had sent and received from the
Bureau of Prisons. I was spending a small fortune on postage
and copies and an even larger one on telephone calls. I didn't
care.

Any and every organization that was related to the judicial system or prison reform received a phone call or a letter.
From the American Civil Liberties Union to Families against
Mandatory Minimums to Citizens United for Rehabilitation of
Errants, every organization either told me that they would try
to help me or suggested other organizations and individuals
who might be able to persuade the Bureau of Prisons to reconsider its position and let me visit Nicolás again.

Every letter that I, the Senators, the Congressmen or the
various organizations received from the Bureau of Prisons
reiterated the same message: I could not see Nicolás until he
was released from prison in November, 1999. Anyone else
could visit him, just not me. This meant that there was
nobody who visited him.

We sent each other photographs of ourselves for Christmas presents, and Nicolás called Christmas morning and serenaded me in Spanish. At 11:30 on New Year's Eve I uncorked
and drank half a bottle of champagne while we talked and
laughed over the telephone.

"Happy New Year, Mami," Nicolás said in English as he
awakened me on New Year's Day. "I love you."

"Happy New Year, honey," I answered.

He was right: we were surviving; we were doing okay in
spite of everything. No one could tell by looking at us what we
were going through. Nicolás had promised that he would start
eating if I would stop crying, so outwardly we appeared fine.
And if he had trouble eating sometimes, and if I cried myself
to sleep a few times a week, we didn't mention it to each
other. We supported each other emotionally and spiritually.
Whenever I weakened and started to feel depressed, he made
me strong and made me laugh. And whenever I heard discour-

agement in his voice, I cheered him up and told him how much I and his family needed him.

By the middle of January, Nicolás was getting more and more discouraged. All of his appeals had been denied. I tried to convince him that although we still couldn't see each other, we were making progress. I read him the copy of the letter that the executive director of the ACLU Prison Project had mailed to the chief counsel of the Bureau of Prisons. The letter described our separation as "unjust and bizarre."

A week later, I received a letter from the Bureau of Prisons informing me that I could apply again for visitation after a year. I wasn't foolish enough to assume that it would automatically be granted, but at least I could tell myself that I'd only have to wait one year instead of six years until Nicolás and I could be together again.

There was nothing to do now but wait and see if any of the people and organizations I had contacted would be able to help us. I had finally started teaching again: at Havana Middle School in a small town just north of Tallahassee. Although I missed Nicolás more than ever, my days were busy and my mind was occupied with something other than visiting him.

Every afternoon when I got home from work, I checked my mailbox to see if I had received any answers to the countless letters I had sent out over the last three and a half months. Usually there was at least one or two letters from Congressmen or Senators telling me that they were still awaiting word from the Bureau of Prisons. As soon as I entered my bedroom, I played back the messages on my answering machine, hoping for some good news.

On January 24, exactly three years to the day that he was arrested, Nicolás called and told me that he was about to be transferred again. When I started crying he reminded me that it really wouldn't make any difference in our situation because we only communicated through letters and the telephone anyway. I agreed that he had a point, but I still wanted to know that he was relatively close.

A few days later, he called and told me that the Bureau of Prisons had changed its mind and had informed him that he would not be transferred. I breathed a sigh of relief. Although our situation was awful, I was used to it and didn't want to change the status quo...unless it was to visit him again.

Less than a week passed when Nicolás called at his usual time in the evening, laughing as he said hello. When I asked him what was so funny, he replied that he was calling from FBI Marianna, where he had just been transferred that afternoon. I was elated. Marianna was just a little over an hour away from Tallahassee, and if I received permission to visit him after a year had passed, he would be closer.

At least we were both in the state of Florida.

The red light on my answering machine was flashing as I walked into my room on Friday, February 18. I automatically hit the replay button as I started taking off my coat and shoes. Suddenly I heard the now familiar voice of Pauline Sullivan, a co-founder of CURE (Citizens United for Rehabilitation of Errants), one of the organizations I had contacted four months earlier.

"This message is for Carol Córdoba," she started. "This is Pauline Sullivan from CURE. I've been talking to the Justice Department and I just got a call back today, and they said that your visits with your husband have been reinstated."

"Oh, my God...thank you, thank you," I started sobbing aloud as I immediately called her back to confirm the message. It was true, she assured me after I stopped crying enough to thank her. She informed me that I'd probably be getting a letter from the Bureau of Prisons any day.

Not only did I get a letter directly from the Bureau of Prisons, but over the next few days, almost each and every Congressman and Senator that I had contacted over the last four months sent copies of the letters that they had also received from the Bureau, along with letters telling me how glad they were that they had been able to help. Their case-workers and secretaries and assistants also left messages on my answering machine in order to tell me the good news before the letters arrived.

I didn't know which individual or organization was the one that finally convinced the Bureau of Prisons to place me back on Nicolás' approved visitors' list. In my mind it was the accumulated efforts of all of them: strangers who didn't even know us but had helped bring us together.

Nicolás took it matter-of-factly when he called and I told him the good news. Maybe he was afraid to get too excited, thinking that the Bureau might change its mind again or transfer him to the opposite end of the country before I could see him. Maybe it was because he had been so pessimistic in the beginning that it was hard for him to believe that we had actually done it.

After my several frantic phone calls to FCI Marianna, trying to find out if I could visit Nicolás the next day, his unit counselor telephoned me and said I could visit the following weekend.

I tried unsuccessfully to reason to myself that after waiting almost four whole months, another week wasn't going to kill me.

The following Saturday, I entered the visiting room at FCI Marianna and sat down to wait for Nicolás to enter.

For the past few months, I had envisioned a scene somewhat like the one in "Gone With the Wind," when Rhett Butler sweeps Scarlett O'Hara into his arms and carries her up the broad spiral staircase and into their bedroom. While I realized that the visiting room didn't have any spiral staircases, I had imagined our long-awaited reunion so often in my mind that I expected it to be at least as romantic as what took place on the screen.

Finally, there he was.

"Hi, Mami," he said, kissing me as if he had just seen me the day before.

"So much for romantic reunions," I said to myself.

I could hardly believe it. At last we were together again. I had survived.

It was Presidents' weekend and there was no school that Monday, so I visited Nicolás for three days in a row. The weather was mild and sunny, and we were able to sit outside on a concrete bench with our arms wrapped around each other. Wordlessly, we gazed into each others' eyes and stole more than a kiss or two, trying to make up for all the days and weeks and months we had been apart. We both realized that we had been changed by the separation, but instead of becoming estranged by it, we had grown even closer and become even more in love with each other than ever.

I had my own apartment, I was teaching again and visiting Nicolás every Saturday and Sunday. We were finally living, if not a normal life, at least a life that was as normal as possible, considering the circumstances. Foolishly, I thought that this idyllic situation would last until Nicolás was released from prison.

Exactly one month after I was placed back on Nicolás' approved visiting list, he called and told me that he had just been informed that he was going to be transferred to Pennsylvania.

This time I didn't panic. The next day during my lunch break, the only time I could leave the school, I drove to the closest public telephone, outside a convenience store two miles away. Nobody at work knew about Nicolás, and I didn't want my conversation to be overheard. Feeding three rolls of quarters into the phone, I first called the Southeast Regional Designator of the Bureau of Prisons, the person who decides which institution each inmate is sent to. Then, when she couldn't or wouldn't change Nicolás' impending transfer, I called every Senator, Congressman, and organization that had helped us before. As soon as I got home from work, I wrote a letter to each person I had called, stating why it would be a financial as well as emotional hardship if they transferred Nicolás to Pennsylvania.

I knew that Nicolás' penal classification level was low, and that because of this he was supposed to be in a low security institution, but as I reasoned in my letter, there were other, closer, institutions. It certainly seemed that the Bureau of Prisons was doing everything in its power to prevent us from seeing each other. After writing all the letters and speaking to everyone who could possibly help, there was nothing to do but wait. Although I was receiving letters from Congressmen and Senators telling us that they were still working on it, we weren't hopeful.

Luckily, the next week was my spring vacation and I took advantage of it to visit Nicolás almost every day. We knew that if the transfer went through as planned, I wouldn't be able to visit him for months.

On April 13, Nicolás sent not one, but two bouquets of flowers to the school where I was teaching. It was our first wedding anniversary. Not only was I unable to be with him because I was working, but also because there were no visits allowed on Wednesdays.

Two weeks later, Nicolás called at the usual time. He said he was leaving in the morning and that he'd call me as soon as he got to Pennsylvania. At seven the following morning, Nicolás woke me up to say goodbye and tell me he loved me.

I didn't even cry. I had gone through so much over the last few months just to be able to visit him again, I was emotionally drained. If Pennsylvania was the only place I could see Nicolás, then I'd have to go to Pennsylvania. At least I was allowed to see him. I counted my blessings, remembering how only a few months ago I had been pleading with the Bureau of Prisons to let me visit Nicolás one day a year.

At nine o'clock, Nicolás called to say goodbye again. The carton containing his personal property was already on the bus and he was waiting for them to call him. When, after two hours had passed and the phone hadn't rung, I was certain that he was on his way to Pennsylvania.

"Oh well," I said to myself, as I prepared to go shopping. "At least I tried."

As I opened the door to leave, the telephone rang again.

"Hi, Mami."

"Papi, you're crazy," I told him, thinking he was calling to say goodbye again.

But instead of saying goodbye, he told me that he had just gotten off the bus. He had been standing in line with the other inmates who were being transferred, when just as he was about to step up into the bus, an officer called out "Córdoba!" and told him to get off the bus. His transfer had just been canceled.

It was a like a miracle...and we hadn't even prayed for one.

A few weeks later, we lost our visiting privileges for the next six months.

It happened during Memorial Day weekend. Nicolás and I were sitting outside playing cards. We were joking and laughing as I told him how much I was looking forward to my summer vacation, which was just a week away, in which I was hoping to make up for the all the months when we weren't able to see each other. An officer approached us and requested that I give her the raincoat that I had just taken off. She told me that since I wasn't wearing it anymore, she would hold it for me until I left, as it wasn't permitted for me to just hang on to it.

When I reminded her that I usually placed it on the concrete, in the corner of the patio area, to sit in the shade when all the benches outside were occupied, she said that I wasn't permitted to do that either, even though I had been doing exactly that for the past three weekends.

Nicolás hadn't understood what she had said, and when I handed my coat to her, he thought that she was confiscating it. After I translated her words to him, he insisted upon going inside to ask her to clarify the reason she had requested my coat. Ten minutes later she opened the door to the patio, where I was still sitting at the table waiting for Nicolás to return. Smiling broadly, she beckoned me to come inside. Thinking that everything had been cleared up and that Nicolás had decided to sit inside, I gathered the cards together and quickly walked towards the visiting room.

As soon as I entered, she told me that I had to leave.

I looked around for Nicolás to kiss him before I left or at least say goodbye, but he was nowhere to be found. He had been taken out in handcuffs and placed in Segregation.

It was October before I saw him again.

There are many ways, depending on the severity of the offense, that the Bureau of Prisons can discipline an inmate who has broken one or more of the rules. These are all spelled out, with specific infractions receiving specific punishments. An inmate can be placed in Segregation for a short or an extended period of time, or some or all of his earned "Good Conduct Time," the fifty-four days that an inmate earns annually in order to reduce the amount of time he spends in prison, can be taken away. These punishments are meted out for severe infractions of the rules. Loss of privileges is the customary punishment for less serious offenses.

Nicolás was accused of refusing to obey an order and of speaking in an insolent manner. It was just his word against the word of the Hispanic officer sitting at the desk in the visiting room who took offense to the way Nicolás was speaking and called for a lieutenant to take Nicolás to Segregation. With no one to refute the officer's words, or testify on Nicolás' behalf, Nicolás lost his visitation privileges for six months.

In addition, he was punished by being removed from the cell that he shared with only one other inmate and placed in a common area shared by one hundred men. When he got out of Segregation, he was not permitted to buy anything from the commissary or use the gym or go to the rec yard for one month.

The only punishment I received was that I couldn't visit my husband. It was beginning to seem that every time we took one step forward, we took three steps backward. In spite of the fact that the Congressmen trying to help us were told "The Unit Disciplinary Committee imposed these sanctions in an effort for Mr. Córdoba to assume responsibility for his actions and correct his behavior," I was also suffering.

This time the letters and the phone calls didn't help.

From the last week of May until the second week of December, the only time we saw each other was one weekend in October, after Nicolás had repeatedly requested permission to see me at least once during the six months.

Through my daily letters and his nightly phone calls, we kept the lines of communication open. We talked about what we had done during the day and what we had seen on television or read in the newspaper. I found myself with too many things to do and not enough time to do them, and he had almost nothing to do and all day to do it. When I told him that sometimes I wished I could change places with him, he became upset and told me I was crazy.

I sent him poems that I wrote just for him, and he serenaded me in Spanish over the telephone. He sent me articles from newspapers and magazines, and I drew funny pictures for him of what I had seen and what I had done. We both sent photographs of each other every few weeks.

The only way he could fall asleep at night was to watch television until two o'clock in the morning and fall exhausted into bed. Because I had to wake up at five-thirty to get ready for work, I couldn't follow his example. Instead, I swallowed two antihistamine tablets every night at eight o'clock. They weren't habit-forming and acted like sleeping pills. Within an hour of taking them, I was usually sound asleep.

It wasn't easy, but we survived.

When people on the "outside" think of a prison, if they think of it at all, they picture the drab cement block buildings and barbed-wire fences depicted in the movies. They envision hardened convicts in black and white uniforms pacing behind the bars of their cells. I know they think this way, because I also did. Indeed, until I started working at FCI Otisville, I didn't even think of prisons or the inmates and their families. It was a world that didn't even exist as far as I was concerned.

Now it is my entire life. Until Nicolás is released, prison and how it affects those who are incarcerated and their families will remain my entire life.

Unless you have a husband, son or anyone you love in prison, it is difficult, if not impossible, to imagine what it is like to be a wife of a man in prison. It's driving twelve hours to be with him for six hours. It's standing and waiting outside the prison entrance in the cold and the heat and the rain and the snow. It's spending $3.00 to buy five barbecued chicken wings from the vending machine in the visiting room, when you know you can buy a whole chicken for $2.25 in the supermarket.

It's not complaining about anything to your husband, because he can't do anything to help you and he'll only get upset because he knows that he can't help you.

It's seeing happy couples on the street, laughing and holding hands, while telling yourself that you have to wait for years to hold your husband's hand and walk together like that. It's denying the passionate desires and needs of your body and mind for five, ten, fifteen or more years. It's expressing all the love and longing you feel for your husband in a few farewell kisses while an officer is standing beside you, watching and telling you that you have to leave.

It's going everywhere alone, eating every meal alone and sleeping alone every night for years. It's having no one to say good morning to and no one to kiss you good night.

It's staggering out of bed to get some aspirin, because there's no one to take care of you when you're sick. It's having nobody to tell your troubles to because nobody understands what you're going through.

It's having no one to hug you after a hard day and no one's shoulder to lean on when you're tired or discouraged. It's having to make every decision every day by yourself. It's having no one to call when your car breaks down. It's having no one to hold you tight during a thunderstorm.

It's having no one to put suntan lotion on your back or to zip up the back of your dress or to tell you if your slip is showing. It's having no one to help you bring the groceries into the house when you come back from the supermarket, and no one to fix a fancy dinner for.

It's having no one to help you decorate the Christmas tree or to drink champagne with on New Year's Eve. It's having to spend your birthday and his birthday and your anniversary apart. It's having no one to pray beside you in church.

It's lying and telling him that you're "doing all right," when all you want to do is cry and tell him how much you miss him.

And worst of all, it's having to walk away and leave while the person you love most in this entire world has to stay behind.

People say that when a husband is incarcerated, especially for many years, as in our case, the marriage either falls apart or gets stronger. Unfortunately, this is all too true.

Nicolás best described our relationship and how we feel about each other, when we attended a Marriage Encounter seminar at FCI Tallahassee. In front of the twenty-five couples gathered there he said in Spanish to the tumultuous applause of all at the end of his declaration, "My wife and I met when I was already an inmate. We married when I was an inmate. I have known other women in my life...some maybe prettier, all younger...but she is the love of my life."

And he knows that's the way I feel about him. To all outward appearances, we are as different as two people could possibly be, but we're the same where it counts: inside.

Because Nicolás and I met in prison, we have never lived together. We've never even had a private minute together. And though we've been married for years, we realize that there are more things about each other that we don't know than we know.

One day, hopefully soon, he'll find out that I snore like a buzz saw and I'll discover that he doesn't like to shave every day. We've never seen each other undressed and he's never seen me without makeup. I've never seen him in anything but clothes issued by the prison. We realize that we have a lot to learn about each other and that these first years of our marriage, in which we've been forced to live apart, have been almost like a long, too long, engagement.

We still don't know a lot about each other—that will take time. But we do know that we love each other, more than ever, and that nothing is impossible.

The Immigration and Naturalization Service has decreed that Nicolás will be deported back to Colombia after he finishes serving his sentence. They say that despite his marriage to an American citizen, he is a convicted felon and will not be permitted to remain here. This means that his lifelong dream of living in the United States, the one that he risked his life for, will be denied to him forever.

I already have a resident visa to live in Colombia. If that's the only place where we can live together, that's where I'll go. Hopefully, he'll be permitted to stay in this country.

When his sentence is almost finished, maybe we'll have a better chance of convincing the Immigration and Naturalization Service to let him stay. Right now, the only thing we can do is wait.

A few months after Nicolás and I met, a friend told our fortune by consulting the ancient Chinese manuscript, *I Ching*. I had never heard of it before, but it seemed to predict exactly what Nicolás and I would be facing in the future when it said, "Waiting is not merely empty hoping. It has the inner certainty of reaching a goal."

We have a goal: we want to be together as husband and wife. Unless we win an appeal or the law is changed, we will have to wait until November 5, 1999.

So we wait and hope.